AMERICA'S
CHILDREN

A VOLUME IN THE CENSUS MONOGRAPH SERIES

AMERICA'S
CHILDREN

by

ELEANOR H. BERNERT

Research Associate
University of California, Los Angeles

for the
SOCIAL SCIENCE RESEARCH COUNCIL
in cooperation with the
U. S. DEPARTMENT OF COMMERCE
BUREAU OF THE CENSUS

JOHN WILEY & SONS, INC., NEW YORK
CHAPMAN & HALL, LIMITED, LONDON

301.43
B45e

To
Jamie and Tony

FOREWORD

The statistical results compiled by the Bureau of the Census constitute a tremendous mass of detailed information about the population of the United States and its characteristics and economic activities. To meet the requirements of government agencies, business concerns, and investigators of social problems and to satisfy the needs of individual citizens, facts must be gathered and published, showing the distribution of the population in each large and small political unit with respect to age, sex, color, marital status, occupation, income, education, national origin, and other characteristics. This information provides the basis for apportionment of representatives in Congress, for answering many questions by direct reference, and for formulating many plans, at least in preliminary form.

It is the first business of the Bureau of the Census to put into print the census results that directly answer as many such questions as possible. Along with these results, similar data from one or two previous censuses are usually included. Limitations of time, space, and money prevent any extensive statement of the relations between particular results, the long-term trends of significant totals and subtotals, the shifting proportions of the people belonging to different categories, various interesting and important relations such as those between income, occupation, and age. It is not that the Bureau of the Census fails in any sense to appreciate the value and need for such analyses, but rather that it must concentrate on its basic concern with the summary statistics that constitute its unique contribution to knowledge.

When plans for the 1950 Census were made, the need for more extensive analysis was recognized and a series of census monographs similar to those issued after the 1920 Census was proposed. Because of the pressures caused by the depression in the early 1930's and by defense and war in the early 1940's, plans for monographs based on those censuses could not be carried out. Late in the 1940's interested persons from business, research, and government agencies expressed the need for a series that would provide analyses of the most significant results of the 1950 Census. The Social Science Research Council, with the assistance of Russell Sage Foundation, took the lead in stimulating the formulation of suitable plans and in June 1950 appointed a Committee on Census Monographs to cooperate with the Bureau in organizing this project. The members of the Committee are:

Ralph G. Hurlin, Russell Sage Foundation (Chairman)

Robert W. Burgess, formerly Western Electric Company, since February 1953 Director of the Bureau of the Census

John D. Durand, United Nations

Ernest M. Fisher, Columbia University

F. F. Hill, Cornell University

Frederick F. Stephan, Princeton University

Conrad Taeuber, Bureau of the Census

Ralph J. Watkins, Dun & Bradstreet, Inc.

Paul Webbink, Social Science Research Council

J. Frederic Dewhurst, Twentieth Century Fund, and William F. Ogburn, University of Chicago, were members of the Committee during the first year and a half.

It is essential in any sound census monograph program to obtain the co-operation of authors with a broad understanding not only of the statistical information provided by the regular tabulations of the current census but also of the results of earlier censuses and other relevant knowledge and points of view from other sources and even from other countries. The preparation of a monograph should include broad exploration of new questions suggested by the new information, as well as narrowing the elements of doubt and controversy on old questions. The Social Science Research Council Committee early undertook, in consultation with leading figures in various professional fields, to develop a suggested list of monograph titles and authors and persuaded experts in the subject areas selected to undertake the preparation of memoranda outlining and discussing the topics proposed. Then, in 1951, arrangements were made for continuing cooperation between the Committee and the Bureau concerning the selection of topics, proposals of authors and consultants, and editorial supervision.

Throughout the conduct of the project there has been close collaboration with a number of interested Federal agencies and with universities and research organizations, which provided staff and facilities to help bring the project to completion. They and the Council, which also obtained necessary funds from the Rockefeller and Russell Sage Foundations, provided assistance without which the monographs could not have been prepared.

The task of preparing monographs is an essential part of the broad function of making the information secured by censuses fully available to satisfy the needs and interests of the community and to constitute a broad base for further studies in the social sciences. As Director of the Census and President of the Social Science Research Council, respectively, we wish to record our full approval of the monograph project. It is not implied, of course, that the views expressed in these reports are necessarily those of the Bureau of the Census, the Department of Commerce, or the

Social Science Research Council. The views are those of the individual authors, each of whom has been given the freedom to interpret available materials in the light of his technical knowledge and competence. This freedom of the individual authors is an essential element in making the most useful analyses and interpretations generally available to the community.

ROBERT W. BURGESS, DIRECTOR
BUREAU OF THE CENSUS

PENDLETON HERRING, PRESIDENT
SOCIAL SCIENCE RESEARCH COUNCIL

PREFACE

This is a book about children and youth in the United States in relation to some of their social and economic characteristics. It is a statistical analysis based chiefly on the 1950 Census of Population and a few more recent sample surveys of the Nation's population. The aim of the study is to distill from a mass of statistical materials some picture of the interrelatedness of selected characteristics of children, such as geographic location, education, work activity, color, etc. The scope of the study and the characteristics investigated are necessarily defined and limited by the data utilized. Chapter 1 discusses these limitations and definitions in greater detail.

I am grateful to the Social Science Research Council and the Bureau of the Census for making this study possible and to the Council's Committee on Census Monographs for its patience in supporting and encouraging the study through its long path from beginning to end. I am particularly indebted to the Russell Sage Foundation for allowing me the use of its office and staff facilities, especially for the expert typing services of Mary B. McGark and Dorothy Jung. I am also grateful to Dr. Leonard Broom of the Department of Anthropology and Sociology, University of California, Los Angeles, for making possible the use of the library and departmental facilities.

The manuscript was critically reviewed by Reuben Hill of the University of North Carolina, Dr. Conrad Taeuber of the Bureau of the Census, Dr. Ralph Hurlin of the Russell Sage Foundation, and Paul Webbink of the Social Science Research Council. Their criticisms and suggestions helped in the elimination of many errors and misinterpretations and in the expansion of many other areas of analysis. From the early preparation to the final stages of the study the advice of Howard G. Brunsman, Henry S. Shryock, Jr., and Paul C. Glick, all of the Bureau of the Census, helped considerably in the proper use and interpretation of the data. The many discussions with Robert O. Carleton, formerly with the Bureau of Applied Social Research, Columbia University, yielded the model of analysis employed in Chapter 8. The overall and continuing assistance of James N. Ypsilantis, University of Massachusetts, and his particular contributions to Chapters 5 and 6 warrant especial and grateful acknowledgment. The full responsibility for the shortcomings of the study is, of course, mine.

Malibu, California　　　　　　　　　　　　　　　　ELEANOR H. BERNERT
December 1957.

CONTENTS

CHAPTER 1

INTRODUCTION

Knowledge of the numbers of children and youths in the United States and their social and economic characteristics is greater now than ever before and is accumulating rapidly. With it have come considerable understanding of the problems and needs peculiar to young people and a variety of programs and policies of care related to them. Basic to many of these activities is the need for a social-economic perspective. This study is focused upon such a perspective in an attempt to provide up-to-date knowledge of the demographic characteristics of young people, the interrelations of these characteristics, and their probable future trends.

Demographic research in recent years has thrown considerable light on the changing characteristics of the Nation's population and the probable course of their future development. It is the purpose of this monograph to review some of these developments and to consider their significance and implications in relation to the young age groups. Specifically, the inquiry will include an examination of the 1950 Census statistics with a view toward more clearly identifying the differences among children in the varying segments of the Nation and presenting as objectively as possible an analysis of the demographic factors which bear upon these differences.

In any population the child and youth group is composed of those who are in the various stages of transition from the complete dependency of the young to membership in the adult community of individual responsibility. For such a group no age limits can be set that will not depart from the facts of individual cases. Generally throughout this volume, the following age groups are considered:

0–4 years, comprising the preschool ages;
5–9 years, representing early school ages;
10–14 years and 15–19 years, representing the middle and latter school ages, respectively;
20–24 years, constituting those at the threshold of their working lives and/or marriage.

Modifications in these age limits are used throughout the text as the subject matter of discussion varies; combinations and refinements of these groups are also used when it is deemed significant and where the data allow.

1

Age assumes significance largely in terms of what the society makes of it—often ascribing to age groupings particular functions and limited areas of activity. Similarly, the sex distinction decrees for each many associated functions. The conditions of age and sex together "set up involuntary groupings to which under the rule of biology and culture are adjusted (a person's) routines and functions, habits and personality."[1] Age-sex distinctions form a primary basis of classification and analysis in the following presentation of the social and economic variations among the Nation's youngsters.

There are many social milieux in the United States. Among those discussed in this volume are certain regions of the Nation—the Northeast, the North Central, the South, and the West. The reference is not entirely geographic. Regional variations in the demographic characteristics of children and youth are presented also, and perhaps fundamentally, because of the different patterns of life existing in these sections,[2] some of which are revealed by the data themselves and most of which obtain only indirect reflection.

In the Northeast Region industrial activity has long colored its culture pattern.[3] The processing of goods, rather than their raw production has been foremost in its economic activities. Partially as a result of its industrial activity it is an area of in-migration and is largely urban in population concentration. During the earlier decades of the century it received a large influx of foreign-born and more recently of native farm and other rural youths. Birth rates have been comparatively low and incomes high, with respect to the size of the dependent age groups.

In the North Central Region, an advanced family-farm agriculture and a considerable degree of urban-industrial development exist. Here there are fewer extreme variations in the ratio of population to resources, a sizable, though smaller, foreign-born group than in the Northeast, and a recent large influx of southern Negroes.

The South as a region has been given much attention, particularly from the standpoint of the relationship between population and welfare.[4] It is perhaps the most distinctive and the most studied of the four major regions referred to here. In this area an essentially agrarian culture still predominates; it is the area with the highest fertility rates in the Nation and the lowest per capita income; it is also an area where the biracial problem is more critical than elsewhere in the country.

---

[1] Rupert B. Vance and Nadia Danielevsky, *All These People, The Nation's Human Resources in the South*, University of North Carolina Press, Chapel Hill, 1945, p. 39.

[2] For further discussion of the Nation's regions see Howard W. Odum and Harry E. Moore, *American Regionalism; A Cultural-Historical Approach to National Integration*, Henry Holt and Company, New York, 1938; and Vance and Danielevsky, *op. cit.*

[3] The brief descriptions presented here are summarized chiefly from Paul Landis, *Population Problems—A Cultural Interpretation*, 2nd ed., prepared by Paul Hatt, American Book Company, New York, 1954, pp. 363 ff.

[4] For example, see Odum and Moore, *op. cit.* and Vance and Danielevsky, *op. cit.*

In the West there are the mountain areas which are almost entirely rural, characterized generally by sparse resources and sparse population settlements living in the open country or in agricultural trade centers. The West also includes the Pacific States, the Far West—an area of great population influx. It has drawn people of all levels of life, from the pleasure seeker to the migratory worker and the middle class elders approaching retirement age. The culture pattern of the area is becoming increasingly urban and increasingly dominated by metropolitan centers, a trend which was accentuated by the expansion of war industries. Since much of the area's agriculture is nourished through irrigation developments, much of the "rural" life is industrialized.

More closely related to the social and economic lives of population groups than regional divisions are the rural and the urban divisions. These display, in all regions of the Nation, distinctly different kinds of social climates. An understanding of the characteristics and conditioning processes of both rural and urban life is particularly important because of the interchange of population between the two, especially of the youth group.[5] The one extreme is represented by the stable, isolated rural community, where all of life is built about the family and where there is, in a very specific sense, no individuality; the other, by the metropolitan community which is individualistic, competitive, and casual.

> In the more transient areas of the metropolitan community the child reaches adolescence with the ability to shed experiences readily. He has no deep roots in any social soil. His values are likely to be a confusion of superficial experiences with many behavior patterns and systems of authority. The farm child developed in the other extreme environment is so deeply rooted in the mores, traditions, and folkways of the familistic groups that he has little equipment to function anywhere outside the immediate social habitat. The transfer to another group during the period of adolescence or youth is likely to constitute a supreme crisis, since his emotional life, his system of values, his life objectives and goals, are likely to be in rather rigid conformity with the goals of the familistic group which have little place in the normal society of the larger world outside the neighborhood.[6]

In the United States today most children develop in social milieux somewhere between these two extremes. Actually, there appears to be no clearcut distinction between urban and rural.

---

[5] Charles E. Lively and Conrad Taeuber, *Rural Migrations in the United States*, U. S. Government Printing Office, Washington, D. C., 1939; Eleanor H. Bernert, *Volume and Composition of Net Migration from Rural Farm Population, 1930–1940*, U. S. Department of Agriculture, Bureau of Agricultural Economics (mimeographed), January 1944. For bibliographical references on wartime rural-urban migration, see Eleanor H. Bernert and Gladys K. Bowles, *Farm Migration, 1940–45*, U. S. Department of Agriculture, Bureau of Agricultural Economics (mimeographed), September 1947. More recent estimates of the rural-urban migration of young people may be found in *Net Migration From the Rural-Farm Population, 1940–1950*, U. S. Department of Agriculture, Agricultural Marketing Service, Statistical Bulletin No. 176, June 1956.

[6] Paul Landis, *Adolescence and Youth, The Process of Maturing*, McGraw-Hill Book Company, New York, 1952, p. 94.

Although city and country are opposite poles of life, it does not follow that they are separate. As civilization has advanced they have grown ever more interdependent. Even people who live remote from cities use its services, are affected by its functions, and come to share its problems. Their mode of life, irrespective of the immediate community in which they live, is more and more taking on urban features. Modern technology has reduced the importance of *where* we live, and enhance the importance of *how* we live.

While he may still cherish the illusion of independence, the farmer even in what he plants, how he cultivates the soil, the tools he uses, and the prices he gets for his product, cannot be oblivious to the city. His physical well-being, his housing, his health, the education of his children, his politics, his taxes, his social security, his income and his standard of living, his ideas, and his attitudes are shaped as much or possibly even more by what goes on in the cities than by what transpires in his own immediate surroundings.

On the other hand, urban life in many respects still bears the imprint of an earlier agrarian society, symbolized by the manor and the village. We still find all gradations of life between the two poles of the rural folk society and the urban industrial civilization. Moreover, since the populations of the cities themselves are in large measure recruited from the countryside, we should not expect to find abrupt and discontinuous variations between urban and rural modes of life and types of personality. Our urban institutions and ways of living and the outlook characteristic of the urbanite still bear the vestiges of the rural atmosphere from which they have sprung.[7]

For statistical purposes, the Bureau of the Census has employed the criteria of number of inhabitants and density in defining its urban and rural residence groups[8] and has enumerated persons living within certain officially designated limits. Such a definition of these residence categories is employed in this volume because of the data utilized, but the meaning of the findings of the study lies in relating them to the socially derived characteristics of the areas.

It must be acknowledged that numbers and density of population are useful ways of roughly distinguishing between urban and rural population groupings. However, they must be viewed within a matrix of social, economic, political, and geographic facts.

Rural and urban areas present considerable differences in the organization of the social life and institutions which comprise each. In comparison with rural life, the city has more widely divergent human groupings and a more complicated institutional arrangement.

Economically the rural household is more self-sufficient than the urban household. The rural community, moreover, generally consists of a more homogeneous population, so that the same social groups and institutions come more nearly to satisfy the needs and to enlist the participation of all the people in the community.

The rural community is generally small enough so that every one in it can know everyone else intimately. The controls thus exercised over people are direct, personal,

[7] Louis Wirth, *Urban and Rural Living, Planning Post-War Ways of Life for American Youth*, National Council for the Social Studies and the National Association of Secondary School Principals, National Education Association, Washington, D. C., 1944, pp. 9–10.

[8] See *1950 Census of Population*, Vol. II, *Characteristics of the Population*, Part 1, U. S. Summary, Introduction, pp. 9–11, 21–22, 33–35.

and emotional. In contrast, the city contains heterogeneous people who know little about one another and whose contact with one another is segmental, indirect, utilitarian. The services which urbanites need are generally bought and paid for in the market. Urbanites are bound together less by a common past and a wide range of common interests than by the pecuniary nexus and the coincidence of some single, transitory aim that a few happen to have in common for the time being.

Whereas in the small rural settlement most of the inhabitants will be related to one another, belong to the same race and stock, have the same religion, and be of approximately the same economic status and engaged in the same occupations, urbanites are broken up into countless isolated, overlapping and conflicting fragments, owing partial allegiance to many social groups and institutions and no undivided allegiance to any. The family and the church stand out as the dominant institutions in the rural community, whereas they lead a precarious existence in the city. The functions that the family performs in simpler communities are divided among many institutions in the city, among them the school, the health and welfare agencies, organized recreational institutions, social clubs, professional services and a host of commercial, public and philanthropic agencies. The same is true of the urban church. Its members may have little in common except association for formal worship. The church in the city takes on a variety of services and secular functions. Its members are not stable, and it is often manned by a staff of highly trained professional personnel. The control of the church over its members in the city is highly tenuous. The city, moreover, generates a variety of creeds which have to exist side by side in an atmosphere of toleration or even indifference.[9]

Rural education has been traditionally associated with the one room schoolhouse. Though this may no longer be the common association, compared with the more differentiated and specialized educational services of the large city, rural education has not progressed as far. The school year is generally shorter, teachers are apt to be less well trained and more poorly paid, less cognizance is given the backward or gifted pupil, fewer children continue their education to higher levels (see Chapter 5), and often experimentation or change in methods of education is difficult to accomplish. More recently, the consolidation of many small school districts and the development of consolidated schools have made it possible for some rural areas to offer more advanced educational services. Since many young people who are educated in rural schools later migrate to the cities and meet the competition and problems of urban living, the implications of the educational differentials are far-reaching.

The population of any given area may be viewed functionally as those people who comprise the home population, the school population, the labor force, and those who are retired or eligible for retirement. The children and youth discussed in this book are viewed similarly—from the standpoint of the home (Chapter 4), the school (Chapters 5 and 6), and their work (Chapters 7 and 8). In addition, some attention is given to children as dependents in relation to the population of productive ages (Chapters 2 and 3).

In outline, this book is divided into pairs of chapters, the first of which

[9] Wirth, *op. cit.*, pp. 29–30.

is generally a descriptive presentation of the data and the second of which is a more detailed analysis of some of the correlates of the variable being considered. It is the purpose of the concluding chapter of the volume to bring together (and to bring up to date, wherever possible) the findings of the earlier chapters and in some instances to elaborate upon the implications of these findings. In the appendices are placed the methodological notes and the basic tables not elsewhere readily available. For definitions of terms such as school enrollment, years of school completed, median school years, employment status, labor force participation rates, urban and rural residence, farm population, standard metropolitan areas, urbanized areas, and the like, see *1950 Census of Population*, Vol. II, *Characteristics of the Population*, Part 1, U. S. Summary, Introduction, pp. 2, 9–11, 21–22, 27–28, 33–35, 44–47, 49–53.

Census statistics utilized here represent cross-classified descriptions of the population of the Nation at a given period of time. As such they contain very little of a longitudinal view of population groups, of the developmental history of individuals, or of motivations in group or individual behavior. Thus the aspects of child and adolescent life discussed in this volume are necessarily bounded by the detail and accuracy of available data. Though references are made to earlier findings, this volume does not present an analysis of the migration of young people. The 1950 Census questions in themselves limited migration period to one year, scarcely long enough to provide a strong basis for detailed analysis and generalization. Similarly, military service, an important aspect in the life of young people today, is not viewed as a central subject of discussion in this volume and is viewed only tangentially in its effect upon the education and labor force participation of youngsters. Also, the demographic correlates of marriage, household status, etc., are viewed only with reference to their roles in the major areas selected for analysis.

CHAPTER 2

THE SIZE AND DISTRIBUTION
OF THE CHILD AND YOUTH POPULATION

A. Trends in the size of the child and youth population

A discussion of the social and economic characteristics of a specified age group or groups, such as those comprising children and youth, may be more sharply focused and more readily understood when viewed within the setting of the total age structure, for it is the shifting proportions of the various age groups and their interrelations which create many of the most pressing concerns for any particular group. Thus, it is with the recognition of the importance of the age *interdependencies* that before turning to the primary interest of this study, namely, an analysis of the demographic characteristics of children and youth, we present a brief description of some of the most significant changes in the total age profile of the Nation.

In the past half-century, from 1900 to 1950, the total population of the United States almost doubled, from 76.0 million persons in 1900 to 150.7 million persons in 1950. During these years, and even before the turn of the century, the Nation's population underwent a process of aging, and there is little indication that this process will cease in the near future.

The extent of this aging may be seen at a glance by examining the trend in the median age of the Nation's population. As far back as 1820 one half of the people of the country were under 17 years of age, by 1900 the median age had reached 22.9 years, and it increased steadily at each decennial count until it reached 30.2 years in 1950.[1] The 1940–1950 decade, however, brought a slackening of the aging tendency because of the large rise in births immediately following the close of World War II.

While the age structure of the population was undergoing this general shift, varying changes were taking place among the different age groups, of which the younger groups are of particular interest here. For the purpose of viewing some of the more particular changes without getting lost in a welter of detail, some broad age groups are considered: children 0 to 4 years of age, roughly comprising the preschool ages; children 5 to 9 years of age, representing the early school ages; youth 10 to 14 and 15 to 19

---

[1] *1950 Census of Population*, Vol. II, *Characteristics of the Population*, Part 1, U. S. Summary, table 39.

years old comprising the middle and later school ages; young adults 20 to
24 years of age, generally constituting those at the threshold of their working lives and/or marriage; adults 25 to 44 years old comprising the peak
working years; persons 45 to 64 years old representing the later years of
working life; and the aged, 65 years of age and over.

In 1950 the total population of the United States of 150.7 million persons was distributed among these age groups as follows: 0 to 4 years, 16.1
million; 5 to 9 years, 13.2 million; 10 to 14 years, 11.1 million; 15 to 19
years, 10.6 million; 20 to 24 years, 11.5 million; 25 to 44 years, 45.2 million; 45 to 64 years, 30.6 million; and 65 years of age and over, 12.3 million persons.

The data in table 1 indicate clearly that up to the 1920–1930 decade
the population in each of the eight age groups had increased during every
decennial period.   By the 1920's, however, the long-established decline in
the birth rate was manifested in the slight decline in the number of children under 5 years of age.   This decline was accelerated in the succeeding
decade when the Nation was undergoing its worst economic depression, so
that considerable losses in the population of school children aged 5 to 14
years were added to those of preschool children.   These earlier declines in
the number of preschool and early school children moved up in the age
structure during the 1940's and were reflected in the later school and
early working years.   The increasing birth rate during the war years and
the "baby boom" immediately following the close of the war resulted in a
considerable increase in the number of preschool children and a sizable,
though less marked, increase in the number of children aged 5 to 9 years
by 1950.

TABLE 1.—PERCENT INCREASE IN THE POPULATION, BY AGE: 1900 TO 1950

[Minus sign (−) denotes decrease]

Age	1900 to 1950	1940 to 1950	1930 to 1940	1920 to 1930	1910 to 1920	1900 to 1910
All ages................	98.3	14.5	7.2	16.1	14.9	21.0
Under 5 years..................	76.3	53.3	-7.9	-1.1	8.9	15.9
5 to 9 years..................	48.7	23.5	-15.3	10.6	16.8	10.4
10 to 14 years................	37.6	-5.3	-2.2	12.8	16.8	12.7
15 to 19 years................	40.5	-13.9	6.8	22.5	4.0	20.0
20 to 24 years................	56.5	-0.9	6.6	17.2	2.4	23.5
25 to 44 years................	112.3	14.0	9.7	15.6	16.7	25.9
45 to 64 years................	194.6	17.5	21.8	25.7	26.9	29.1
65 years and over............	298.3	36.0	36.0	34.5	24.9	28.2

Source: Derived from *1950 Census of Population*, Vol. II, *Characteristics of the Population*, Part 1, U. S. Summary,
table 39.

While these shifts were occurring among the lower age groups and
young adults, the numbers of persons in their peak productive years increased at steadily declining rates up to the 1940–1950 decade, at which
time a slight increase in rate appeared.   The size of the population in later
working years increased during each decennial period, also at steadily declining rates.   Those of retirement age increased in numbers during each

decade of the 50-year span so that by 1950 persons in this age group numbered almost 300 percent more than in 1900.

As a result of these shifts in the age distribution of the population the relative share of preschool children declined persistently through 1940 amounting to 12 percent of the total population in 1900 and 8 percent in 1940. By 1950, as a result of the marked increase in births during the 1940 decade, their share increased to 11 percent. (See table 2 and figure 1.) The trend in the relative share of children in the early, middle, and later school years is less consistent, but by 1950 the proportion of population in each of the groups was less than in 1900 and only the youngest, those aged 5 to 9 years, showed an increase over 1940. Only among persons in later working life and of retirement age did the relative share of the total population increase persistently from the turn of the century to its midpoint.

TABLE 2.—PERCENT DISTRIBUTION OF THE POPULATION, BY AGE: 1900 TO 1950

Age	1950	1940	1930	1920	1910	1900
All ages...............	100.0	100.0	100.0	100.0	100.0	100.0
Under 5 years.................	10.7	8.0	9.3	10.9	11.6	12.1
5 to 9 years.................	8.8	8.1	10.3	10.8	10.6	11.7
10 to 14 years...............	7.4	8.9	9.8	10.1	9.9	10.6
15 to 19 years...............	7.0	9.4	9.4	8.9	9.9	9.9
20 to 24 years...............	7.6	8.8	8.9	8.8	9.8	9.7
25 to 44 years...............	30.0	30.1	29.4	29.6	29.2	28.0
45 to 64 years...............	20.3	19.8	17.5	16.2	14.6	13.7
65 years and over...........	8.2	6.9	5.5	4.7	4.3	4.1

Source: *1950 Census of Population*, Vol. II, *Characteristics of the Population*, Part 1, U. S. Summary, table 39.

Figure 2 shows clearly the half-century change in the age profile of the Nation by 5-year age groups. Particularly marked are the heavy losses of population in each of the age groups up to about age 30 and the increasingly heavy gains beyond that point. These superimposed age pyramids also contrast graphically the pattern of age structure of the two populations. The structure in 1900 was fairly regular and simple with a gradual slope from each age group to the next older one. In contrast, the 1950 profile is quite irregular particularly under age 25, reflecting the wide fluctuations in the number of births since 1930.

B. Distribution of the child and youth population, 1950

Regional variations. There have long been notable differences in the distribution of children and youth among the several geographic regions of the United States. The highest proportion of children under 5 years of age in 1950 was found in the South (11.8 percent) and the lowest proportion was found in the Northeast (9.5 percent). The proportion in the North Central Region was 10.5 percent and in the West 11 percent. The same rank order among the regions is found for the proportion of children

FIGURE 1.—CHANGES IN DISTRIBUTION OF POPULATION AMONG SELECTED AGE GROUPS:
1900 TO 1950

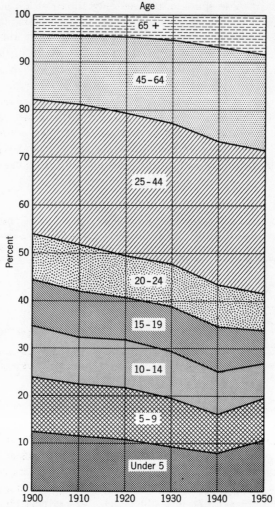

Note: Based on data in table 2.

5 to 9 years of age: 7.8 percent in the Northeast, 8.4 percent in the North
Central, 8.6 percent in the West, and 9.9 percent in the South (table 3).

In the 10 to 19 years of age group there is a marked difference between
the two extremes of the Northeast and the South. The proportion of
youths in this age group amounted to only 12.8 percent in the Northeast
as contrasted with 16.7 percent in the South. Between the two are the proportions of youths in the North Central States (13.8 percent) and in the West
(13.4 percent).

FIGURE 2.—AGE-SEX DISTRIBUTION OF THE POPULATION: 1950 AND 1900

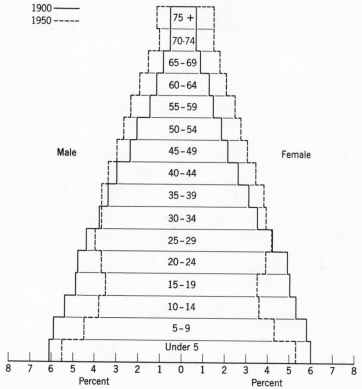

Source: *1950 Census of Population*, Vol. II, *Characteristics of the Population*, Part 1, U. S. Summary, table 39.

TABLE 3.—PERCENT DISTRIBUTION OF THE POPULATION, BY AGE, BY REGIONS: 1950

Area	Total population (all ages)	Percent of the population, by age				
		All ages	Under 14 years	14 to 19 years	20 to 64 years	65 years and over
United States................	150,697,361	100.0	25.8	8.4	57.7	8.2
Northeast........................	39,477,986	100.0	22.9	7.7	60.8	8.7
North Central....................	44,460,762	100.0	25.2	8.1	57.9	8.9
South...........................	47,197,088	100.0	28.9	9.8	54.5	6.9
West............................	19,561,525	100.0	25.5	7.8	58.6	8.2

Source: Derived from *1950 Census of Population*, Vol. II, *Characteristics of the Population*, Part 1, U. S. Summary, tables 62 and 155.

The proportion of young adults aged 20 to 24 years showed hardly any variation among the four major regions of the Nations: 7.4 percent in the Northeast, the North Central, and the West, and 8.1 percent in the South.

Adults 25 to 64 years of age varied from 46.6 percent in the South to 53.7 percent in the Northeast and about 51 percent in both the North Central and the West. The proportion of the aged population, 65 years and

over, was greatest in the two northern regions (8.9 percent in the North
Central and 8.7 percent in the Northeast) and smallest in the South (6.9
percent). In the West, the aged population comprised 8.2 percent of the
total.

If we view these age groupings from the point of view of the economic
functioning of the various groups, we find that the Northeast Region appears to be in the most favorable position with respect to the supporting
capacity of its population, with less than 23 percent of its population too
young to participate in the labor force (under 14 years of age) and over 60
percent in the productive ages of 20 to 64 years. The South, on the other
hand, is in the least favorable position to support its dependent children
with almost 30 percent of its population under 14 years of age and only 55
percent aged 20 to 64 years. If we add to the dependent population group
adolescents 14 to 19 years of age and the aged, 65 years of age and over,
we find that the dependency burden of the Northeast Region amounts to
somewhat less than 40 percent of the total population as compared with
over 45 percent in the South.

The total dependency loads (including children, adolescents, and the
aged) in each of the other regions amounts to 42 percent in both the North
Central and Western States.

In table 4, it is noted that over one third of the Nation's children reside
in the South and that less than one fourth live in the Northeast Region. Less
than 30 percent of the Nation's children live in the North Central States
and only 12 or 13 percent of them reside in the West.

TABLE 4.—REGIONAL DISTRIBUTION OF THE POPULATION, BY AGE: 1950

Area	All ages	Under 14 years	14 to 19 years	20 to 64 years	65 years and over
United States.............	100.0	100.0	100.0	100.0	100.0
Northeast......................	26.2	23.3	23.8	27.6	28.1
North Central..................	29.5	28.8	28.3	29.6	32.4
South.........................	31.3	35.1	36.0	29.6	26.5
West..........................	13.0	12.8	11.9	13.2	13.0

Source: Derived from *1950 Census of Population*, Vol. II, *Characteristics of the Population*, Part 1, U. S. Summary,
tables 62 and 155.

With respect to the smaller geographic divisions of the Nation, the data
indicate that the age structure in the Middle Atlantic area (New York, New
Jersey, and Pennsylvania) is the most economically favorable with less than
one fourth of its population under 14 years of age and 8 percent over 65
years of age. In contrast, in the East South Central area (Kentucky, Tennessee, Alabama, and Mississippi) almost 30 percent of the population may
be numbered among the child dependents and 7 percent among the aged.
In addition, the other two southern divisions (South Atlantic States comprised of Delaware, Maryland, Virginia, West Virginia, North Carolina,
South Carolina, Georgia, and Florida, and the West South Central States of

Arkansas, Louisiana, Oklahoma, and Texas) are roughly in the same position as the East South Central States with respect to the functional age structures of their populations.

On a state basis, the States of Mississippi and South Carolina carry the heaviest child-aged dependency loads (almost 40 percent each) and New York and New Jersey the least (with about 30 percent each).[2]

Rural-urban variations. In viewing the Nation's children and youth with respect to the demographic balance between the dependent and productive population segments, rural-urban variations[3] become quite important. It is well known that the total age structure of the urban population is more favorably balanced in regard to supporting capacity than is either the rural-nonfarm and rural-farm populations.

Over 60 percent of the urban population in 1950 was in the productive age group of 20 to 64 years. This contrasts with 50 percent in rural-farm areas and only 54 percent in rural-nonfarm areas (table 5). In addition, the child and youth dependent groups in urban areas comprised a considerably lower proportion (31 percent) of the total population than in either the rural-farm (42 percent) or rural-nonfarm (38 percent) populations. Variations in the aged dependency load among the three residence groups were minimal.

TABLE 5.—PERCENT DISTRIBUTION OF THE POPULATION, BY AGE, URBAN AND RURAL: 1950

Area	Total population (all ages)	Percent of the population, by age				
		All ages	Under 14 years	14 to 19 years	20 to 64 years	65 years and over
United States.................	150,697,361	100.0	25.4	8.5	57.9	8.2
Urban.............................	96,467,686	100.0	23.0	7.6	61.2	8.2
Rural nonfarm.....................	31,181,325	100.0	28.7	9.0	53.6	8.6
Rural farm........................	23,048,350	100.0	31.1	11.3	50.0	7.5

Source: *1950 Census of Population*, Vol. II, *Characteristics of the Population*, Part 1, U. S. Summary, table 38.

If the residential classification is graduated on a continuum from a high degree of urbanization[4] to a high degree of ruralization, the relationship of the proportion of children and youth in a given population and the size class of the residential area is portrayed more vividly. Table 6 and figure 3 indicate the consistent pattern of an increasing proportion of children and youth as the size of the urbanized area of residence declines. In urbanized areas of 3 million inhabitants or more in 1950, 28 percent of the total population were under 20 years of age; in areas of 1 to 3 million inhabitants, 30 percent were less than 20 years old; in areas of 250,000 to

[2] *1950 Census of Population*, Vol. II, *Characteristics of the Population*, Part 1, U. S. Summary, table 63.

[3] For definitions see *1950 Census of Population*, Vol. II, *Characteristics of the Population*, Part 1, U. S. Summary, Introduction, pp. 2, 9–11, 21–22, 27–28, 33–35.

[4] *Ibid.*

1,000,000, 31 percent were numbered among the children and youth; and in the smallest category of urbanized areas (less than 250,000 inhabitants) 32 percent were in this group.

TABLE 6.—PERCENT DISTRIBUTION OF THE POPULATION IN URBANIZED AREAS BY AGE, BY SIZE OF PLACE: 1950

Size of place	Total population (all ages)	Percent by age						
		All ages	Under 5 years	5 to 13 years	14 to 19 years	20 to 24 years	25 to 64 years	65 years and over
Total urbanized areas...........	69,114,600	100.0	10.0	12.6	7.3	7.8	54.4	7.8
Central cities................	48,303,720	100.0	9.6	12.1	7.2	8.1	54.9	8.2
Fringe........................	20,810,880	100.0	11.1	14.0	7.4	7.3	53.2	7.1
Areas of 3,000,000 or more........	21,184,020	100.0	9.2	12.0	6.8	7.3	56.8	7.9
Central cities................	14,208,750	100.0	8.7	11.4	6.8	7.6	57.5	7.9
Fringe........................	6,975,270	100.0	10.3	13.1	6.9	6.7	55.3	7.7
Areas of 1,000,000 to 3,000,000...	16,608,450	100.0	10.0	12.8	7.2	7.8	54.6	7.6
Central cities................	10,106,460	100.0	9.4	12.0	7.1	8.0	55.6	8.0
Fringe........................	6,501,990	100.0	11.0	13.9	7.4	7.4	53.2	7.1
Areas of 250,000 to 1,000,000.....	17,380,080	100.0	10.5	12.7	7.4	8.2	53.3	7.8
Central cities................	12,991,920	100.0	10.1	12.1	7.4	8.4	53.8	8.3
Fringe........................	4,388,160	100.0	11.9	14.5	7.6	7.5	52.0	6.5
Areas of less than 250,000........	13,942,050	100.0	10.6	13.4	7.9	8.2	51.9	8.0
Central cities................	10,996,590	100.0	10.2	12.9	7.8	8.3	52.4	8.5
Fringe........................	2,945,460	100.0	12.0	15.2	8.2	7.8	50.3	6.5

Source: *1950 Census of Population*, Vol. IV, *Special Reports*, Part 5, Chapter A, Characteristics by Size of Place, table 1.

FIGURE 3.—AGE DISTRIBUTION OF THE POPULATION IN URBANIZED AREAS: 1950

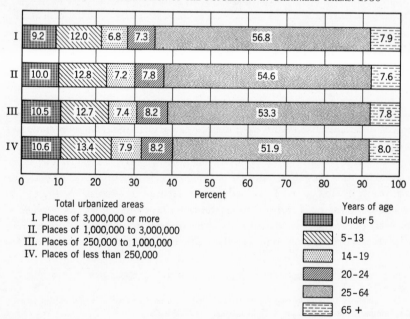

Total urbanized areas
I. Places of 3,000,000 or more
II. Places of 1,000,000 to 3,000,000
III. Places of 250,000 to 1,000,000
IV. Places of less than 250,000

Years of age
Under 5
5-13
14-19
20-24
25-64
65 +

Note: Based on data in table 6.

Figure 4 provides a more detailed picture of the distribution of children and youth by the size of residence area shown separately for central cities and fringe areas.[5] First, in both the central cities and in the fringe areas surrounding them the proportion of children and youth in the total population increases as the size of the urbanized area decreases. Further, the proportion of population among the preschool children (under 5 years old), among the children of school age (5 to 13 years), and among youths aged 14 to 19 years is greater in the fringe areas than in the central cities for each size class of urbanized areas.

FIGURE 4.—AGE DISTRIBUTION OF THE POPULATION IN CENTRAL CITIES AND FRINGE AREAS: 1950

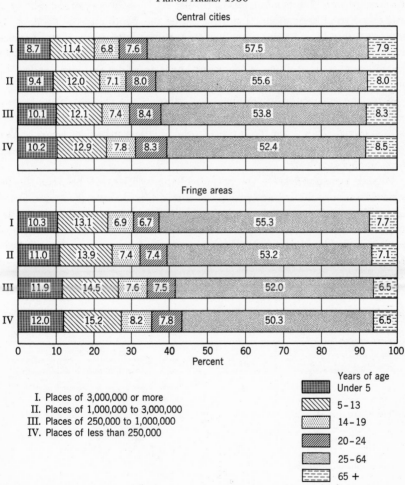

I. Places of 3,000,000 or more
II. Places of 1,000,000 to 3,000,000
III. Places of 250,000 to 1,000,000
IV. Places of less than 250,000

Years of age
Under 5
5 - 13
14 - 19
20 - 24
25 - 64
65 +

Note: Based on data in table 6.

[5] *Ibid.*

Complementary to the varying proportion of children and youth, the productive population (20 to 64 years) declines in proportion to the total population as the size of area decreases in both central cities and fringe areas. In all size classes, adults of productive ages comprise a smaller proportion of the total population in fringe areas than in the central cities.

As the size of area declines the proportion of the aged population increases in the central cities and declines in the fringe areas, though the variations are negligible in size.

In terms of the supporting capacity of a given age structure, it appears that central cities in urbanized areas of 3 million inhabitants or more have, on the average, the most advantageous age distribution. These central cities carry a child dependency load (under 14 years of age) of about 20 percent and a total dependency load, including the youth and the aged, of 35 percent (table 6). At the other extreme, the age structure of the population in the fringe areas of less than 250,000 inhabitants includes a child dependency ratio of about 27 percent and a total dependency load of 42 percent.

With the exception of populations living on the fringes of the largest urbanized areas, child dependency and total dependency increased steadily in the central cities from the largest to the smallest urbanized areas. Also in the fringes the dependency ratios increased from the largest urbanized areas to the smallest.

Outside urbanized areas the pattern of the relationship between the dependent and productive age groups becomes less definite (see table 7 and figure 5). In the larger areas (places of 2,500 inhabitants or more) the pattern is similar to that found in urbanized areas, that is, an increasing proportion of the child and youth dependency group with declining size of place. However, when the population base gets below 2,500 persons, no consistent pattern is detected.

TABLE 7.—PERCENT DISTRIBUTION OF THE POPULATION OUTSIDE URBANIZED AREAS BY AGE, BY SIZE OF PLACE: 1950

Size of place	Total population (all ages)	Percent by age						
		All ages	Under 5 years	5 to 13 years	14 to 19 years	20 to 24 years	25 to 64 years	65 years and over
Places of 25,000 or more.........	7,108,050	100.0	10.5	13.2	8.5	9.0	50.3	8.5
Places of 10,000 to 25,000........	8,204,070	100.0	10.5	13.8	8.5	8.5	49.8	8.8
Places of 2,500 to 10,000.........	11,822,340	100.0	11.0	14.7	8.7	7.9	48.5	9.2
Places of 1,000 to 2,500..........	6,440,550	100.0	11.0	15.5	8.8	7.1	47.3	10.3
Nonfarm......................	6,311,310	100.0	11.1	15.5	8.7	7.1	47.3	10.3
Farm.........................	129,240	100.0	8.5	17.2	10.5	5.0	47.7	11.1
Incorporated places of less than 1,000............................	4,010,580	100.0	10.3	15.6	8.7	6.2	45.9	13.5
Nonfarm......................	3,795,630	100.0	10.3	15.5	8.5	6.2	45.7	13.6
Farm.........................	214,950	100.0	9.5	17.7	10.9	5.7	45.1	11.1
Other rural.....................	43,588,440	100.0	12.2	18.7	10.4	7.0	44.4	7.4
Nonfarm......................	20,929,410	100.0	12.9	17.5	9.3	7.9	45.1	7.2
Farm.........................	22,659,030	100.0	11.5	19.8	11.4	6.1	43.8	7.5

Source: Same as table 6.

FIGURE 5.—AGE DISTRIBUTION OF THE POPULATION OUTSIDE OF URBANIZED AREAS: 1950

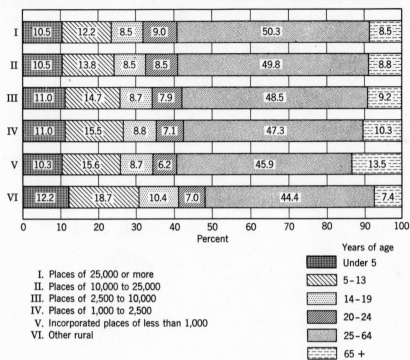

I. Places of 25,000 or more
II. Places of 10,000 to 25,000
III. Places of 2,500 to 10,000
IV. Places of 1,000 to 2,500
V. Incorporated places of less than 1,000
VI. Other rural

Years of age
Under 5
5–13
14–19
20–24
25–64
65 +

Note: Based on data in table 7.

Color variations. The age structure of the nonwhite population is appreciably different from that of the white population. As is evident from figure 6, children and youth comprise considerably greater proportions of the nonwhite population than of the white. Concurrently the population of productive ages among the nonwhites is proportionately less than it is among the whites. The aged population, on the other hand, is relatively larger for the whites than for the nonwhites, largely reflecting the longer expectation of life for the white population.

The heavier child and youth dependency loads of the nonwhite population are shown in table 8 where we find 30 percent of the nonwhite and 25 percent of the white population under 14 years of age, and 10 percent of the nonwhite and 8 percent of the white 14 to 19 years old. The population of productive ages (20 to 64 years) accounts for 54 percent of the total nonwhite and 58 percent of the total white population.

If we add to the population under 20 years of age those 65 years old and over, we find the demographic balance between the dependent and productive age segments of the white population slightly more favorable than that of the nonwhite population; for every dependent white person there are 1.4 persons of productive age; for every dependent nonwhite person there are only 1.2 persons of productive age.

FIGURE **6.**—AGE-SEX DISTRIBUTION OF THE WHITE AND NONWHITE POPULATION: 1950

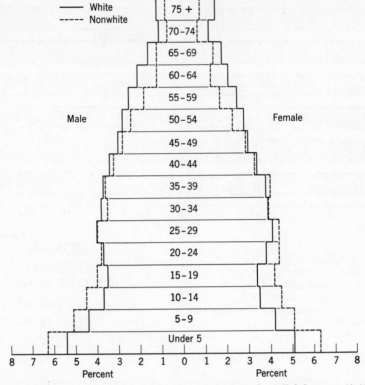

Source: *1950 Census of Population*, Vol. II, *Characteristics of the Population*, Part 1, U. S. Summary, table 39.

TABLE **8.**—AGE DISTRIBUTION OF THE POPULATION, BY COLOR: 1950

Color	Total population (all ages)	Percent of the population, by age				
		All ages	Under 14 years	14 to 19 years	20 to 64 years	65 years and over
Total......................	150,697,361	100.0	25.8	8.4	57.7	8.2
White........................	134,942,028	100.0	24.9	8.3	58.4	8.4
Nonwhite.....................	15,755,333	100.0	30.0	9.9	54.4	5.7

Source: Derived from *1950 Census of Population*, Vol. II, *Characteristics of the Population*, Part 1, U. S. Summary, table 38.

C. Summary

In April 1950 there were 150,697,000 persons of all ages in the United States, representing an almost twofold increase since the turn of the century when the population numbered 75,995,000 persons. As compared with 1940, when there were some 131,700,000 persons in the Nation, our population increased by 14 percent during the last decennial period. Concurrently the number of children and youths under 20 years of age increased by 6 million, from 45 to 51 million, reversing the earlier downward trend in the size of the child population.

When this increase is examined more closely it becomes evident that the rise has not been uniform among the age groups, the most striking growth having occurred among children under 5 years of age. In 1950 there were almost 6 million more youngsters in this age group than in 1940, representing an increase of approximately 55 percent. These young people are swelling the Nation's school population, requiring even greater expansion of facilities and personnel than the expansion that has been effected with such difficulty in recent years. A sizable increase also occurred among the 5- to 9-year-olds, but those between 10 and 20 years of age were fewer in 1950 than in 1940. This decline in the number of teen-agers tends to reduce the number of new workers entering the labor force and the number of young men available for military service.

Variations in the balance between dependent and productive age groups indicate that there are fewer adults in the South to share the responsibilities of caring for their children than in the other regions of the Nation. In the South there are fewer than 1.5 adults of productive ages to every child and youth under 20 years of age, as compared with 2 producers per child dependent in the Northeast, 1.8 in the North Central, and 1.8 in the West.

Generally, lighter dependency ratios occur in urban areas (2 adults of productive ages for each child and youth dependent) than in rural-nonfarm areas (1.4 persons in the productive ages for every child dependent) or in rural-farm areas (1.2 adults of productive ages for every child dependent). Age structure balances are functionally more favorable in the largest urbanized areas than in the smaller, becoming less favorable as size of place declines.

The childhood dependency ratio for the nonwhite population is greater than that for the white population.

CHAPTER 3

CORRELATES OF CHILDHOOD DEPENDENCY

Probably the most important single key to the social and economic progress of a nation is the achievement of a satisfactory standard of education for its citizens. As one of the foundation stones of democracy, educational opportunity, at least at the primary and secondary level, is assumed to be open to all children on an equal basis. The facts, however, do not support the assumption of equal opportunity for all. In the United States, various regions, States, and communities within States are inadequately supplied with educational facilities primarily because of economic inequalities. Most effective in seriously hampering the attainment of a satisfactory standard of education in a given area is its childhood dependency load, that is, large numbers of children in proportion to the numbers of adults who support them and who pay the bills for their education.

The assumption that persons of particular ages are producers and those not within the specified range are dependents is a useful one in reaching an approximation to a measure of dependency. Although in each age group, except for the very young and very old, there are persons who take part in the production of goods and services and some who only consume what is produced by others, an approximate measure defined by age limits does provide some indications of the burdens of dependency. Such a measure as is used in the analysis which follows cannot be considered with regard to the supporting capacity of a person's or family's finances, but rather from the view of the supporting capacity of a specified area or population group. It provides presumptive evidence of the favorableness of the economic conditions of the area. It implies a given number of elders to care for and attend to the needs of a given number of children.

In Chapter 2 the total age structure of a given population was viewed with respect to the relationship between dependent and productive age groups. In general it was found that the dependency loads of the nonwhite population exceeded those of the white population, that rural-farm areas are demographically in the least favorable position with respect to supporting their children and youth, and that the dependency burdens of urban areas are the lightest. It was also pointed out in Chapter 2 that the balance between dependent and productive ages indicates that the South carries the heaviest and the Northeast the lightest child and youth dependency loads in the Nation.

In this chapter we carry the dependency analysis one step further by examining some correlates of dependency, on a State-by-State basis.[1] For the purposes of this examination child and youth dependency is defined as the ratio of persons 0 to 19 years of age to persons 20 to 64 years old. This measure has been correlated with some fifteen variables measuring on a State basis—family income, educational attainment of adults, school enrollment rates, retardation of youths in school, expenditures for schooling, teen-age labor force participation, urbanization, fertility, dilapidation and overcrowding in housing, and others.

In general, the problem of childhood dependency may be summarized as follows: a high ratio of children and youth to adults of productive ages correlates highly with low family income and poor housing conditions, low expenditures for schooling, and poor educational performance.

As indicated in figure 7, the greatest concentration of childhood dependency loads is in the States of the South.[2] In Mississippi and South Carolina the dependency ratios are as high as 86 and 87 children and youth per 100 adults in the productive ages. Similarly high ratios occur in New Mexico and Utah, 84 and 80, respectively. These high dependency ratios contrast sharply with those of the industrial Northeast where the ratios for New York and New Jersey run as low as 46 and 47 young people per 100 adults of productive age. Ratios below 50 are also found in Illinois and Connecticut. Low childhood dependency burdens ranging from 50 to 60 occur in the Pacific States and Nevada, the North Atlantic States (excluding Maine), Pennsylvania, Ohio, Indiana, Michigan, Missouri, and Kansas. High dependency ratios, comparable to those of the South, are also found in North Dakota, Idaho, and Arizona.

In examining figure 8, it is immediately apparent that with respect to State variations in family income the Nation may be divided into a South–non-South dichotomy. The lowest median family income occurred in Mississippi where it was less than $1,200 per year in 1949. Similarly low median incomes (less than $2,000) were found in Arkansas, Alabama, Georgia, South Carolina, and Tennessee. These contrast with median family incomes of $3,500 and more in New Jersey and Connecticut, Illinois and Michigan, California, Nevada and Washington. Similarly high median incomes ($3,000 to $3,499) were found throughout the States of the Northwest (Oregon, Idaho, Utah, Montana, Wyoming, and Colorado), States bordering on the Great Lakes (New York, Pennsylvania, Ohio, Indiana, and Minnesota), and in Iowa, Maryland, Delaware, Rhode Island, and Massachusetts.[3]

---

[1] See also U. S. Department of Health, Education, and Welfare, Social Security Administration, "Age of Population and Per Capita Income, by State, 1953," *Social Security Bulletin*, December 1954, pp. 20–22.

[2] In all references to the South, the State of Florida stands out as an exception. More detailed analyses of Florida as an exceptional southern State may be found in Rupert B. Vance, *Human Geography of the South; A Study in Regional Resources and Human Adequacy*, University of North Carolina Press: Chapel Hill, 1932, pp. 55, 237–238, 357, 502–504.

[3] These income data represent only cash incomes and therefore are understatements for farm areas where part of the income is in forms other than cash.

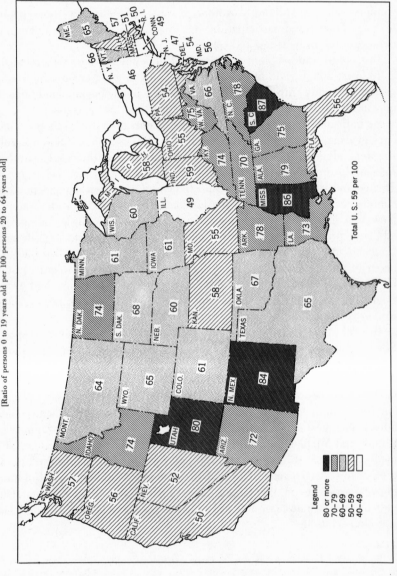

FIGURE 7.—CHILD AND YOUTH DEPENDENCY, BY STATES: 1950

[Ratio of persons 0 to 19 years old per 100 persons 20 to 64 years old]

Total U. S.: 59 per 100

Legend

80 or more
70–79
60–69
50–59
40–49

Note: Based on data in appendix table E–1.

FIGURE 8.—MEDIAN FAMILY INCOME IN 1949, BY STATES: 1950

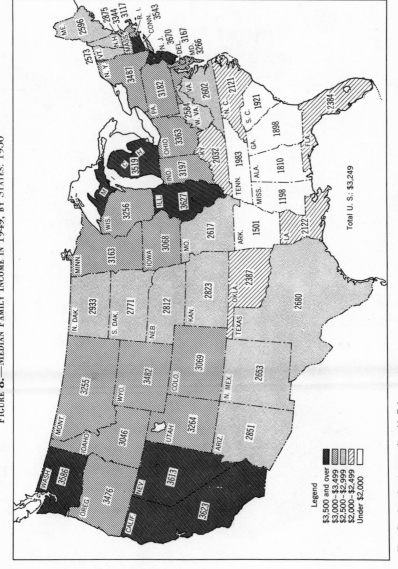

Legend
$3,500 and over
$3,000–$3,499
$2,500–$2,999
$2,000–$2,499
Under $2,000

Total U. S.: $3,249

Note: Based on data in appendix table E-1.

FIGURE 9.—EXPENDITURES PER PUPIL IN AVERAGE DAILY ATTENDANCE IN FULL-TIME PUBLIC
ELEMENTARY AND SECONDARY SCHOOLS, BY STATES: 1949–1950

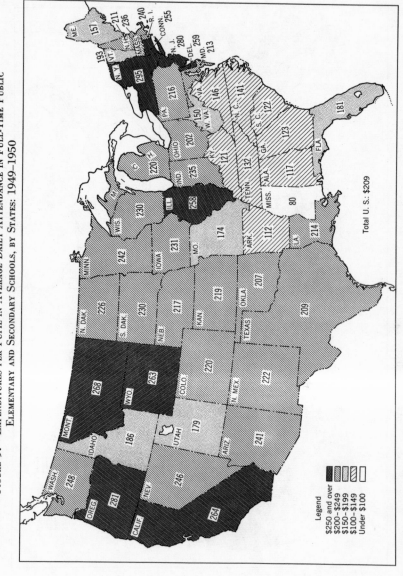

Legend

$250 and over
$200–$249
$150–$199
$100–$149
Under $100

Total U. S.: $209

Note: Based on data in appendix table E–1.

In comparing figures 7 and 8 it is evident that, generally, in those States where childhood dependency is greatest, median family income is lowest; that is, where the demographic burden is heaviest, the economic supporting capacity is least.

Of course, there is only an indirect relationship between income as conceived above and resources for tax purposes from which school funds must be drawn. Variations in actual school expenditures are given in figure 9, where, again, the South–non-South dichotomy is immediately apparent. In the Southern States of high demographic dependency and low income occur also the lowest expenditures per pupil attending public schools. The State of Mississippi spends less than $80 annually per pupil attending its public schools. Relatively low expenditures are also found in Arkansas, Alabama, Georgia, South Carolina, Kentucky, Tennessee, North Carolina, and Virginia, where less than $150 per year is spent on each pupil. West Virginia, Missouri, and Florida, Idaho and Utah, Maine and Vermont provide between $150 and $200 a year for each pupil attending their public schools. The remaining thirty-two States of the Nation expend from $200 to $300 per pupil in public school attendance. These expenditures range from $207 and $209 in Oklahoma and Texas to $295 in New York.

The unequal school opportunities, resulting in large measure from inequalities in dependency burdens and economic resources, as suggested by these illustrative materials, are further evidenced in figure 10, showing the relative educational performances of youths enrolled in school. Again the Nation is divided into a South–non-South dichotomy: Retardation in the age-grade progress of boys 14 to 17 years old is higher in the South than in the other States of the Nation. In Mississippi alone, 45 percent of the young boys of these ages who are enrolled in school are more than one grade behind their expected age-grade position.[4] Throughout the other States of the South, with the exception of Oklahoma and Florida, retardation of two or more grades in age-grade progress varies from 20 to 40 percent of the total youths enrolled in school. That is, 20 to 40 percent of the school boys in these States are enrolled in grades which are two or more behind those of the average of their age mates throughout the Nation. This high rate of retardation contrasts with such relatively low rates as 4 percent in Nebraska, 14 percent in Oklahoma and Maine, and 19 percent in Florida.

In relating school performance to childhood dependency burdens we find that there is a decided tendency for high retardation in school progress to occur in those States where dependency is high, although Idaho and Utah provide evidence that high childhood dependency loads need *not* be

---

[4] Established on the basis of expected age-grade positions of males 14 to 17 years old in the United States as a whole. See Appendix B.

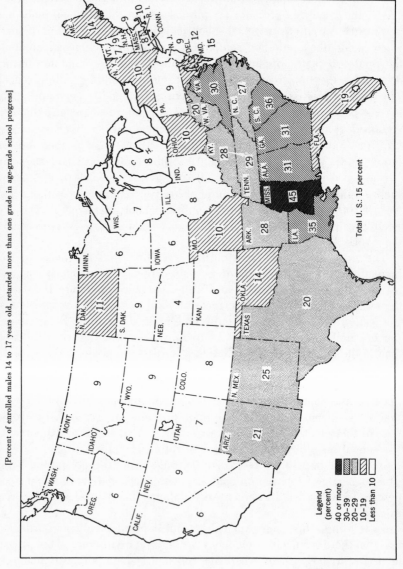

FIGURE 10.—RETARDATION IN SCHOOL PERFORMANCE FOR MALES 14 TO 17 YEARS OLD: 1950

[Percent of enrolled males 14 to 17 years old, retarded more than one grade in age-grade school progress]

Total U. S.: 15 percent

Legend
(percent)
40 or more
30–39
20–29
10–19
Less than 10

Note: Based on data in appendix table E-1.

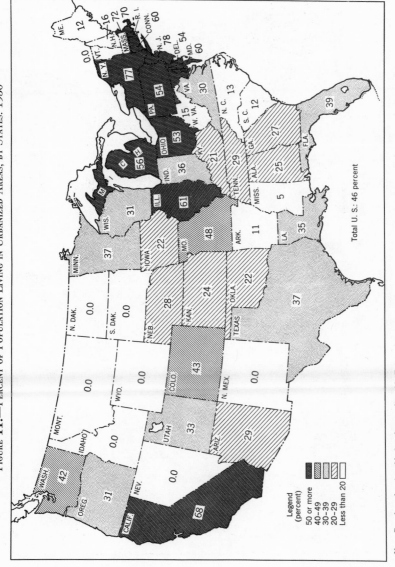

FIGURE 11.—PERCENT OF POPULATION LIVING IN URBANIZED AREAS, BY STATES: 1950

Legend
(percent)

50 or more
40–49
30–39
20–29
Less than 20

Total U. S: 46 percent

Note: Based on data in table 9 and appendix table E-1.

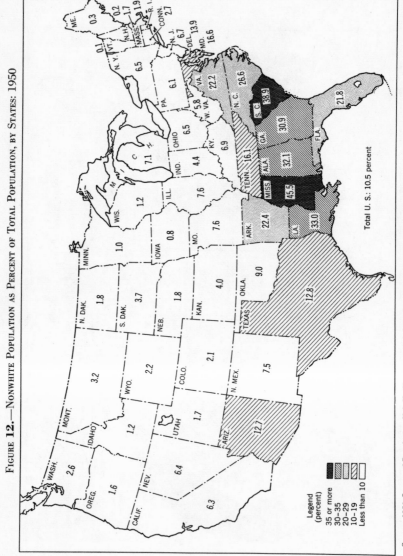

FIGURE **12.**—NONWHITE POPULATION AS PERCENT OF TOTAL POPULATION, BY STATES: 1950

Total U. S.: 10.5 percent

Legend
(percent)

35 or more
30–35
20–29
10–19
Less than 10

Source: *1950 Census of Population, Vol. II, Characteristics of the Population, Part 1, U. S. Summary,* table 59.

accompanied by high retardation in educational performance. Though dependency is high in these States, family income is also high. In the southern belt, high dependency and high retardation are accompanied by low family incomes. The level of school expenditures per pupil is also higher in the States of Idaho and Utah than throughout most of the Southern States.

That inequalities in State dependency loads and economic resources are, in part, a function of variations in degree of urbanization is suggested in figure 11. In those States where a large proportion of the population reside in urbanized areas[5] childhood dependency burdens tend to be low. This relationship between low demographic dependency and high urbanization occurs in fourteen States (Connecticut, Massachusetts and Rhode Island, New York, New Jersey and Pennsylvania, Maryland and Delaware, Ohio, Michigan, Illinois and Missouri, and Washington and California). Exceptions occur in Oregon, for example, where both the percentage of population living in urbanized areas and the dependency ratio are below the national averages and in Colorado where relative urbanization and dependency are high.

The southern belt of high demographic dependency and low financial supporting capacity is also characterized by a high percentage of total population which is nonwhite. The population of Mississippi is 45 percent nonwhite and the populations of South Carolina, Georgia, Alabama, and Louisiana are between 30 and 40 percent nonwhite (figure 12). These same five States rank among the highest with respect to dependency and retardation and among the lowest with respect to income. The nonwhite populations in States outside of the South comprise only small proportions of their total populations (less than 10 percent).

Generally, as is indicated in figures 7–12, those states of the Nation which are characterized by high dependency ratios may also be characterized by low family income, low expenditures for schooling, a low degree of urbanization, and poor educational performance. Streams of migration from the states of comparative disadvantage (previously centered in the South) to areas of relatively greater opportunity make the differences in the training and welfare services offered to young people a matter of nationwide concern. To the extent that public support for educational and welfare programs is derived chiefly from state resources, these differences among the Nation's children and youth are likely to persist. The exceptions are few in number. The chief exception, illustrating the influence of other factors, is the case of Utah. It has one of the highest dependency ratios among the states. Its average family income is about at the national average, but it is below the national average in relation to expenditures per pupil and to the extent of urbanization. However, it has one of the lowest scores on the retardation index that is used here.

---

[5] For definition see *1950 Census of Population*, Vol. II, *Characteristics of the Population*, Part 1, U. S. Summary, Introduction, pp. 21–22.

A summary of the interstate variations and the interrelations among the above-discussed items as well as others is presented in table 9, in the form of product moment correlations. It is again evident from examination of these data that high dependency loads are correlated with low family income ($r_{1.3} = -.75$), low expenditures for schooling ($r_{1.5} = -.73$), low degree of urbanization ($r_{1.14} = -.71$), high retardation in school performance ($r_{1.6} = .70$), high percentage failure in the AFQT literacy test ($r_{1.7} = .64$), poor housing conditions ($r_{1.11} = .78$, $r_{1.13} = .82$), and, of course, high fertility ($r_{1.15} = .92$).

TABLE 9.—INTERCORRELATIONS OF 16 VARIABLES FOR THE 48 STATES

Identification of variable	Identification of variable															
	1	2	3	4	5	6	7	8	9	10	11	12	13	14	15	16
1.........	...	-.75	-.45	-.50	-.73	.70	.64	.47	.32	.02	.78	-.66	.82	-.71	.92	-.36
2.........	-.75	...	.71	.58	.88	-.84	-.84	-.23	-.23	.24	-.89	.50	-.71	.47	-.54	.08
3.........	-.45	.71	...	.55	.59	-.73	-.75	.00	-.16	.33	-.64	.05	-.45	.12	-.20	.20
4.........	-.50	.58	.55	...	.54	-.72	-.66	.05	-.20	.33	-.60	.15	-.61	.20	-.31	.49
5.........	-.73	.88	.59	.54	...	-.76	-.75	-.18	-.20	.15	-.79	.42	-.59	.40	-.50	.13
6.........	.70	-.84	-.73	-.72	-.76	...	.94	.06	.10	-.47	.92	-.28	.80	-.29	.43	-.49
7.........	.64	-.84	-.75	-.66	-.75	.94	...	.00	.07	-.48	.88	-.24	.72	-.22	.34	-.45
8.........	.47	-.23	.00	.05	-.18	.06	.00	...	.77	.31	.27	-.66	.30	-.63	.64	.06
9.........	.32	-.23	-.16	-.20	-.20	.10	.07	.77	...	.05	.19	-.39	.18	-.42	.41	.04
10.........	.02	.24	.33	.33	.15	-.47	-.48	.31	.05	...	-.37	-.30	-.25	-.26	-.29	.37
11.........	.78	-.89	-.64	-.60	-.79	.92	.88	.27	.19	-.37	...	-.49	.86	-.47	.55	-.39
12.........	-.66	.50	.05	.15	.42	-.28	-.24	-.66	-.39	-.30	-.49	...	-.56	.84	-.73	-.02
13.........	.82	-.71	-.45	-.61	-.59	.80	.72	.30	.18	-.25	.86	-.56	...	-.52	.67	-.57
14.........	-.71	.47	.12	.20	.40	-.29	-.22	-.63	-.42	-.26	-.47	.84	-.52	...	-.81	.02
15.........	.92	-.54	-.20	-.31	-.50	.43	.34	.64	.41	-.29	.55	-.73	.67	-.81	...	-.19
16.........	-.36	.13	.20	.49	.13	-.49	-.45	.06	.04	.37	-.39	-.02	-.57	.02	-.19	...

Identification of variable:
1. Persons under 20 years old per 100 persons 20 to 64 years old.
2. Median family income.
3. Median grade of school completed by persons 25 years old and over.
4. Percent of persons 5 to 19 years old enrolled in school.
5. Current expenditure (excluding interest) per pupil in average daily attendance in full-time public elementary and secondary day schools, 1949–50.
6. Percent of enrolled males 14 to 17 years old retarded more than one grade in age-grade school progress.
7. Percent of selective service registrants who failed Armed Forces Qualification Test, July 1950–June 1951.
8. Percent of persons 14 and 15 years old in the labor force.
9. Percent of persons 16 and 17 years old in the labor force.
10. Percent of dwelling units which are owner occupied.
11. Percent of dwelling units which are dilapidated.
12. Percent of dwelling units with television.
13. Percent of dwelling units with 1.51 or more persons per room.
14. Percent of population living in urbanized areas.
15. Persons under 5 years old per 100 women 20 to 44 years old.
16. Persons 65 years old and over per 100 persons 20 to 64 years old.

Source: See appendix table E-1.

Interstate variations in the educational attainment of adults, in the labor force participation of young teen-agers, in the extent of owner-occupied dwellings, and in aged dependency are not highly correlated with variations in child and youth dependency.[6] The product moment correlation between dependency and the educational attainment of adults indicates

---

[6] Of peripheral interest may be the high negative correlation between the percentage of dwelling units with television and childhood dependency ($r_{1.12} = -.66$). Further examination of this relationship shows that it is due, to a large extent, to the high correlation between urbanization and television ($r_{12.14} = .84$).

that where dependency is high the attainment levels of adults tend to be low, but the degree of the relationship is not very high ($r_{1.13} = -.45$). Though we would expect young teen-agers to enter the labor force more readily in States where the dependency ratio is high, product moment correlations between the variables (dependency and participation of 14- and 15-year-olds and dependency and participation of 16- and 17-year-olds) are positive but small: $r_{1.8} = .47$ and $r_{1.9} = .32$. It is apparent from an examination of the inter-correlations of labor force participation and the other variables presented that economic activity on the part of young teen-agers is to a considerable extent a function of ruralization, which cuts across State lines and thus is not reflected in these correlations.[7]

Examination of the intercorrelations of those variables which are highly correlated with childhood dependency presents a familiar picture:

Where income is high and dependency is low, public expenditures for schooling tend to be relatively high, housing conditions are relatively good, and the educational performance of young people is good. Where income is low and childhood dependency high, expenditures for schooling are low; housing conditions are poor; enrollment rates tend to be low; and the educational performance of young people is startlingly poor.

The relationship among States between family income and school funds is of course high and positive ($r_{2.5} = .88$), and where each of these is high, retardation in school performance and failure in a general literacy test are low: $r_{2.6} = -.84$, $r_{2.7} = -.84$, $r_{5.6} = -.76$ and $r_{5.7} = -.75$. Furthermore, retardation is highly and positively correlated with housing dilapidation ($r_{6.11} = .92$) and overcrowding ($r_{6.13} = .80$). Poor housing, in turn, is part of that matrix of factors comprising low income ($r_{11.2} = -.89$, $r_{13.2} = -.71$), low school expenditures ($r_{11.5} = -.79$, $r_{13.5} = -.59$), and high fertility ($r_{11.15} = .55$ and $r_{13.15} = .67$).

Such a matrix of interrelated components is well known, and the meaning is significant. With a high ratio of children to adults and a low income for family units, people can hardly afford to keep their children in well-equipped schools and to support other necessary services for health, recreation, protection, etc. A penalty is paid in the form of lost opportunities for social and economic advancement. Dependent students may be regarded as assets, the value of which, in regard to their potential future productivity, increases with each addition to their care and schooling. States, and other communities of the Nation, cannot offer equal opportunities to their children; those States which can afford the least carry the heaviest dependency loads.

Although considerable progress has been made in the past decade or more in reducing these dependency–resources inequalities (many States in

---

[7] See Chapter 8 for an analysis of demographic factors related to the labor force participation of young people.

the Rocky Mountain and Great Plains areas and some in the South have undertaken additional financial responsibility for their schools), it is clear from the data presented that equitable schooling opportunity among States still does not exist.

CHAPTER 4

LIVING AND FAMILY ARRANGEMENTS

A. Living arrangements

Almost all children under 18 years of age (98 percent or 36.7 million) were living with one or both parents or other relatives in 1950. About 800,000 children were not living with relatives, but as foster children, institutional residents, etc.[1] Among children who were living in households about 90 percent were living with one or both parents, 5 percent with one or both grandparents and about 2 percent were residing with other relatives (table 10). A larger proportion of younger children than older ones were residing with grandparents.

A considerably larger percent of nonwhite than white youngsters were living with relatives other than parents (20 percent as compared with 6 percent), reflecting chiefly the continued importance of the Negro grandmother in the rearing of children.[2] The tendency of children to be living with relatives other than parents is discernibly greater in rural-farm than in either rural-nonfarm or urban areas.

The vast majority of children under 18 (94 percent) who were living with one or both parents had a home in which no in-laws or other persons outside the immediate family resided. However, there were over 2.5 million children whose parents shared their residences with other persons, primarily relatives (table 11). Among the 45 million children who were living with parents, about 90 percent (40.5 million) were living with both parents, 1 percent (700,000) with the father only, and 8 percent (3.4 million) with the mother only.[3]

B. Broken families

Though the family as an institution has changed in many respects in the past several decades, it is still regarded as the central mechanism for the transmission of culture and as the most practical means of caring for chil-

---

[1] U. S. Bureau of the Census, *Current Population Reports*, Series P-20, No. 32, table 3.

[2] E. Franklin Frazier states, "The Negro grandmother's importance is due to the fact . . . that she has been the 'oldest head' in a maternal family organization," and furthermore, that, "The Negro grandmother has not ceased to watch over the destiny of the Negro families as they have moved in ever increasing numbers to the cities. . . ." *The Negro Family in the United States*, University of Chicago Press, Chicago, 1939, pp. 153 and 159.

[3] Metropolitan Life Insurance Company, *Statistical Bulletin*, Vol. 36, No. 2, February 1955, p. 5, reports that in 1953 there were 7 million children living with only one parent or with neither parent.

dren until they may assume their responsibilities in adult society.[4]   Generally, to fulfill this purpose a division of labor of family members is required, with the husband-father as provider and the wife-mother as homemaker.   Circumstances which interfere with or alter the performance of these roles often create problems which not only threaten the survival of the family but also give rise to problems of adjustment for the children.[5]

TABLE **10.**—PERCENT DISTRIBUTION OF CHILDREN UNDER 18 YEARS OLD IN HOUSEHOLDS BY RELATIONSHIP TO HEAD, BY AGE AND COLOR, URBAN AND RURAL: 1950

Area, age, and color	Total	Head or wife of head	Child	Grand-child	Other relative	Lodger	Resident employee
UNITED STATES							
All Classes							
Total, under 18 years....	100.0	0.3	90.8	5.8	2.2	0.8	0.1
Under 5 years................	100.0	...	89.4	8.1	1.6	0.8	...
5 to 9 years.................	100.0	...	92.0	5.6	1.6	0.7	0.1
10 to 14 years...............	100.0	0.1	92.3	4.1	2.6	0.8	0.1
15 to 17 years...............	100.0	2.3	88.7	3.0	4.3	1.4	0.3
White							
Total, under 18 years....	100.0	0.3	92.5	4.7	1.7	0.7	0.1
Under 5 years................	100.0	...	91.4	6.8	1.1	0.6	...
5 to 9 years.................	100.0	...	93.7	4.5	1.2	0.6	...
10 to 14 years...............	100.0	0.1	94.0	3.2	2.0	0.7	0.1
15 to 17 years...............	100.0	2.3	90.1	2.4	3.7	1.2	0.3
Nonwhite							
Total, under 18 years....	100.0	0.4	78.1	13.5	6.0	2.0	0.1
Under 5 years................	100.0	...	74.5	18.0	5.2	2.2	0.1
5 to 9 years.................	100.0	...	79.7	13.7	5.0	1.5	0.1
10 to 14 years...............	100.0	0.1	81.2	10.4	6.5	1.7	0.1
15 to 17 years...............	100.0	2.5	78.2	7.3	9.0	2.7	0.3
URBAN							
Total, under 18 years....	100.0	0.3	90.6	5.8	2.3	1.0	...
Under 5 years................	100.0	...	89.2	8.1	1.7	1.0	...
5 to 9 years.................	100.0	...	91.9	5.6	1.7	0.8	...
10 to 14 years...............	100.0	0.1	92.3	4.0	2.7	0.9	...
15 to 17 years...............	100.0	2.1	88.9	2.9	4.5	1.5	0.1
RURAL NONFARM							
Total, under 18 years....	100.0	0.4	91.6	5.2	2.0	0.7	0.1
Under 5 years................	100.0	...	91.1	6.9	1.4	0.5	0.1
5 to 9 years.................	100.0	...	92.9	5.0	1.4	0.6	0.1
10 to 14 years...............	100.0	0.1	92.8	4.0	2.4	0.7	0.1
15 to 17 years...............	100.0	3.4	87.8	3.1	4.2	1.1	0.2
RURAL FARM							
Total, under 18 years....	100.0	0.3	90.2	6.5	2.2	0.6	0.2
Under 5 years................	100.0	...	87.7	10.1	1.7	0.4	0.1
5 to 9 years.................	100.0	...	91.2	6.5	1.6	0.5	0.1
10 to 14 years...............	100.0	0.1	92.3	4.5	2.3	0.7	0.1
15 to 17 years...............	100.0	2.0	89.0	3.1	3.9	1.2	0.6

Source: Derived from *1950 Census of Population*, Vol. II, *Characteristics of the Population*, Part 1, U. S. Summary, table 107.

---

[4] There is considerable literature covering a vast area of information, knowledge, and opinion on this topic.   See for example, Willard Waller, *The Family—A Dynamic Interpretation*, Revised by Reuben Hill, The Dryden Press, New York, 1951; Robert E. L. Faris, "Interaction of Generations and Family

TABLE **11.**—HOUSEHOLD STATUS OF CHILDREN UNDER 18 YEARS OLD LIVING WITH ONE
OR BOTH PARENTS: 1950

Household status[1]	All children living with one or both parents (thousands)	Percent living with--		
		Both parents	Father only	Mother only
Total....................................	44,623	90.8	1.5	7.7
Parents with own household....................	41,986	93.1	1.3	5.7
Parents without own household.................	2,637	54.7	5.6	39.7
In families................................	268	63.8	3.7	32.5
In subfamilies.............................	2,369	53.7	5.9	40.5

[1] Children living with "parents with own household" are children in primary families; the father or mother is head of the household. Children living with "parents without own household" are children in secondary families (unrelated to household head) or in subfamilies (related to household head).

Source: U. S. Bureau of the Census, *Current Population Reports*, Series P–20, No. 32, "Children and Youth: 1950," table 13.

In 1950 there were over 2.5 million children under 18 years of age who lived in families which had been broken by widowhood and divorce (1.7 million by widowhood and 900,000 by divorce) and whose parents had not yet remarried. In addition there were 1.5 million children who were living with one parent apart from the other parent for reasons including separation because of marital discord, service in the Armed Forces, civilian employment elsewhere, and extended hospitalization.[6] About 400,000 married parents were living apart; 75 percent of these were separated because of marital discord.[7]

Of the 37.5 million families in the United States whose head had ever married, less than 20 million, about 53 percent, had one or more children under 18 years old in 1950. Approximately 7 percent of these families were broken by widowhood, divorce, or separation (table 12). Widowhood accounted for the largest single proportion of broken families (45 percent), although the combined reasons of divorce and separation due to marital discord represent an approximately equal magnitude (42 percent). The increasing role of divorce and separation in the incidence of broken families is revealed in a comparison of these data with similar data for 1930.

Stability," *American Sociological Review*, Vol. XII, No. 2, April 1947, pp. 159–164; Ray H. Abrams, (Ed.) "The American Family in World War II," *The Annals of the American Academy of Political and Social Science*, Vol. 229, September 1943; Paul C. Glick, *American Families*, John Wiley and Sons, 1957.

[5] For example, the relationship of broken homes to such problems as juvenile delinquency and child dependency has received much attention for many decades. See for example, Ernest Mowrer, *Family Disorganization*, University of Chicago Press, Chicago, 1927; Clifford Shaw and H. D. McKay, "Social Factors in Juvenile Delinquency" in White House Conference on Child Health and Protection, *The Adolescent in the Family*, D. Appleton-Century Company, New York, 1934, pp. 212–236; T. Earl Sullenger, *Social Determinants in Juvenile Delinquency*, John Wiley and Sons, New York, 1936; James H. S. Bossard, *The Sociology of Child Development*, Harper and Brothers, New York, 1948 and 1954.

[6] U. S. Bureau of the Census, *Current Population Reports*, Series P–20, No. 32, table 13. See also Paul C. Glick, "Population Changes: Their Effect on Children and Youth," paper presented at the Midcentury White House Conference on Children and Youth in Washington, D. C., Dec. 4, 1950 (Mimeographed), p. 10.

[7] *1950 Census of Population*, Vol. IV, *Special Reports*, Part 2, Chapter A, General Characteristics of Families, table 7.

In the earlier decade, more than half (57 percent) of the broken families were the result of widowhood, whereas divorce constituted only 6 percent and separation only 11 percent of the total.[8]

TABLE 12.—BROKEN FAMILIES BY MARITAL STATUS OF HEAD, URBAN AND RURAL: 1950

Area and marital status of head of family	Number (thousands)	Percent distribution		Area and marital status of head of family	Number (thousands)	Percent distribution	
		All families	Broken families			All families	Broken families
UNITED STATES				RURAL NONFARM			
All families with children..........	19,784	100.0	...	All families with children..........	4,270	100.0	...
Both parents present....	18,316	92.6	...	Both parents present....	3,972	93.0	...
Broken families.........	1,467	7.4	100.0	Broken families.........	299	7.0	100.0
Widowed..............	658	3.3	44.9	Widowed..............	152	3.6	50.8
Divorced.............	309	1.6	21.1	Divorced.............	50	1.2	16.7
Separated............	308	1.6	21.0	Separated............	51	1.2	17.1
Spouse absent........	192	1.0	13.1	Spouse absent........	46	1.1	15.4
URBAN				RURAL FARM			
All families with children..........	12,397	100.0	...	All families with children..........	3,117	100.0	...
Both parents present....	11,367	91.7	...	Both parents present....	2,979	95.6	...
Broken families.........	1,030	8.3	100.0	Broken families.........	139	4.4	100.0
Widowed..............	419	3.4	40.7	Widowed..............	88	2.8	63.3
Divorced.............	247	2.0	24.0	Divorced.............	12	0.4	8.6
Separated............	239	1.9	23.2	Separated............	19	0.6	13.7
Spouse absent........	125	1.0	12.1	Spouse absent........	20	0.6	14.4

Source: Derived from *1950 Census of Population*, Vol. IV, *Special Reports*, Part 2, Chapter A, General Characteristics of Families, table 7.

The percentage of broken families with children among urban residents is higher than among rural-nonfarm and rural-farm residents: 8 percent as compared with 7 percent and 4 percent, respectively (table 12). Widowhood accounts for the majority of broken homes in both rural areas while in urban areas the combined result of divorce and separation comprise the largest proportion (47 percent) of broken homes with children.

Women bear the major burden of broken homes not only because of their longer length of life but also because children usually remain with the mother when a marriage is disrupted by divorce or separation. Of the total number of disrupted families with children in 1950, 80 percent (involving some 3.4 million children) were headed by women as compared with 700,000 children living with fathers only.[9]

---

[8] It is likely that the figure for "divorced" is an understatement for some of the divorced heads may have reported themselves as "single" or "married, spouse absent." See Mortimer Spiegelman, "The Broken Family—Widowhood and Orphanhood" in Louis I. Dublin (Ed.), "The American People," *The Annals of the American Academy of Political and Social Science*, Vol. 188, November 1936, pp. 117–130. Data on divorce 1920–1950 are presented and analyzed by Mabel A. Elliott, "The Scope and Meaning of Divorce" in Howard Becker and Reuben Hill (Eds.), *Family, Marriage and Parenthood*, D. C. Heath and Company, Boston, 1955, pp. 669–708.

[9] According to a Metropolitan Life Insurance Company report, *op. cit.*, in 1953 there were 4.1 million children living with their mothers only and 600,000 with their fathers only.

From both the social and the individual points of view the number of children in broken families is an important factor in the guiding progress of readjustment. The size of broken families has been found to vary with the reason for disruption.[10] In Spiegelman's earlier study it was found that in the unbroken families 68 percent had one or more dependent children (under 21 years old) and that this magnitude was considerably greater than in any of the various types of broken families. Contrary to this observation, the 1950 data show that only 55 percent of the unbroken families had one or more dependent children (under 18 years old), whereas in families with female heads disrupted by divorce and separation, over 60 percent had one or more dependent children: 63 percent for the divorced group and 65 percent for the separated (table 13). Though the data are not strictly comparable they do suggest that the role of children as restraints upon family disruption has been somewhat weakened.

Only 41 percent of the men separated from their wives had dependent children living with them as compared with 65 percent in the case of wives separated from their husbands, reflecting the tendency of children to remain with their mothers. Among the divorced, the corresponding figures were 47 percent for families with male heads and 63 percent for families with female heads. Roughly the same percentage of families disrupted by widowhood included children under 18 years of age whether the father or the mother was the deceased parent: 22 percent in the former and 25 percent in the latter. In families disrupted by separation due to other than marital discord, again there is a greater tendency for the mother to assume responsibility for the children: 65 percent of such fatherless families had one or more dependent children as compared with 37 percent of the motherless families, reflecting largely the bulk of families disrupted by Armed Forces service and civilian employment elsewhere. Nor are the largest families found invariably in unbroken homes, as observed in some earlier studies.[11]

Among the unbroken families in 1950, only 15 percent included 3 or more children under 18 years old. In contrast, over 20 percent of the families with female heads which had been disrupted by separation contained 3 or more dependent children, suggesting again the weakening role of children as restraints upon family disruption. In addition, 19 percent of the fatherless families which were separated for reasons other than marital discord contained 3 or more children. The smallest families are found among the widowed with male or female heads, for usually widowhood occurs late in the family cycle and often the children have left the parental home and established their own units.[12]

---

[10] Spiegelman, *op. cit.*, pp. 123–125.

[11] Spiegelman, *op. cit.*, p. 125.

[12] Paul C. Glick, "The Family Cycle," *American Sociological Review*, Vol. XII, No. 2, April 1947, pp. 164–174.

TABLE **13.**—PERCENT DISTRIBUTION OF FAMILIES BY NUMBER OF OWN CHILDREN UNDER 18 YEARS OLD, BY MARITAL STATUS AND SEX OF HEAD, URBAN AND RURAL: 1950

Area and number of own children under 18 years old	All families with head ever married	Families with male head ever married					
		Total	Married, wife present	Separated	Other married, wife absent	Widowed	Divorced
United States...........	100.0	100.0	100.0	100.0	100.0	100.0	100.0
No children under 18..........	47.3	46.0	45.3	58.7	61.3	78.1	63.2
1 child under 18.............	21.4	21.6	21.9	19.4	15.5	11.1	20.0
2 children under 18...........	16.8	17.5	17.8	11.2	11.8	5.1	10.9
3 or more under 18............	14.5	14.9	15.1	10.7	11.3	5.6	6.0
Urban....................	100.0	100.0	100.0	100.0	100.0	100.0	100.0
No children under 18..........	49.9	48.5	47.8	61.0	63.0	81.4	65.2
1 child under 18.............	22.1	22.4	22.7	18.7	16.0	9.9	20.1
2 children under 18...........	16.7	17.4	17.7	11.4	12.2	4.4	9.8
3 or more under 18............	11.3	11.6	11.8	8.9	8.9	4.3	4.9
Rural nonfarm..............	100.0	100.0	100.0	100.0	100.0	100.0	100.0
No children under 18..........	43.1	42.0	41.4	49.9	53.8	72.6	53.6
1 child under 18.............	21.3	21.6	21.7	25.2	16.0	13.9	23.1
2 children under 18...........	17.7	18.2	18.5	10.8	13.3	6.0	14.0
3 or more under 18............	17.9	18.2	18.4	14.1	16.9	7.4	9.4
Rural farm.................	100.0	100.0	100.0	100.0	100.0	100.0	100.0
No children under 18..........	41.5	40.5	39.6	59.2	63.6	73.0	66.2
1 child under 18.............	18.2	18.4	18.6	14.7	13.0	12.3	14.6
2 children under 18...........	16.2	16.6	16.9	10.6	8.8	6.5	12.1
3 or more under 18............	24.1	24.5	25.0	15.6	14.6	8.3	7.1

Area and number of own children under 18 years old	Families with female head ever married				
	Total	Separated	Other married, husband absent	Widowed	Divorced
United States...........	100.0	100.0	100.0	100.0	100.0
No children under 18..........	61.7	34.3	34.8	74.7	36.6
1 child under 18.............	18.2	28.1	27.6	12.4	32.7
2 children under 18...........	10.0	16.9	19.0	6.2	17.8
3 or more under 18............	10.1	20.7	18.6	6.6	13.0
Urban....................	100.0	100.0	100.0	100.0	100.0
No children under 18..........	62.6	35.7	37.0	76.8	37.9
1 child under 18.............	18.9	29.1	29.1	12.2	33.7
2 children under 18...........	9.9	16.7	18.6	5.8	17.3
3 or more under 18............	8.6	18.5	15.3	5.1	11.1
Rural nonfarm..............	100.0	100.0	100.0	100.0	100.0
No children under 18..........	57.4	28.7	28.1	69.2	28.5
1 child under 18.............	17.3	24.9	26.4	13.6	27.9
2 children under 18...........	11.0	18.5	21.0	7.3	20.8
3 or more under 18............	14.3	27.9	24.5	9.9	22.8
Rural farm.................	100.0	100.0	100.0	100.0	100.0
No children under 18..........	62.9	27.2	34.1	70.1	36.3
1 child under 18.............	13.4	20.3	17.9	11.7	25.6
2 children under 18...........	8.9	15.1	16.8	7.1	18.1
3 or more under 18............	14.8	37.4	31.2	11.0	20.1

Source: *1950 Census of Population*, Vol. IV, *Special Reports*, Part 2, Chapter A, General Characteristics of Families, table 7.

Invariably, a larger proportion of urban families are among those which have been disrupted for various reasons than of either the rural-nonfarm or rural-farm families. Childless, or with one, two, or three or more dependent

children, the rural-farm family appears to be more stable than corresponding families in either of the other two residential areas.[13]

Further indication that the presence of children does not necessarily act
as a restraint upon family disruption is borne out also in the residential
comparisons.   In urban areas, only 52 percent of the unbroken families
had one or more children under 18 years of age as compared with about
60 percent in each of the rural areas (table 13).   In all three residential
areas a markedly larger proportion of divorced and separated families
headed by women included dependent children.   Among the divorced
families with female heads 63 percent of the urban, 72 percent of the
rural-nonfarm, and 64 percent of the rural-farm cases contained one or
more children under 18 years of age.   Among the fatherless families separated because of marital discord, 64 percent of the urban, 71 percent of
the rural-nonfarm, and 73 percent of the rural-farm families had dependent
children.

The size of families is generally greater in rural-farm areas than in either
of the other two areas and smallest in urban areas.   This residential pattern generally persists among the various types of broken families.   In
almost every type of disrupted family a larger percentage of the rural-farm
families includes three or more dependent children than in either of the
other two areas.[14]   Invariably, a smaller proportion of the urban families
includes three or more children than are corresponding families in either
of the rural areas.

In summary, it might be pointed out again that the child population in
the United States has been experiencing an unprecedented growth and it is
expected to continue to grow.   Concurrently there is an increasing number
of children being reared in disrupted families.   Any break in the home is
likely to be a critical experience in the life of the child.   In some instances
it may draw the remaining members of the family closer together, making
for greater integration.   It is more likely, however, especially in cases of
divorce and separation, to create problems of adjustment for the child (and
parents), often leading to further disintegration of the family unit and
possibly of the personality of the child.   Often, also, a large proportion of
the broken family units are not self-supporting, giving rise to many other
derivative problems.

---

[13] U. S. Bureau of the Census, *Current Population Reports*, Series P–20, No. 32, table 7.   There has
been some discussion, although little evidence points either way, to the effect that whereas the
rural family less frequently ends in disruption, there is a relatively greater lack of psychological and
emotional units in the rural as compared with the city family.   See Paul Landis, *The Adolescent in the
Family*, D. Appleton-Century Company, New York, 1934, p. 250, for further discussion; also A. R.
Mangus, "Personality Adjustment of Rural and Urban Children," *American Sociological Review*, Vol.
XIII, No. 5, October 1948, pp. 566–575.

[14] An exception is noted in separated families with wife absent.   See table 13.

C. Income of families and working mothers

There is considerable evidence demonstrating that families with larger numbers of children tend to be in the lower income brackets than those with fewer children.[15] In 1950, for example, the average number of children per family having children ranged from 2.4 for families with an income of less than $1,000 per year in 1949 to 1.9 where the annual family income was $6,000 or more.[16]

In 1949 the median family income was approximately $3,100. The median income for families with one child approached $3,200 as compared with less than $3,000 for families having three or more children.[17] Over 10 percent of the families with one or two children had incomes exceeding $6,000 in 1949 as compared with 8 percent in families with 3 or more children. At the lower end of the income scale almost 30 percent of the families with 3 or more children had incomes of less than $2,000 in 1949 as compared with 22 percent of the families with only one child.[18]

Figure 13 demonstrates further that the responsibility for rearing children in the United States is unequally distributed. Almost half of the Nation's families had no children under 18 years old living at home in 1950 and half of the children were in one seventh of the families—those families comprising three or more children apiece.

Half of the urban families had no children as compared with 43 percent and 41 percent of the rural-nonfarm and rural-farm families. Forty-three percent of the urban children lived in large families of 3 or more children as compared with 57 percent and 67 percent of the rural-nonfarm and rural-farm children, respectively. About a quarter of the rural-farm families contained 3 or more children as compared with about 10 percent of the urban families.

---

[15] For further discussion and references see United Nations Department of Social Affairs, *The Determinants and Consequences of Population Trends*, A Summary of the Findings of Studies on the Relationships between Population Changes and Economic and Social Conditions, Population Studies No. 17, Chapter V, especially pp. 86–88, United Nations, New York, 1953.

[16] U. S. Bureau of the Census, *Current Population Reports*, Series P–20, No. 32, table 11. Data are not available for examining this relationship while controlling for age of head of family (that is, different stages in the family cycle). However, some recent fertility–income data reveal that the traditional pattern of higher fertility in groups of lower economic position is demonstrated *only* among married women 45 years old and over in 1951. Among women 15 to 44 years old, standardized for age, fertility was quite similar at the various income levels. See U. S. Bureau of the Census, *Current Population Reports*, Series P–20, No. 46, table 4.

[17] U. S. Bureau of the Census, *Current Population Reports*, Series P–20, No. 32, table 11. Median income in 1949 for families having 3 children amounted to $3,185; for families with 4 children, $2,878; for families with 5 children, $2,533; and for families with 6 or more children, $2,175. (*Current Population Reports*, Series P–60, No. 7, table 6.) The total annual cost of the city worker's family (consisting of employed father, housewife not gainfully employed, and 2 children under 15 years old) budget in 34 large cities in 1950 ranged from $3,453 in New Orleans to $3,933 in Milwaukee. (U. S. Department of Labor, Bureau of Labor Statistics, *Family Budget of City Worker*, October 1950, Bulletin No. 1021.)

[18] U. S. Bureau of the Census, *Current Population Reports*, Series P–20, No. 32, table 11. Data for 1952 demonstrate the same pattern of differentials, while showing generally higher income levels. *Current Population Reports*, Series P–60, No. 15, table 4.

FIGURE **13.**—PERCENT OF FAMILIES HAVING AN ESTIMATED PERCENT OF CHILDREN UNDER 18 YEARS OLD IN FAMILIES WITH 1, 2, AND 3 OR MORE CHILDREN, URBAN AND RURAL: 1950

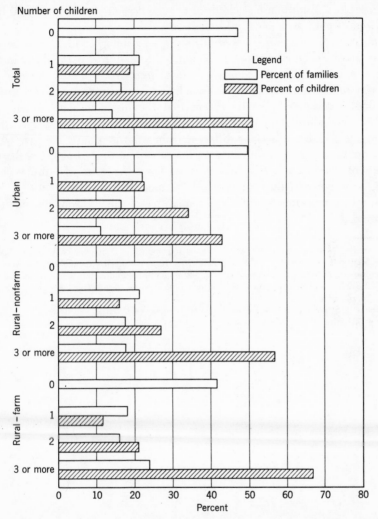

Source: *1950 Census of Population,* Vol. IV, *Special Reports,* Part 2, chapter A, General Characteristics of Families, table 7. Estimates of the number of children in families having 3 or more children were derived on the assumption that the total number of children in families of all sizes would be equal to the totals given in *1950 Census of Population,* Vol. II, *Characteristics of the Population,* Part 1, U. S. Summary, table 107.

Often for the purpose of raising the family income, both parents enter the labor market. In 1950 about 15 percent or approximately 6.5 million children under 18 years old were in families (numbering 7.5 million) where both parents were members of the labor force.[19] About 1.7 million working mothers had children of preschool age (under 6 years old); 2.9 million had children of school age only (6 to 17 years old); and 800,000

---

[19] U. S. Bureau of the Census, *Current Population Reports,* Series P–20, No. 32, table 11.

were mothers of preschool and school age children.[20] In families where the husband was present 1.4 million working mothers had children under 6 years old, 2.2 million had children of school age only, and 650,000 had children of both preschool and school ages.

Undoubtedly the employment of mothers of young children outside the house involves the readjustment of family life patterns, particularly in the care of children. There are many aspects from which to view the absence of the mother from the home and such facts as time and duration are of obvious importance. To the extent that the hours of employment are limited and adjusted to domestic and maternal requirements, the effect upon young children may be different from what is usually the case when working hours are not adjusted to household needs. Furthermore, the effects of the additional income derived from the mother's employment must be weighed against the costs of the mother's absence, as well as the substitute arrangements and the personalities of the children and mothers involved.[21]

---

[20] U. S. Bureau of the Census, *Current Population Reports*, Series P–50, No. 29, table 4. Figures for 1955 indicate some increases in these magnitudes. In husband and wife families there were 2.0 million working mothers with children under 6, 3.2 million with children 6 to 17 only, and 1.1 million with children in both age groups. U. S. Bureau of the Census, *Current Population Reports*, Series P–50, No. 62, table 3.

[21] James H. S. Bossard, in *The Sociology of Child Development*, Harper and Brothers, New York, 1948, p. 381, discusses this further.

CHAPTER 5

SCHOOL ENROLLMENT AND THE EDUCATIONAL ATTAINMENT OF CHILDREN AND YOUTH

A. Trends in school enrollment, 1910 to 1950

Since the turn of the century, and perhaps even earlier, the educational systems of the United States and people's attitudes toward the desirability of education have undergone considerable change. Opportunities for free schooling have increased; better equipped schools have been constructed; the training of school personnel has been expanded and improved upon; schools have assumed an ever-increasing responsibility for many phases of child care, training, and health.

Changes in both the institutional and attitudinal aspects of education parallel the social and economic changes of the time. The rapid development of machine industry which required less child labor, the improved economic status of the American family which facilitated the substitution of schooling for the employment of children, the urbanization of the population, and the rise of science and the growth of new occupations which required advanced training have all led to an approaching realization of the ideal of universal education and longer periods of formal schooling.

The expanding population of the Nation has brought with it great increases in school enrollment. The expansion in the school enrollment of children and youth, however, has far outpaced the increase in their total numbers. While the population aged 5 to 20 years [1] increased by 25 percent (from 29.8 million persons to 37.2 million persons, between 1910 and 1950), the population enrolled in school increased by almost 54 percent (from 17.6 million pupils in 1910 to 27.0 million in 1950) [2] (table 14). As is clearly indicated in table 15, the expansion in school enrollment has resulted not only from an increase in the size of the school age population but also from the fact that a larger proportion of them now attend school; whereas less than 60 percent of the persons aged 5 to 20 years were in school in 1910, about 73 percent were in school in 1950.

---

[1] Before the 1940 Census, enrollment data are available for persons only through 20 years of age. Therefore, for the historical discussions, the school age population is comprised of persons 5 to 20 years of age. In the presentation of the 1950 data which is discussed later, the 5- to 24-year-olds are considered as population of school age.

[2] Excluding kindergarten in 1950. Children enrolled in kindergarten were reported separately in the 1950 Census and were not counted as enrolled in school.

TABLE 14.—PERCENT INCREASE IN THE POPULATION 5 TO 20 YEARS OLD AND IN SCHOOL ENROLLMENT, BY AGE, FOR EACH DECADE, 1910 TO 1950, AND BY AGE AND SEX, 1910 TO 1950

[Minus sign (−) denotes decrease]

Age and school enrollment	1940 to 1950	1930 to 1940	1920 to 1930	1910 to 1920	1910 to 1950		
					Total	Male	Female
POPULATION							
Total, 5 to 20 years old.....	0.3	-3.3	15.4	11.6	25.0	25.6	24.4
5 and 6 years old.................	30.9	-16.4	7.1	15.2	35.0	36.3	33.7
7 to 13 years old.................	6.0	-8.0	12.4	18.2	29.6	30.4	28.7
14 and 15 years old..............	-11.6	3.2	19.7	9.5	19.6	20.6	18.5
16 and 17 years old..............	-14.7	4.9	21.8	4.8	14.3	15.5	13.2
18 to 20 years old...............	-11.6	8.4	23.4	-0.4	17.7	16.4	19.1
ENROLLED IN SCHOOL							
Total, 5 to 20 years old.....	3.0	-2.1	25.6	21.1	53.5	56.1	50.9
5 and 6 years old[1]................	19.6	-16.7	12.8	36.7	53.6	54.8	52.3
7 to 13 years old.................	6.8	-8.3	18.2	24.4	44.0	45.3	42.8
14 and 15 years old..............	-8.6	4.6	33.0	16.7	48.4	50.9	45.9
16 and 17 years old..............	-7.5	25.9	62.4	4.5	97.6	105.5	90.3
18 to 20 years old...............	2.8	19.7	78.8	-3.6	112.2	129.2	95.0
Percent enrolled...........	2.7	1.3	8.7	8.6	22.8	24.2	21.2
5 and 6 years old.................	8.6	-0.5	5.4	18.5	13.6	13.5	14.0
7 to 13 years old.................	0.7	-0.3	5.2	5.2	11.1	11.4	10.9
14 and 15 years old..............	3.4	1.4	11.1	6.5	24.1	25.1	23.1
16 and 17 years old..............	8.4	19.9	33.6	-0.5	72.9	77.9	68.1
18 to 20 years old...............	16.5	10.3	44.6	-2.6	80.9	97.4	63.3

[1] Enrollment figures for the years prior to 1950 include some kindergarten enrollment which is excluded from the 1950 figures.

Source: Derived from *1950 Census of Population*, Vol. II, *Characteristics of the Population*, Part 1, U. S. Summary, table 110.

TABLE 15.—PERCENT OF THE POPULATION 5 TO 20 YEARS OLD ENROLLED IN SCHOOL, BY AGE AND SEX: 1910 TO 1950

Age and sex	1950	1940	1930	1920	1910
Total, 5 to 20 years old.......	72.7	70.8	69.9	64.3	59.2
5 and 6 years old[1]....................	39.3	43.0	43.2	41.0	34.6
7 to 13 years old....................	95.7	95.0	95.3	90.6	86.1
14 and 15 years old..................	93.1	90.0	88.8	79.9	75.0
16 and 17 years old..................	74.5	68.7	57.3	42.9	43.1
18 to 20 years old...................	27.5	23.6	21.4	14.8	15.2
Male, 5 to 20 years old..........	73.4	71.2	70.2	64.1	59.1
5 and 6 years old[1]....................	38.8	42.3	42.5	40.4	34.2
7 to 13 years old....................	95.6	94.8	95.1	90.4	85.8
14 and 15 years old..................	93.1	89.7	88.9	79.5	74.4
16 and 17 years old..................	74.2	68.2	56.5	40.3	41.7
18 to 20 years old...................	30.6	25.7	22.4	14.8	15.5
Female, 5 to 20 years old........	72.0	70.4	69.7	64.5	59.4
5 and 6 years old[1]....................	39.8	43.7	43.9	41.6	34.9
7 to 13 years old....................	95.8	95.2	95.5	90.8	86.4
14 and 15 years old..................	93.1	90.4	88.8	80.4	75.6
16 and 17 years old..................	74.8	69.2	58.0	45.5	44.5
18 to 20 years old...................	24.5	21.6	20.4	14.7	15.0

[1] Enrollment figures for the years prior to 1950 include some kindergarten enrollment which is excluded from the 1950 figures.

Source: Same as table 14.

Increases in both the numbers and proportions of those enrolled in school, 1910 to 1950, occurred in all age groups, although more markedly in the older ones. While the total school age population grew most notably at the younger ages (5 to 6 years and 7 to 13 years), increased enrollment rates have been greatest at the older ages (16 to 17 years and 18 to 20 years). Between 1910 and 1950, for example, the population 7 to 13 years of age[3] increased by 30 percent, and the number enrolled in school increased by 44 percent. Among those 18 to 20 years of age, the population increased by only 18 percent while their school enrollment more than doubled in size (112 percent).

Males contributed more heavily to the increased enrollment at the older ages than did females, a 129 percent growth as compared with a 95 percent growth for males and females, respectively. The greatest change seems to have occurred in the 1920–1930 decade when the school enrollment of the 18- to 20-year-olds increased by almost 80 percent and the proportion attending school increased by almost 45 percent (table 14).

The increased emphasis on schooling at all age levels, and especially at the older ages, is again demonstrated in table 15 and in figure 14 where we find a general and rather consistent tendency toward higher enrollment rates over each decade. The major interruption of this tendency seems to have occurred in the 1910–1920 decade when World War I withdrew from school the older youths who later did not have the benefits of a G.I. Bill.[4]

B. Variations in school enrollment, 1950

Variations by age, sex, and color. School enrollment of young persons of school age is largely dependent upon customs which regulate the issue of who goes to school and for how long and which relate to legal regulations pertaining to school attendance and labor force participation, the necessity and opportunity to find work, the availability of facilities which enable youths to attend school, and progress made in advancing from one grade to the next.

About 28 million persons 5 to 24 years of age were enrolled in the schools of the Nation in April 1950. The number enrolled in 1950 exceeded by approximately 1.4 million the number enrolled in 1940.

As indicated in table 16, over 95 percent of all children 7 to 13 years of age (compulsory school ages in nearly all States) were enrolled in

---

[3] Those aged 5 and 6 years are excluded from more detailed consideration because of the lack of comparability in the figures.

[4] The slightly higher enrollment rates in 1930 as compared with 1940 for the 7- to 13-year-olds in table 15 and the 10-, 11-, 12-, and 13-year-olds in figure 14 may be explained in part by the fact that in the 1940 and 1950 census enumerations the enrollment question referred to a shorter time period (roughly March 1 to April 1 in 1940 and February 1 to April 1 in 1950), and indications are that, particularly in 1940, in some areas many schools closed early because of floods, lack of funds, etc. See *1950 Census of Population*, Vol. II, *Characteristics of the Population*, Part 1, U. S. Summary, Introduction, p. 45, Comparability.

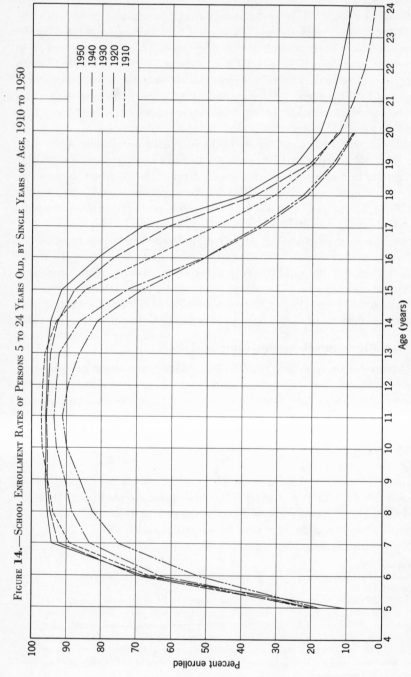

FIGURE 14.—SCHOOL ENROLLMENT RATES OF PERSONS 5 TO 24 YEARS OLD, BY SINGLE YEARS OF AGE, 1910 TO 1950

Source: *1950 Census of Population*, Vol. II, *Characteristics of the Population*, Part 1, U. S. Summary, table 110.

school. Among the 14- and 15-year-olds, 93 percent were enrolled in school. For each succeeding age group enrollment rates dropped sharply. At ages 16 and 17 years, enrollment declined to 75 percent, reflecting the relaxation of compulsory education at these ages and the concomitant increasing eligibility for wider labor force participation. In addition to those who drop out from school, many boys and girls have completed their secondary education at 16 or 17 years of age. Each of these factors is even more pertinent at the older ages.[5]

TABLE **16.**—POPULATION 5 TO 24 YEARS OLD ENROLLED IN SCHOOL, BY AGE, COLOR, AND SEX: 1950

[Numbers in thousands]

Age and school enrollment	All classes			White			Nonwhite		
	Total	Male	Female	Total	Male	Female	Total	Male	Female
POPULATION									
Total, 5 to 24 years old..	46,493	23,297	23,195	40,886	20,567	20,319	5,607	2,730	2,877
5 and 6 years old...........	5,495	2,796	2,699	4,828	2,464	2,365	666	332	334
7 to 13 years old...........	16,778	8,529	8,249	14,690	7,485	7,205	2,088	1,043	1,044
14 and 15 years old........	4,267	2,169	2,099	3,738	1,907	1,830	530	261	268
16 and 17 years old........	4,174	2,109	2,065	3,655	1,855	1,800	519	254	265
18 and 19 years old........	4,342	2,136	2,206	3,836	1,896	1,940	505	240	265
20 to 24 years old.........	11,437	5,559	5,878	10,138	4,960	5,178	1,299	600	700
ENROLLED IN SCHOOL									
Total, 5 to 24 years old..	28,176	14,601	13,575	24,901	12,971	11,930	3,276	1,631	1,645
5 and 6 years old...........	2,159	1,085	1,074	1,901	959	942	258	126	132
7 to 13 years old...........	16,055	8,150	7,906	14,094	7,173	6,920	1,962	976	985
14 and 15 years old........	3,972	2,019	1,953	3,500	1,787	1,713	471	231	240
16 and 17 years old........	3,109	1,566	1,543	2,776	1,404	1,372	334	162	172
18 and 19 years old........	1,401	751	650	1,268	687	581	133	64	69
20 to 24 years old.........	1,480	1,031	449	1,362	960	402	119	72	47
Percent enrolled, 5 to 24 years old...........	60.6	62.7	58.5	60.9	63.1	58.7	58.4	59.7	57.2
5 and 6 years old...........	39.3	38.8	39.8	39.4	38.9	39.8	38.7	38.0	39.5
7 to 13 years old...........	95.7	95.6	95.8	95.9	95.8	96.0	94.0	93.6	94.3
14 and 15 years old........	93.1	93.1	93.1	93.6	93.7	93.6	88.9	88.5	89.6
16 and 17 years old........	74.5	74.2	74.8	76.0	75.7	76.2	64.4	63.8	64.9
18 and 19 years old........	32.3	35.2	29.5	33.1	36.2	29.9	26.3	26.7	26.0
20 to 24 years old.........	12.9	18.5	7.6	13.4	19.4	7.8	9.2	12.0	6.7
ENROLLED IN SCHOOL AND KINDERGARTEN									
Persons 5 and 6 years old:									
Number in kindergarten....	904	461	442	840	430	410	64	32	33
Percent in kindergarten.	16.5	16.5	16.4	17.4	17.4	17.4	9.6	9.5	9.8
Number in school and kindergarten.............	3,063	1,546	1,516	2,741	1,389	1,352	322	158	165
Percent in school and kindergarten...........	55.7	55.3	56.2	56.8	56.4	57.2	48.3	47.6	49.4
Persons 5 to 24 years old:									
Number in school and kindergarten.............	29,080	15,062	14,017	25,741	13,401	12,340	3,340	1,663	1,678
Percent in school and kindergarten...........	62.5	64.7	60.4	63.0	65.2	60.7	59.6	60.9	58.3

Source: Derived from *1950 Census of Population*, Vol. II, *Characteristics of the Population*, Part 1, U. S. Summary, tables 109 and 111.

The percentage of males and the percentage of females under 18 years of age enrolled in school were about the same, but for older groups a con-

[5] For an accounting of the nonschool population of school ages see Appendix A.

siderably higher proportion of males than females were enrolled. With-
drawals from advanced schooling (primarily for the purpose of marriage
and secondarily for entering the labor force) undoubtedly account, in large
part, for the lower enrollment rates among females at these older ages. In
addition, the G.I. Bill and other postwar developments encouraged the con-
tinuation of education among many young men including a sizable group
who otherwise may not have had an opportunity to continue.[6]

Nonwhites at each age level have lower enrollment rates than whites,
with the differences reaching a peak at those ages when labor force participation begins to compete with school enrollment. Almost 95 percent of
white youths 14 and 15 years old were enrolled in school as compared with
less than 90 percent of the nonwhite youths (table 16). Whereas 76 percent of the white youths 16 and 17 years of age were attending school in
1950, only 64 percent of the nonwhite youths were enrolled.

Color differences among males are slightly higher than among the
females, particularly at the college age levels. The differences between the
females at these ages amount to only 4 percent for the 18- and 19-year-
olds and 1 percent for the 20- to 24-year-olds; among the males enrollment
rates differ by 9 percent and 7 percent, respectively, for the two age groups,
pointing to higher rates of labor force participation among nonwhite male
youths.[7] At the earlier ages, color differences in enrollment rates by sex
are less divergent.

Variations by region and rural-urban residence. An inspection of
the variations in school enrollment rates for the four major regions of the
United States portrays primarily a similarity among the three non-South
regions (Northeast, North Central, and West) and a divergence in the
South (table 17). Enrollment rates in the South at each age level are considerably lower than those in other regions; in the three non-South regions,
enrollment rates are generally highest in the West.[8] Aside from the differences among 5- and 6-year-olds which are due primarily to local variations in the legal age for school entrance, the major regional divergences
in school enrollment occur at those ages when the element of compulsory
attendance begins to become weaker. In the South, less than 90 percent
of the young people 14 and 15 years old are enrolled in school, as compared with about 95 percent in areas outside the South. The differences
increase at ages 16 and 17 years: 65 percent in the South as compared with
about 80 percent in the non-South. At the college-age levels, the variations again become smaller, averaging about a 5 percent difference for both
the 18- and 19- and 20- to 24-year-olds.

---

[6] For a further discussion of the war and postwar effects upon advanced education see Dael Wolfle,
America's Resources of Specialized Talents, The Report of the Commission on Human Resources and
Advanced Training, Harper and Brothers, New York, 1954, Chapter III.

[7] See Chapter 7, table 37 and figure 22.

[8] An exception is noted among the 5- and 6-year-olds.

TABLE **17.**—POPULATION 5 TO 24 YEARS OLD ENROLLED IN SCHOOL, BY AGE AND SEX,
FOR REGIONS: 1950

[Numbers in thousands]

Age and school enrollment	Northeast			North Central			South			West		
	Total	Male	Female	Total	Male	Female	Total	Male	Female	Total	Male	Female
POPULATION												
Total, 5 to 24 years old...............	11,114	5,526	5,587	13,250	6,627	6,623	16,373	8,210	8,163	5,756	2,934	2,823
5 and 6 years old.....	1,271	649	622	1,547	789	758	1,956	992	964	720	366	354
7 to 13 years old.....	3,877	1,973	1,905	4,815	2,451	2,363	6,015	3,048	2,967	2,070	1,057	1,014
14 and 15 years old...	986	501	484	1,219	621	598	1,558	789	769	505	256	249
16 and 17 years old...	997	503	494	1,179	596	583	1,511	762	748	487	248	240
18 and 19 years old...	1,057	504	553	1,214	581	632	1,539	772	767	532	279	253
20 to 24 years old....	2,926	1,396	1,530	3,276	1,588	1,689	3,794	1,847	1,947	1,441	729	713
ENROLLED IN SCHOOL												
Total, 5 to 24 years old...............	6,776	3,534	3,242	8,170	4,235	3,936	9,641	4,952	4,689	3,590	1,881	1,708
5 and 6 years old.....	565	286	279	616	309	307	680	339	341	299	151	147
7 to 13 years old.....	3,706	1,884	1,822	4,643	2,361	2,281	5,705	2,884	2,821	2,002	1,020	981
14 and 15 years old...	937	477	459	1,153	588	566	1,398	707	691	483	246	237
16 and 17 years old...	787	398	389	932	468	464	989	493	496	401	206	194
18 and 19 years old...	359	193	165	403	215	188	446	235	211	192	107	85
20 to 24 years old....	422	295	127	423	294	129	423	293	130	213	149	64
Percent enrolled, 5 to 24 years....	61.0	64.0	58.0	61.7	63.9	59.4	58.9	60.3	57.4	62.4	64.1	60.5
5 and 6 years old.....	44.5	44.1	44.9	39.8	39.2	40.5	34.8	34.2	35.4	41.5	41.3	41.5
7 to 13 years old.....	95.6	95.5	95.6	96.4	96.3	96.5	94.8	94.6	95.1	96.7	96.5	96.7
14 and 15 years old...	95.0	95.2	94.8	94.6	94.7	94.6	89.7	89.6	89.9	95.6	96.1	95.2
16 and 17 years old...	78.9	79.1	78.7	79.1	78.5	79.6	65.5	64.7	66.3	82.3	83.1	80.8
18 and 19 years old...	34.0	38.3	29.8	33.2	37.0	29.7	29.0	30.4	27.5	36.1	38.4	33.6
20 to 24 years old....	14.4	21.1	8.3	12.9	18.5	7.6	11.1	15.9	6.7	14.8	20.5	9.0
ENROLLED IN SCHOOL AND KINDERGARTEN												
Persons 5 and 6 years: Number in kindergarten............	286	145	141	358	184	174	98	50	48	163	82	80
Percent in kindergarten..........	22.5	22.3	22.7	23.1	23.3	23.0	5.0	5.0	5.0	22.6	22.4	22.6
Number in school and kindergarten...	851	431	420	974	493	481	778	389	389	462	233	227
Percent in school and kindergarten.	67.0	66.4	67.5	63.0	62.5	63.5	39.8	39.2	40.4	64.2	63.7	64.1
Persons 5 to 24 years: Number in school and kindergarten...	7,062	3,679	3,383	8,528	4,419	4,110	9,739	5,002	4,737	3,753	1,963	1,788
Percent in school and kindergarten.	63.5	66.6	60.6	64.4	66.7	62.1	59.5	60.9	58.0	65.2	66.9	63.3

Source: Derived from *1950 Census of Population*, Vol. II, *Characteristics of the Population*, Part 1, U. S. Summary, tables 150 and 151.

Particularly interesting regional differences occur at ages 5 and 6 years where again we find that the Northeast, West, and North Central Regions have higher school enrollment rates than does the South. If kindergarten enrollment is excluded from consideration, the regional differences vary by 5 to 10 percent with the Northeast exhibiting the highest rates (45 percent) and the South the lowest (35 percent). If kindergarten enrollment is included, the divergence of the South from the other three regions becomes considerably more extreme. Whereas only 40 percent of the 5- and 6-year-olds in the South are enrolled in school and kindergarten, about 65 percent of the children of these ages are enrolled in school and kindergarten in areas outside the South. In the South, only 5 percent of the 5- and 6-year-olds are enrolled in kindergarten, whereas in the other regions over 22 percent are enrolled in kindergarten.[9]

A comparison of enrollment rates by rural-urban residence (table 18) shows that for each age group there is a higher proportion of children and youth in school in urban areas than in either rural-nonfarm or in rural-farm areas and, in turn, for each age group enrollment rates are higher in rural-nonfarm areas than in rural-farm areas. The differences at the compulsory

TABLE 18.—POPULATION 5 to 24 YEARS OLD ENROLLED IN SCHOOL, BY AGE AND SEX, URBAN AND RURAL: 1950

[Numbers in thousands]

Age and school enrollment	Urban			Rural nonfarm			Rural farm		
	Total	Male	Female	Total	Male	Female	Total	Male	Female
POPULATION									
Total, 5 to 24 years old....	27,533	13,483	14,050	10,396	5,315	5,081	8,565	4,500	4,065
5 and 6 years old............	3,151	1,599	1,552	1,301	664	637	1,043	533	509
7 to 13 years old............	9,350	4,720	4,630	3,920	2,002	1,919	3,507	1,807	1,700
14 and 15 years old..........	2,334	1,171	1,164	963	490	473	970	508	462
16 and 17 years old..........	2,333	1,144	1,189	925	472	452	916	492	423
18 and 19 years old..........	2,685	1,235	1,450	932	497	435	724	404	320
20 to 24 years old...........	7,679	3,615	4,065	2,354	1,190	1,164	1,404	755	649
ENROLLED IN SCHOOL									
Total, 5 to 24 years old....	16,540	8,592	7,948	6,191	3,202	2,989	5,445	2,807	2,638
5 and 6 years old............	1,296	651	645	480	242	238	383	192	191
7 to 13 years old............	8,990	4,535	4,455	3,744	1,908	1,836	3,321	1,707	1,614
14 and 15 years old..........	2,217	1,116	1,100	889	454	435	866	448	418
16 and 17 years old..........	1,842	924	917	651	329	322	617	312	304
18 and 19 years old..........	980	518	462	239	135	103	182	98	84
20 to 24 years old...........	1,215	847	368	188	134	54	77	51	26
Percent enrolled, 5 to 24 years old.................	60.1	63.7	56.6	59.6	60.2	58.8	63.6	62.4	64.9
5 and 6 years old............	41.1	40.7	41.6	36.9	36.4	37.4	36.7	36.0	37.5
7 to 13 years old............	96.1	96.1	96.2	95.5	95.3	95.7	94.7	94.5	94.9
14 and 15 years old..........	95.0	95.3	94.5	92.3	92.7	92.0	89.3	88.2	90.5
16 and 17 years old..........	79.0	80.8	77.1	70.4	69.7	71.2	67.4	63.4	71.9
18 and 19 years old..........	36.5	41.9	31.9	25.6	27.2	23.7	25.1	24.3	26.3
20 to 24 years old...........	15.8	23.4	9.1	8.0	11.3	4.6	5.5	6.8	4.0
ENROLLED IN SCHOOL AND KINDERGARTEN									
Persons 5 and 6 years old:									
Number in kindergarten......	747	380	367	113	58	55	45	24	21
Percent in kindergarten...	23.7	23.8	23.6	8.7	8.7	8.6	4.3	4.5	4.1
Number in school and kindergarten....................	2,043	1,031	1,012	593	300	293	428	216	212
Percent in school and kindergarten..............	64.8	64.5	65.2	45.6	45.2	46.0	41.0	40.5	41.7
Persons 5 to 24 years old:									
Number in school and kindergarten....................	17,287	8,972	8,315	6,304	3,260	3,044	5,490	2,831	2,659
Percent in school and kindergarten..............	62.8	66.5	59.2	60.6	61.3	59.9	64.1	62.9	65.4

Source: Same as table 16.

---

[9] These regional differences also hold within each residential group. See *1950 Census of Population*, Vol. IV, *Special Reports*, Part 5, Chapter B, Education, table 1.

school ages are, of course, negligible; they widen at 14 and 15 years of age and reach a peak at ages 16 and 17 when competition between school attendance and labor force participation is at its highest.

With respect to the 5- and 6-year-olds it appears that kindergarten enrollment is largely an urban phenomenon. Almost 25 percent of the urban children of these ages were enrolled in kindergarten as compared with 9 percent of the rural-nonfarm children and only 4 percent of the rural-farm children.

Among males at each age level, enrollment rates in urban areas are higher than those in rural areas, and rural-nonfarm enrollment rates are consistently higher than those in farm areas.[10]   Among females, the residential pattern of enrollment is generally the same with one notable deviation: It appears from the data that rural-farm females are more tenacious in their school enrollment than are the males.   Whereas farm chores are withdrawing young men from school, farm employment opportunities for young women are such that their school enrollment rates remain high.   In urban areas, on the other hand, male rates at each age level above the compulsory school ages exceed female enrollment rates.   In rural-nonfarm areas the differences are less definitive; enrollment rates for those under age 16 are roughly the same for both sexes, at 16 and 17 years old the female rate exceeds the male, and thereafter male rates remain higher.   The very high marriage rates for rural-nonfarm women aged 18 years and over, coupled with a sizable increase in their labor force participation at age 18, may account in large part for the rapid drop in school enrollment.

Summary and conclusions.   In the age range from 7 to 13 years, school enrollment in 1950 was nearly universal, with about 96 percent enrolled in April of that year.   (Almost 99 percent of this group were enrolled in October of the preceding year.)   This may be attributed to compulsory school attendance laws which, in practically all States, encompass these ages.   Among those 14 and 15 years old the enrollment rate was 93 percent, although most State laws on compulsory education allow children who have reached 14 years of age to secure work permits only if they have completed a stipulated minimum education.   Starting with youths 16 and 17 years of age, enrollment rates were lower for each successive age group.

Enrollment rates for males and females were practically the same for all ages under 18 years.   Among youths 18 years old and over, males had substantially higher enrollment reflecting in part veteran enrollment and in part preferential attitudes favoring advanced education for males.

In each of the age groups, the enrollment rate for the white population was higher than that for the nonwhite.   Enrollment rates were most frequently highest in urban areas and lowest in rural-farm areas.   Enrollment in the South was considerably lower than enrollment in other regions of the Nation.

---

[10] College students living at the college are enumerated there.   The fact that there are so few rural-farm college students is reflected in the residential differentials at the upper ages.

Many factors contribute to these sex, color, and residential differentials in enrollment, few of which have received close examination. In one study which examines the relative impact of selected demographic characteristics upon differential school enrollment rates of young persons 14 to 17 years of age,[11] the analyst concluded the following:

1. Labor force participation is the most important single factor differentiating the enrollment rates between the 14- and 15-year-olds and the 16- and 17-year-olds. The effect of this factor upon male enrollment at each age group is greater than upon female enrollment.

2. The greater concentration of nonwhites in the South is the most important single factor differentiating national white-nonwhite enrollment rates. This is true for each age-sex group considered.

3. The greater concentration of nonurban residents in the South is the most important single factor differentiating national rural-urban enrollment rates. This held true for each age-sex group with the exception of the older males (16 and 17 years old). For this group the greater concentration of nonurban residents participating in the labor force is the most important differentiating factor.

4. The higher rate of labor force participation among southern females of these ages is the most important factor differentiating their enrollment rates and those of females of these ages elsewhere in the country.

5. The greater concentration of southern males 14 and 15 years old residing in nonurban areas is the most important factor differentiating the enrollment rates between southern and nonsouthern males of these ages.

6. The greater concentration of southern males 16 and 17 years old who are in the labor force is the most important factor differentiating between southern and nonsouthern enrollment rates for males of these ages.

Thus the choice between remaining in school and participating in the labor force is perhaps the most important single factor affecting the secondary schooling of our young teen-agers. The impact of this choice is reflected in differential school enrollment rates; the resulting picture is a familiar one: High enrollment rates are generally associated with being white, urban, and nonsouthern. Conversely, low enrollment rates and high labor force participation are usually associated with being nonwhite, rural, and southern.

C. Variations in educational attainment, 1950

The average educational attainment[12] of young people in the United States (5 to 24 years old) varies as demographic characteristics and region

---

[11] Murray Gendell, "Demographic Correlates of School Enrollment of Youths, 14–17 Years Old," unpublished paper, Columbia University, Department of Sociology, 1954. Characteristics considered were: color, labor force participation, region, and rural-urban residence. Males and females 14 to 15 years old and 16 to 17 years old were analyzed separately. The definition and derivation of the "impact" measure is the same as that described in Appendix D.

[12] Measured by median grade of school completed.

of residence vary. As shown in table 19, the average attainment of young females exceeds that of males; educational attainment is considerably higher for white children and youth than for the nonwhite; in urban areas, the median grade of school completed is higher than in rural areas; and young persons in the South generally attain markedly lower educational levels than do young people residing in the North and West.

TABLE **19.**—MEDIAN YEARS OF SCHOOL COMPLETED BY THE POPULATION 5 TO 24 YEARS OLD, BY COLOR, RESIDENCE, AND REGION, BY SEX: 1950

Area and color	Male	Female	Area	Male	Female
Total...............	6.6	7.3	Northeast...................	7.4	8.1
			North Central..............	7.2	7.9
White.....................	6.9	7.5	South......................	5.7	6.4
Nonwhite..................	4.9	5.9	West.......................	7.1	7.4
Urban.....................	7.3	8.1			
Rural nonfarm.............	6.1	6.5			
Rural farm................	5.6	5.9			

Source: *1950 Census of Population*, Vol. II, *Characteristics of the Population*, Part 1, U. S. Summary, tables 114 and 153.

The relationship between age and educational attainment for young persons is essentially linear in form, as is depicted in figure 15. The pattern of educational attainment generally involves an increment of about one grade of schooling with each increment of one year of age, starting at ages 6 or 7 years and continuing through age 19. At the older ages there occurs a leveling off or even a slight decline in the attainment level with an increase in age.[13]

Though similar in form, the relationship between educational attainment and age differs among the various population groups. At each single year of age (from ages 7 to 24 years) the attainment level is consistently higher for females than for males (figure 16). Sex differentials in attainment, however, are small, particularly at the earlier ages, tending to increase during the high school years. The relatively greater "backwardness" in school progression and higher drop-out rates among males account in large part for this increasing differential.[14]

Age specific educational attainment levels are considerably higher among white youths, male and female, than among nonwhite youths (figure 16). At the earlier ages the color differences in attainment levels are slight, widening perceptibly with increasing age, reaching an approximate three-year differential at the older ages. Again, greater retardation in school progress and higher drop-out rates among the nonwhite youths largely account for this difference at the older ages.

[13] A partial explanation of this decline may be found in the fact that many of these older persons were attending school when the pressures for drop-out, such as the depression and the war, were greater than now.

[14] See Chapter 6 for further discussion.

FIGURE **15.**—MEDIAN YEARS OF SCHOOL COMPLETED BY PERSONS 7 TO 24 YEARS OLD,
BY SINGLE YEARS OF AGE AND SEX: 1950

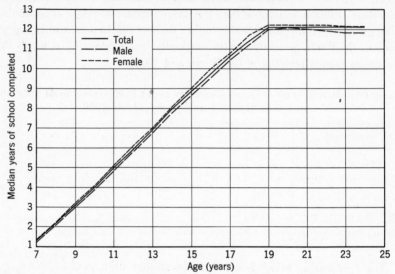

Source: *1950 Census of Population*, Vol. II, *Characteristics of the Population*, Part 1, U. S. Summary, table 114.

FIGURE **16.**—MEDIAN YEARS OF SCHOOL COMPLETED BY PERSONS 7 TO 24 YEARS OLD,
BY SINGLE YEARS OF AGE, COLOR, AND SEX: 1950

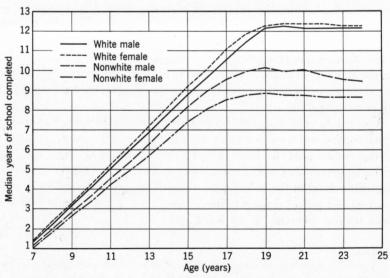

Source: *1950 Census of Population*, Vol. II, *Characteristics of the Population*, Part 1, U. S. Summary, table 114.

In the white and nonwhite population groups, attainment levels for non-white females are higher than for nonwhite males.   However, the sex differentials in educational attainment for white children and youth are considerably smaller than the differentials for the nonwhite group.   For white youths 19 years old, for example, the sex differential in median grade of school completed amounted to only one-tenth of one grade while among nonwhite youths of the same age there was a difference of 1.3 grades.

Urban-rural differences in age specific educational attainment of young people shows that generally the highest attainment levels are achieved by urban residents, for both males and females (figure 17).[15]   In the rural population, higher educational levels were achieved by females, both farm and nonfarm, than by males in either category.   The high levels of attainment among urban children and youth appears to be a function of "urbanness" with only slight sex differences.   In the rural groups educational attainment levels are generally higher for females than for males irrespective of residence, at least among youth of elementary and high school ages (7 to 19 years).

The analysis of regional differences in age specific educational attainment resolves itself largely into a differentiation between the South and the rest of the Nation.   Attainment levels, as measured by median years of school completed, are persistently lower in the South than in any of the regions outside the South (figure 18); the very slight differences among the three non-South regions generally favor the Northeast with attainment levels generally higher than in the other two regions; the North Central States generally show higher levels than the West.[16]

South–non-South differences in attainment levels are small at the younger ages, widening gradually with increasing age.   In the North and West, the sex differentials at each age are consistently small while in the South, sex differences in attainment levels increase slowly with increasing age, maximizing at the post-high school ages.

Tables 20 and 21 summarize the median educational attainment level achieved by 19-year-old youths[17] for the various color, residential, and regional groups for both 1950 and 1940.   From table 20 we see that in the United States in 1950 one half of the 19-year-old population had completed at least a high school education.   Educational attainment for females was slightly higher than for males of the same age.   Although on the aver-

---

[15] See footnote 10.

[16] *1950 Census of Population*, Vol. II, *Characteristics of the Population*, Part 1, U. S. Summary, table 153.

[17] Inspection of figure 15 shows that for the United States population of school age (7 to 24 years), the peak in educational attainment is usually achieved by age 19.   Assuming that children enter school at no later than 7 years of age and that the usual progression through school involves a one-grade advance with a one-year increase in age, age 19 years should represent the completion of twelve grades of school, generally encompassing elementary and high school.

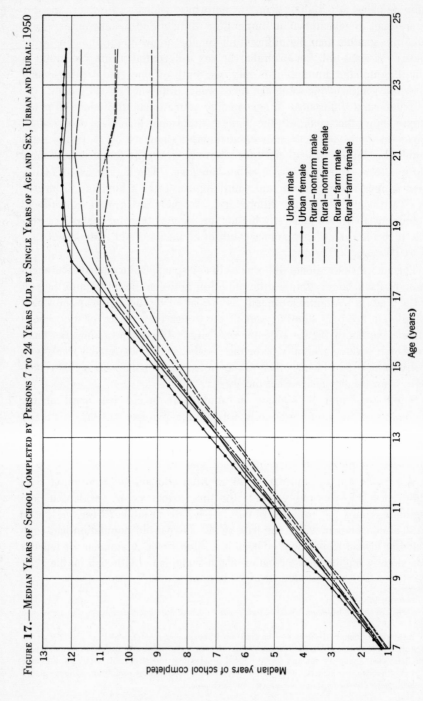

FIGURE 17.— MEDIAN YEARS OF SCHOOL COMPLETED BY PERSONS 7 TO 24 YEARS OLD, BY SINGLE YEARS OF AGE AND SEX, URBAN AND RURAL: 1950

Urban male
Urban female
Rural-nonfarm male
Rural-nonfarm female
Rural-farm male
Rural-farm female

Age (years)

Median years of school completed

Source: 1950 Census of Population, Vol. II, Characteristics of the Population, Part 1, U. S. Summary, table 114.

age (median) white youths had achieved a high school education or better by the time they reached 19 years of age, the achievement level of non-white youths of the same age was strikingly lower; among the nonwhite youths only half of the male 19-year-olds had completed as much as an elementary school education and only half of the females of the same age had completed as much as two years of high school.

FIGURE **18.**—MEDIAN YEARS OF SCHOOL COMPLETED BY PERSONS 7 TO 24 YEARS OLD, BY SINGLE YEARS OF AGE AND SEX, FOR THE SOUTH AND NON-SOUTH REGIONS: 1950

Source: *1950 Census of Population*, Vol. II, *Characteristics of the Population*, Part 1, U. S. Summary, table 153.

TABLE **20.**—MEDIAN YEARS OF SCHOOL COMPLETED BY 19-YEAR-OLDS, BY COLOR AND SEX, URBAN AND RURAL: 1950 AND 1940

Area and year	All classes		White		Nonwhite	
	Male	Female	Male	Female	Male	Female
1950						
Total..................	12.0	12.2	12.1	12.2	8.8	10.1
Urban......................	12.2	12.3	12.3	12.4	10.2	10.9
Rural nonfarm...............	11.1	11.6	11.3	12.0	8.5	10.0
Rural farm.................	9.7	10.9	10.6	11.6	6.8	8.3
1940						
Total..................	11.0	11.8	11.4	12.0	7.3	8.4
Urban......................	11.9	12.1	12.0	12.2	9.2	9.9
Rural nonfarm...............	10.8	11.3	11.1	11.7	7.1	7.9
Rural farm.................	8.9	9.9	9.4	10.8	5.5	6.8

Source: *1950 Census of Population*, Vol. II, *Characteristics of the Population*, Part 1, U. S. Summary, table 114; *1940 Census of Population*, Vol. IV, *Characteristics by Age*, Part 1, U. S. Summary, table 20.

TABLE **21.**—MEDIAN YEARS OF SCHOOL COMPLETED BY 19-YEAR-OLDS, BY COLOR AND SEX,
BY REGIONS: 1950 AND 1940

Region and year	Total		Nonwhite	
	Male	Female	Male	Female
1950				
United States.....................	12.0	12.2	8.8	10.1
Northeast..........................	12.2	12.3	10.6	11.3
North Central.....................	12.2	12.3	10.6	11.3
South..............................	10.4	11.3	8.0	9.4
West...............................	12.1	12.3	11.4	11.5
1940[1]				
United States.....................	11.0	11.8	7.3	8.4
Northeast..........................	11.2	11.9	9.8	10.3
North Central.....................	11.3	12.1	10.0	10.7
South..............................	8.9	9.7	6.5	7.7
West...............................	12.0	12.3	10.9	11.6

[1] The 1940 figures represent the weighted averages of the median year of school completed for the population attending school and the population not attending school.

Source: *1950 Census of Population*, Vol. II, *Characteristics of the Population*, Part 1, U. S. Summary, table 153; derived from *1940 Census of Population*, Vol. IV, *Characteristics by Age*, Part 1, U. S. Summary, tables 37, 38, 41, and 42.

Median educational attainment of 19-year-olds in the four major regions of the United States exceeded twelve years of schooling in all regions but the South. In the South, the median educational attainment level fell below high school completion for both males and females. Educational attainment in the South is one to two years below that of the other regions.

That labor force participation on the part of young people is related to their educational attainment levels is clearly evidenced in table 22. Here we find that the attainment levels for male workers are, in general, appreciably lower than the corresponding levels for males not in the labor force. The reverse is true for females; that is, the median grade of school completed for female workers is generally slightly higher than the corresponding grade for females not engaging in economic activity.[18]

For the 14- and 15-year-old boys there is no difference in the median year of school completed between participants and nonparticipants in the labor force (8.1 years). By the ages of 16 and 17 years, however, the educational attainment for labor force participants (9.2 years) is about one grade lower than for those boys who are not in the labor force (10.1 years). Among the older youths the differences reach one or more grades, with those not engaging in economic activity being favored by higher educational attainment levels.

Among the females of high school age, on the other hand, the differences in the median year of school completed by those who participate in the labor force and those who do not are minimal or none. Among the older girls, however, the data indicate a difference of one half to one year

---

[18] This relationship is regarded from the point of view of the effect of education on labor force participation in Chapter 8.

of schooling, approximately, with labor force participants attaining higher educational levels than those who are not in the labor force.

Interesting deviations from the general pattern occur among nonwhite girls of high school age and southern girls of the same age. In both instances we find that those who work complete fewer years of schooling than those who are not in the labor force. Among the older nonwhite girls and girls residing in the South, attainment levels are greater for labor force participants than for nonparticipants, in keeping with the general pattern among females.

TABLE 22.—MEDIAN YEARS OF SCHOOL COMPLETED BY PERSONS 14 TO 24 YEARS OLD, BY LABOR FORCE PARTICIPATION, AGE, COLOR, AND SEX, BY REGIONS: 1950

Area, age, and color	Male		Female	
	Civilian labor force	Not in labor force	Civilian labor force	Not in labor force
UNITED STATES--TOTAL				
14 and 15 years old......................	8.1	8.1	8.5	8.4
16 and 17 years old......................	9.2	10.1	10.2	10.2
18 and 19 years old......................	10.8	11.8	12.2	11.2
20 and 21 years old......................	11.5	13.2	12.4	11.9
22 to 24 years old......................	11.4	13.4	12.4	11.8
UNITED STATES--NONWHITE				
14 and 15 years old......................	5.7	6.9	6.8	7.5
16 and 17 years old......................	6.9	8.9	8.4	9.3
18 and 19 years old......................	7.8	10.1	10.0	9.8
20 and 21 years old......................	8.3	10.2	10.3	9.7
22 to 24 years old......................	8.3	10.1	10.2	9.1
NORTH AND WEST				
14 and 15 years old......................	8.5	8.4	8.8	8.6
16 and 17 years old......................	9.9	10.2	10.4	10.3
18 and 19 years old......................	11.8	12.0	12.3	11.8
20 and 21 years old......................	12.1	13.4	12.4	12.2
22 to 24 years old......................	12.0	13.8	12.5	12.2
SOUTH--TOTAL				
14 and 15 years old......................	6.9	7.4	7.6	8.0
16 and 17 years old......................	8.0	9.6	9.4	9.7
18 and 19 years old......................	8.8	11.1	11.9	10.4
20 and 21 years old......................	9.4	12.8	12.1	10.5
22 to 24 years old......................	9.7	12.5	12.1	10.3
SOUTH--NONWHITE				
14 and 15 years old......................	5.6	6.5	6.6	7.1
16 and 17 years old......................	6.5	8.4	8.0	8.9
18 and 19 years old......................	7.1	9.8	9.1	9.4
20 and 21 years old......................	7.2	9.8	9.1	9.0
22 to 24 years old......................	7.1	9.2	9.1	8.3

Source: 1950 Census of Population, Vol. IV, Special Reports, Part 5, Chapter B, Education, table 9.

Appreciably greater deviations from the general pattern occur among those nonwhite girls who live in the South, where lower attainment levels for labor force participants are the rule rather than the exception.

The reverse pattern of lower educational attainment for males who participate in labor force activity persists throughout the color and regional variations. A possible exception occurs among 14- and 15-year-old boys residing in the North and West where the data suggest that labor force participants may attain higher educational levels (8.5) than the nonparticipants (8.4).

There has been some overall improvement in the educational attainment of youths in the United States (tables 20 and 21). Between 1940 and 1950 the attainment level of 19-year-old youths increased by about one grade for males and one half grade for females. The greatest advances in attainment occurred in the South and among nonwhite youths. In both groups separately as well as among nonwhites residing in the South there occurred a 1½-grade increase in the attainment level of 19-year-olds between 1940 and 1950.

Other notable increases have occurred among the rural-farm youth and young males in the North; for each the attainment level for the 19-year-olds increased by one grade during the decade.

The overall picture for the decade reflects a general striving toward at least a high school education, with the greatest improvements occurring among those groups which were farthest from this goal in 1940 and the least advancement occurring in those areas where the goal had been achieved by 1940 (in the West and among urban groups).

D. Student labor force[19]

About one in every eight students of high school age was working after school hours in 1950, as compared with only one in twenty-five in 1940. In April of 1950 about 919,000 boys and girls 14 to 17 years old were both enrolled in school and in the labor force, with 840,000 employed and 79,000 looking for work.[20] In 1940 when part-time employment for inexperienced minors was rather scarce only 300,000 students in this age group were in the labor force.[21]

The increase in student workers during the decade 1940 to 1950 occurred at the time when high school enrollment was declining. During the decade the population of high school age and, consequently, the numbers enrolled in school declined markedly—as a result of the low birth rate of the depression years. Thus the increase in the student labor force took place within a smaller student population.

The rise in the proportion of student workers of high school age marks a sharp reversal in the historic downward trend in student labor force activity. From 1900 to 1940 the proportion of teen-age persons in the labor force dropped by about one fourth[22] which was due in part to the adoption and enforcement of child labor and compulsory school attendance

[19] Detailed discussions of the student labor force may be found in Chapter 7, section C.

[20] *1950 Census of Population*, Vol. II, *Characteristics of the Population*, Part 1, U. S. Summary, table 122.

[21] U. S. Bureau of the Census, *Current Population Reports*, Series P–50, No. 23.

[22] See Chapter 7, table 36.

laws. The increase in labor force participation of young people since 1940 has not been at the expense of school enrollment, enrollment rates having been higher in 1950 than in 1940 (table 15).

Student workers of college age also showed an appreciable increase between 1940 and 1950. About 33 percent of the students 18 to 24 years of age were in the labor force in 1950 as compared with 20 percent in 1940.

E. Projections of school enrollment, 1953 to 1965

In the past several years, as a result of the birth boom during the war and early postwar periods, much concern has been expressed regarding the facilities provided by the Nation's schools and the problems of additional facilities to absorb the anticipated increases in enrollment. Projections of these increases in the elementary and high schools, by grade, for the United States as a whole for the period 1953 to 1965, have been prepared by the Bureau of the Census.[23]

These projections indicate that enrollment in our elementary and high schools is expected to increase by more than 1.3 million persons annually, an increase of 4 percent per year up to at least 1959 (table 23). The major burden of the increases will be in the elementary grades for the next few years, although high school enrollments will increase at a considerable rate. Elementary enrollments will reach about 30 millions in 1959 as compared with 23 millions in 1953. During the same period high school enrollments will increase from about 7 million to 9 million.

It is estimated, however, that high school enrollment will increase by approximately 3 percent annually from the middle of the decade through 1964, with the peak growth occurring in the early 1960's. Thus we can expect the large elementary school population of the present decade to advance into the high school grades so that for every three pupils now enrolled in high school there will be four enrolled in 1960 and five by 1965.

Projections for elementary school enrollment after 1959 cannot be estimated with any degree of confidence since they would reflect changes in the cohorts of persons yet to be born. However, on the basis of three different assumptions concerning future fertility[24] we find comparatively little change in elementary school enrollment for the early years of the 1960 decade.

The interest and concern in the sheer numbers of future students and the facilities available to them also involves those in higher education.[25] Past trends in the year-by-year totals of the number of persons who were attend-

---

[23] U. S. Bureau of the Census, *Current Population Reports*, Series P–25, No. 85.

[24] The specific assumptions are given in the footnotes of table 23.

[25] See, for example, National Education Association, *NEA Journal*, "A Symposium—Not a Moment to Lose," November 1954, pp. 492–493.

ing the Nation's colleges and universities have been steadily upward and indicate continued growth.   Just how large college enrollments will be in the future will depend upon the number of young people of college age and upon the complex of factors which determines the percentage which goes to college.   The college age population can be projected quite accurately for it involves the aging of cohorts already born.   The college age population was decreasing in the early 1950's.   For some years it will increase very little and then will increase greatly when children born during and after World War II enter the college ages.[26]   What proportion of this expanding group will go to college is affected by many factors: world conditions, military mobilization, student deferment policies, scholarship programs, etc.

There are two sharply contradictory responses to the anticipated growth in college enrollments.   One group is of the opinion that college enrollments should be greatly increased and that administrators must work toward this end.[27]   Another group warns that even the usual trends are likely to produce more college graduates than the Nation's economy could support[28] or more than can be reasonably well educated.[29]

With respect to future manpower resources one analyst summarized that:

> The United States wastes much of its talent.   College graduating classes could be twice as large as they currently are, and with no loss of quality.   The potential supply gets drained off, in large or small amounts, all the way through the educational system.   Practically all potentially good college students enter, and most of them finish high school, but after high school the loss is large.   Fewer than half of the upper 25 percent of all high school graduates ever earn college degrees; only 6 out of 10 of the top 5 percent do.   Society fails to secure the full benefit of many of its brightest youth because they do not secure the education that would enable them to work at the levels for which they are potentially qualified.[30]

He concludes that a nation which has had the ingenuity to eradicate many life-taking diseases, to conquer the air, to achieve a higher standard of living than has ever existed before in the world can surely overcome the barriers of doubt, unequal opportunity, financial handicap, and inadequate motivation and education which interfere with the fullest development of its talent and leadership.[31]

[26] Dael Wolfle, *America's Resources of Specialized Talent*, The Report of the Commission on Human Resources and Advanced Training, Harper and Brothers, New York, 1954, p. 269.

[27] President's Commission on Higher Education, *Higher Education for American Democracy*, U. S. Government Printing Office, Washington, D. C., 1947.

[28] Seymour E. Harris, *The Market for College Graduates*, Harvard University Press, Cambridge, 1949.

[29] See comments on paper read by Douglas Bush at Annual Convention of American Council on Education, Chicago, 1954 in: Benjamin Fine, "Education in Review," *The New York Times*, October 17, 1954.

[30] Wolfle, *op. cit.*, p. 269.

[31] *Ibid.*, p. 283.

TABLE **23.**—PROJECTIONS OF ELEMENTARY AND HIGH SCHOOL ENROLLMENTS: OCTOBER 1, 1953
TO 1965, AND CURRENT ESTIMATE, OCTOBER 1, 1952

[In thousands. Projections are based on assumptions that the 1960 enrollment rates for children 6 to 13 years old
remained constant to 1965; rates for the 14-to-18 group were assumed to improve annually to 1965 on basis of past
trends, 1910 to 1950; rates for the population 19 to 24 years old remained constant at 1950 level]

October 1 of each year	Total enrollment	Elementary enrollment	High school enrollment	Percent change		
				Total enrollment	Elementary enrollment	High school enrollment
1952.........................	29,058	22,000	7,058	...	...	...
1953.........................	30,569	23,347	7,222	+5.2	+6.1	+2.3
1954.........................	31,934	24,546	7,388	+4.5	+5.1	+2.3
1955.........................	33,293	25,699	7,594	+4.3	+4.7	+2.8
1956.........................	34,623	26,732	7,891	+4.0	+4.0	+3.9
1957.........................	36,024	27,707	8,317	+4.0	+3.6	+5.4
1958.........................	37,461	28,704	8,757	+4.0	+3.6	+5.3
1959.........................	38,821	29,716	9,105	+3.6	+3.5	+4.0
SERIES A AND B[1]						
1960.........................	39,970	30,548		+3.0	+2.8	
1961.........................	41,004	31,023		+2.6	+1.6	
1962.........................	41,960	31,292		+2.3	+0.9	
1963.........................	42,792	31,518		+2.0	+0.7	
1964.........................	43,552	31,725		+1.8	+0.7	
1965.........................	44,013	31,868		+1.1	+0.5	
SERIES C[2]						
1960.........................	39,911	30,489	9,422	+2.8	+2.6	+3.5
1961.........................	40,846	30,865	9,981	+2.3	+1.2	+5.9
1962.........................	41,663	30,995	10,668	+2.0	+0.4	+6.9
1963.........................	42,309	31,035	11,274	+1.6	+0.1	+5.7
1964.........................	42,835	31,008	11,827	+1.2	-0.1	+4.9
1965.........................	43,031	30,886	12,145	+0.5	-0.4	+2.7
SERIES D[3]						
1960.........................	39,801	30,379		+2.5	+2.2	
1961.........................	40,564	30,583		+1.9	+0.7	
1962.........................	41,134	30,466		+1.4	-0.4	
1963.........................	41,442	30,168		+0.7	-1.0	
1964.........................	41,561	29,734		+0.3	-1.4	
1965.........................	41,302	29,157		-0.6	-1.9	

[1] Population projections based on assumption that 1950-53 fertility level continues to 1965.
[2] Population projections based on assumption that 1950-53 fertility level declines from 1953 to about the 1940 level by
1975.
[3] Population projections based on assumption that 1950-53 fertility level declines from 1953 to about the 1940 level by
1960 and continues at that level to 1965.

Source: U. S. Bureau of the Census, *Current Population Reports.* Series P-25, No. 85, "Projections of School Enrollment in the United States: 1953 to 1965," table 1.

CHAPTER 6

VARIATIONS IN AGE-GRADE
SCHOOL PROGRESS *

A. Introduction

Among the many problems confronting educators today is the very serious and prevalent one of the holding power of our secondary schools and the extremely high proportion of youths who leave school as soon as legally compelled attendance ceases. The characteristic American belief in the efficacy of education, reinforced by the limited employment opportunities offered to immature workers in our highly industrialized society, would seem to encourage young people to continue their formal education until they are graduated from a secondary school. Nonetheless, the evidence indicates that in the average public school system about 45 to 55 percent of the students who enter high school drop out before graduation.[1] In addition only 80 percent of all youths ever enter high school.[2]

The concern of educators with this problem has expressed itself, in part, in a series of studies aimed at determining both the reasons for early dropouts from school and the measures schools might take to increase their holding power.[3] Resulting from many of these studies is a conclusion that early withdrawal from school is dependent upon a complex of factors and that no one factor can be singled out as the sole contributor. In many of the studies the investigator has either directly or indirectly observed that

---

* Prepared in collaboration with James N. Ypsilantis and used with permission of the *Teachers College Record*, February 1957.

[1] Dael Wolfle, *America's Resources of Specialized Talent*, The Report of the Commission on Human Resources and Advanced Training, Harper and Brothers, New York, 1954, p. 170; Harold J. Dillon, *Early School Leavers. A Major Educational Problem*, National Child Labor Committee, New York, 1949, p. 9; William L. Gragg, "Some Factors Which Distinguish Drop-outs from High School Graduates," *Occupations*, Vol. XXVII, No. 7, April 1949, p. 457; William L. Gragg, "Survey of Drop-outs," *Clearing House*, Vol. XXVI, No. 7, March 1952, p. 413; Stanley E. Hecker, "Early School Leavers in Kentucky," *Bulletin of the Bureau of School Service*, Vol. XXV, No. 4, June 1953, p. 13.

[2] Wolfle, *op. cit.*

[3] Dillon, *op. cit.*; Ruth E. Eckert and Thomas O. Marshall, *When Youth Leave School*, The Regents Inquiry, McGraw-Hill Publishing Company, New York, 1938; Gragg, "Survey of Drop-outs," *op. cit.*; New York State Education Department, *Improvement of Holding Power Through a Continuous Study of Youth in School*, University of the State of New York Press, Albany, 1952; Sam M. Lambert, "Increasing Education's Holding Power," *Journal of the National Education Association*, Vol. XXXIX, No. 9, December 1950, p. 664.

the complex of factors affecting the decision to leave school early corresponds closely with those factors related to retardation in school progress.[4] Explicit throughout many of these studies is the awareness that youths who are retarded in their age-grade progress ("overageness" is a term used by some investigators) are most vulnerable to early withdrawal from school. Since retardation is a cumulative process, often starting in the elementary grades, early school withdrawal may be viewed as a climatic result of an ongoing process, the basic premises of which might well be examined.[5]

The problem of retardation in this Nation is not a small one; over 4 million pupils 8 to 18 years old were retarded in their age-grade school progress in April 1950. About 1.6 million were *two or more grades* behind their expected performance levels. At the high school ages over one fourth of the school youths were enrolled in grades *below* the ones expected of them; 850,000 of them, or approximately 12 percent, were enrolled in grades that were at least two or more grades below the expected performance of their age mates. Thus, for every eight school youths 14 to 17 years of age, two are lagging behind in their school performance, and one of these two is at least two or more grades behind his age mates who have maintained expected levels of age-grade performance.

As shown in Chapter 5, school enrollment rates have increased steadily over the past half-century. Concomitant with this increase there has been an increase also in the number of years spent in the school systems. Both increases reflect the enactment of compulsory attendance laws and legal restrictions on child labor. The whole tone of the Nation's policy for education has been one of greater emphasis on more schooling for its prospective citizens both in terms of time spent within the school system and of curriculum content. However, variations in school *performance* of the Nation's pupils suggest that there are many who, for a complex of reasons, have not kept pace with the rising standards.[6] The poor performances of many of the Nation's youths raise several questions about our school systems and about how well the curricula in many areas mesh with the age-grade specific expectations of the pupils. Are the standards too high for some of the pupils to meet at their respective age-grade levels? Is the age-grade standard theory fallacious in principle? Is it that schools have become so overcrowded that many pupils are unable to receive the proper attention and training that they need in order to grasp the basic knowledge of the

[4] Virgil Stinebaugh, "Why Pupils Leave School," *American School Board Journal*, Vol. LXXII, No. 3, September 1951, p. 40; Daniel W. Snepp, "Why They Drop Out," *Bulletin of the National Association of Secondary School Principals*, Vol. XXXV, No. 180, October 1951, pp. 137–141; Gragg, "Some Factors Which Distinguish Drop-outs from High School Graduates," *op. cit.*; Dillon, *op. cit.*; J. C. Carlisle and L. A. Williams, "What Pupils Are Being Eliminated?", *Clearing House*, Vol. XIII, No. 4, December 1938, p. 233; Eckert and Marshall, *op. cit.*

[5] Willard S. Elsbree in *Pupil Progress in the Elementary School*, Teachers College, Columbia University, New York, 1943, for example, questions the efficacy of the "grade-standard" theory which implies that knowledge can be parceled out for different grades at different ages.

[6] This is evident despite "social promotion," the actual extent of which is not known.

curriculum at each grade level? Are we faced with the alternatives of lowering standards and easing the curriculum at each grade level to assure a maximum flow of pupils through the school system and/or of strengthening the effectiveness of the school system as it now stands by increasing the facilities at hand in terms of buildings, equipment, and faculties?

Irrespective of the standards and facilities of schools there are many factors operating *outside* the school system that affect the relative progression of pupils, especially those of the home and community. Membership in broken homes, economic pressures leading to part and full-time employment of youths (seasonal and regular), illness and family disinterestedness which result in inadequate attendance, and changes of residence and of school which lead to both loss of time in school and problems of readjustment affect a child's school performance.

The measures of school progression discussed in this chapter reflect the complex of all these as well as other factors and do not single out any one or any group of them. The derived measures of progression (expected, retarded, and accelerated) used here represent merely a categorization of statistical information on school enrollment by age and grade.[7]

The school experience of children in the United States is one in which the pupil enters the school system at a given age level and from then on is expected to proceed from grade to grade at regular intervals. Generally a pupil spends one year in each grade and is promoted from grade to grade with each advance in year.

TABLE **24.**—AGE-GRADE PROGRESS LEVELS CLASSIFIED BY EXPECTED, RETARDED, AND ACCELERATED GRADES, BY SINGLE YEARS OF AGE: 1950

Age	Expected grades	Retarded grades		Accelerated grades
		One grade	More than one grade	
7 years old......................	1 and 2	...	...	3 plus
8 years old......................	2 and 3	1	...	4 plus
9 years old......................	3 and 4	2	1	5 plus
10 years old......................	4 and 5	3	1 - 2	6 plus
11 years old......................	5 and 6	4	1 - 3	7 plus
12 years old......................	6 and 7	5	1 - 4	8 plus
13 years old......................	7 and 8	6	1 - 5	9 plus
14 years old......................	8 and 9	7	1 - 6	10 plus
15 years old......................	9 and 10	8	1 - 7	11 plus
16 years old......................	10 and 11	9	1 - 8	12 plus
17 years old......................	11 and 12	10	1 - 9	13 plus
18 years old......................	12 and 13	11	1 - 10	14 plus

Source: Appendix B-1.

After allowing for variations in age at the time of school entrance and examining the data on enrolled grade by single years of age, this expected age-grade pattern was empirically defined. Deviations below the expected levels were classified as retarded and those above the expected grades were

---

[7] For more detailed and specific data on selection of age-grade standards of performance see Appendix B.

classified as accelerated grades. Since the basic data used for the definition of these categories were based on spring enrollment (April) rather than
fall enrollment and since midterm promotion is not universal, the retarded
category was subdivided into "retarded one grade" and "retarded more
than one grade." Into the first of these subdivisions falls an unknown and
perhaps small number of pupils who entered school at age 8 or later and
whose birthdays occur between autumn and April; had they been enumerated in the fall month they would not have been classified in a retarded
age-grade group. Into the latter of these subdivisions fall those pupils who
are unquestionably backward in their age-grade school progress.

Table 24 summarizes these derived categories of school progression.

B. Variations in expected levels of school progress

On the basis of the age-grade pattern of progress throughout the schools
of the Nation, about three fourths of the pupils between the ages of 8 and
18 years were enrolled in grades expected of them (table 25). The proportion of pupils falling within their expected levels of school performance
varies perceptibly as age, sex, color, and residence vary.

In general, the younger age cohorts have the largest proportion of children enrolled in expected grades. Among pupils 8 to 13 years of age, approximately 77 percent were enrolled in their expected grades, whereas
among the pupils between the ages of 14 and 15 years, only 66 percent
were enrolled in their expected grades. Among youths 16 to 18 years old,
about 70 percent of those remaining in school were performing at the grade
levels expected of them. (The increase in the proportion performing at
expected levels among the older teen-agers as compared with the 14- and
15-year-olds is due in part to the early drop-outs from school, the bulk of
whom are from the ranks of the retarded.[8])

Female pupils have a larger proportion of their members enrolled in expected grades than do male pupils. Well over 75 percent of the female
pupils were performing at expected age-grade levels as compared with only
71 percent of the males (table 25).

Color variations in expected levels of school progress strongly suggest
that the standards of age-grade progress designed without reference to color
differentials are much too high for nonwhite youngsters.[9] On the basis of
the age-grade school performance of all pupils 8 to 18 years old throughout the Nation, barely 50 percent of the nonwhite pupils were performing
at expected grade levels (table 25). Over 75 percent of the white pupils,
on the other hand, were in their expected grades. About 55 percent of
the nonwhite school children 8 to 13 years old were in expected grades as
compared with 80 percent of the white children. At ages 14 years and

---

[8] See section C., ff.

[9] In light of these data a standard of performance based upon the age-grade school experience of nonwhite pupils only was derived. See Appendix C.

over, less than half of the nonwhite youths enrolled in school were in the grades expected of them. Approximately 70 percent of the white youths 14 years of age and over were enrolled in their expected grades.

TABLE **25.**—PERCENT OF SCHOOL ENROLLMENT 8 TO 18 YEARS OLD IN EXPECTED GRADES BY AGE AND SEX, BY COLOR, RESIDENCE, AND REGION: 1950

Area, color, and sex	Total, 8 to 18 years old	8 to 13 years old	14 and 15 years old	16 and 17 years old	18 years old
BOTH SEXES					
Total........................	74.1	77.6	66.4	69.4	70.4
White........................	77.3	80.7	69.9	72.9	74.0
Nonwhite.....................	50.3	55.8	40.2	40.4	37.4
Urban........................	77.9	81.5	70.9	72.7	74.5
Rural nonfarm................	71.8	75.6	63.2	66.7	66.2
Rural farm...................	66.2	69.8	58.2	62.5	57.9
Northeast....................	77.1	80.9	68.9	72.8	74.4
North Central................	81.4	84.2	75.5	77.8	78.5
South........................	63.7	68.4	54.2	56.3	57.4
West.........................	80.2	83.1	75.1	75.6	76.6
MALE					
Total........................	71.1	75.3	62.2	65.5	68.0
White........................	74.5	78.6	65.7	69.1	71.7
Nonwhite.....................	46.0	52.0	35.1	34.5	31.4
Urban........................	75.6	79.8	67.5	69.5	72.4
Rural nonfarm................	68.1	72.7	57.8	61.8	63.7
Rural farm...................	62.5	66.7	53.4	57.8	55.0
Northeast....................	74.9	79.3	65.8	69.8	72.4
North Central................	78.8	82.4	71.5	74.1	75.7
South........................	59.7	64.9	48.6	51.1	54.7
West.........................	78.0	81.5	71.7	72.5	74.1
FEMALE					
Total........................	77.1	80.0	70.8	73.3	73.1
White........................	80.2	83.0	74.3	76.8	76.7
Nonwhite.....................	54.6	59.6	45.2	45.9	43.0
Urban........................	80.2	83.2	74.3	75.9	76.8
Rural nonfarm................	75.6	78.7	68.9	71.6	69.2
Rural farm...................	70.0	73.1	63.2	67.3	61.1
Northeast....................	79.4	82.7	72.2	75.9	76.7
North Central................	84.0	86.1	79.6	81.5	81.6
South........................	67.9	71.9	59.9	61.5	60.2
West.........................	82.5	84.7	78.6	79.0	79.6

Source: Appendix tables E-2, E-3, and E-4.

Rural-urban differences in the proportions of pupils enrolled in expected grade categories are not as great as are the color differences. In general, a larger proportion of urban pupils are enrolled in expected grades than are pupils in rural-nonfarm and rural-farm areas. Among school youths 8 to 18 years old, 78 percent of the urban pupils, 72 percent of the rural-nonfarm pupils, and 66 percent of the rural-farm pupils are enrolled in expected grades. For both sexes of each age group, the proportion enrolled in expected grades is highest in urban areas and higher in rural-nonfarm than in rural-farm areas (table 25).

In applying the general United States standards of age-grade progress to the four major regions of the Nation we find that school youths residing outside the South are more likely to be in expected grades than are those living in the South. In the regions of the North and West about 75 to 80 percent of the pupils were performing at expected grade levels, as compared with less than 60 percent of the school youths in the South (table 25). In the non-South regions, from two thirds to four fifths of the pupils of all age groups were in expected grades, whereas in the South, although two thirds of the 8- to 13-year-olds were enrolled in expected grades, only about 55 percent of those over 14 years of age were in expected grades. Less than 50 percent of the 14- and 15-year-old male pupils in the South were performing at grade levels expected of them.

C. Variations in retardation

About 4 million school children, or approximately 20 percent of the enrolled youths 8 to 18 years old, were retarded in their age-grade school progress in April 1950. More than 1.6 million pupils were two or more grades behind their age mates who were maintaining the expected standards of school performance.[10] An inspection of the age, sex, color, and residential differences in rates of retardation reveals variable patterns of its growth and development and suggests areas of its relative seriousness.

Retardation appears to be a cumulative process, starting at a relatively low rate (about 5 percent) among the 8-year-old pupils, increasing steadily with each increase in age, and reaching a peak of over 25 percent for 15-year-olds (figure 19). After age 15 a slight drop occurs in the percentage of pupils in retarded grades (24 percent and 22 percent for the 16-year-olds and 17-year-olds, respectively). At age 18 a slight increase in retardation is apparent (23 percent).

It is evident from these age variations that retarded pupils remain in school during the ages of compulsory attendance, recruiting additional members into their ranks of slow learners as the years and the majority of their age mates pass by. It has been observed by educators that boredom and indifference generally characterize these grade repeaters and that many are just biding time in anticipation of the legal leaving age. This point is reached usually at age 16, at which juncture a decline in the percentage of retarded pupils is observed for those who are retarded only one grade.[11] However, 16-year-olds who are retarded two or more grades have not yet

---

[10] Appendix table E–2.

[11] In 44 States pupils at age 16 who are retarded only one grade (completed elementary school) may leave school; in the other 4 States (California, New York, Ohio, Pennsylvania), they may leave school if they are working.

completed their elementary schooling; only eleven States allow them to leave school if they are not employed,[12] and an additional twelve States do not require school attendance if they are employed.[13]

The increase in the rate of retardation at age 18 years may be explained in part by the large proportion (55 percent) of these youths who are retarded only one grade (that is, juniors in high school) and who remain in school in anticipation of graduation, just one year away.[14]   On the other hand, 18-year-olds who are two or more grades behind in their age-grade progress (sophomores in high school or under) are more prone to leave school (note the decline in definite retardation at age 18) since the road to graduation is a long one, and perhaps a lonely one, for the majority of their age mates have already been graduated.

FIGURE **19.**—RETARDATION OF SCHOOL ENROLLMENT 8 TO 18 YEARS OLD, BY SINGLE YEARS OF AGE AND DEGREE OF RETARDATION: 1950

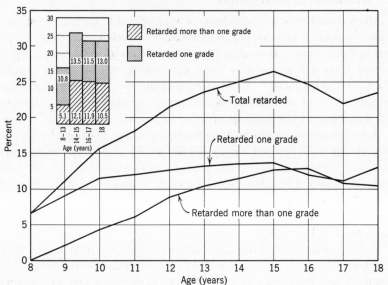

Note: Based on data in appendix table B–2.

[12] Florida, Georgia, Louisiana, Minnesota, Mississippi, Missouri, Montana, North Carolina, Rhode Island, South Carolina, and Vermont.

[13] Alabama, California, Connecticut, Illinois, Iowa, Kentucky, Massachusetts, New Mexico, New York, Ohio, Pennsylvania, and Wisconsin.

[14] Carlisle and Williams report that the most significant difference between slow pupils who leave school and those who remain in school is the difference in their family backgrounds. In general, those who remained in school came from the better-educated native families who encouraged continued schooling. See John C. Carlisle and L. A. Williams, "What Pupils Are Being Eliminated?" *The Clearing House,* Vol. XIII, No. 4, December 1938, pp. 233–234.

Age patterns of retardation differ importantly for those who are retarded only one grade (slightly) and those who are more than one grade behind their age mates in school performance. Rates of slight retardation increase perceptibly between the ages of 8 and 10 years, leveling off thereafter through age 15 years. Definite retardation, on the other hand, increases steadily and markedly between 8 and 15 to 16 years of age, gaining by approximately 2 percent at each single year of age (figure 19). The difference in patterns may be due to the balance between the influx of newly retarded pupils 10 to 15 years old into the group of the slightly retarded and the departure from this group of those who have joined the ranks of definite retardation.

Backwardness in age-grade school progress occurs to a considerably greater extent among males than among females (table 26). While the sex ratio of school children 8 to 15 years old remains fairly constant at 103 males per 100 females, the sex ratios of retarded school children of the same ages amount to 147 for the 8- to 13-year-olds and 152 for pupils 14 and 15 years of age. A sex ratio of almost unity (101) among 16- and 17-year-old pupils contrasts with the ratio of 151 for those pupils who are retarded. Whereas there are about 112 boys for every 100 girls 18 years old who are enrolled in school, there are over 150 retarded boys of this age for every 100 girls.

TABLE 26.—SEX RATIO OF THE POPULATION 8 TO 18 YEARS OLD ENROLLED IN SCHOOL, BY DEGREE OF RETARDATION AND AGE: 1950

[Males per 100 females]

Degree of retardation	Total, 8 to 18 years old	8 to 13 years old	14 and 15 years old	16 and 17 years old	18 years old
Total enrolled..............	103.3	103.1	103.4	101.5	112.0
Total retarded..............	149.1	146.7	152.0	151.0	150.6
One grade..................	143.7	142.4	143.4	146.9	151.1
More than one grade..........	157.6	156.8	162.3	155.2	150.0

Source: Same as table 25.

The predominantly masculine character of retardation increases as the degree of retardation increases. It is evident from table 26 that at each age level except for age 18 the sex ratio among pupils who are retarded two or more grades is markedly higher than the corresponding ratio at the lesser degree of retardation. That the sex ratio of the definitely retarded is the same or even slightly lower than that of those who are retarded one grade at age 18 may be explained, in part, by the fact that males of this age who are only juniors in high school, or lower, are more likely to drop out of school than are females in the same position. Slow learners among females appear more prone to stay in school, biding time until marriage. Labor force opportunities for them are probably less favorable, for it is the better educated girls of this age who are being absorbed into economic activity.[15]

The predominantly masculine character of retardation is also observed for both color groups, the three residence groups, and the four major regions of the Nation (table 27).

TABLE **27.**—SEX RATIO OF THE POPULATION 8 TO 18 YEARS OLD ENROLLED IN SCHOOL
BY DEGREE OF RETARDATION, BY COLOR, RESIDENCE, AND REGION: 1950

[Males per 100 females]

Area and color	Total enrolled	Degree of retardation		
		Total	One grade	More than one grade
Total...........................	103.3	149.1	143.7	157.6
White..................................	104.0	159.0	154.1	168.3
Nonwhite..............................	97.8	125.1	110.8	139.8
Urban.................................	101.8	151.3	150.3	153.5
Rural nonfarm.........................	104.4	150.6	142.2	164.5
Rural farm............................	105.9	144.8	134.9	156.9
Northeast.............................	103.8	158.7	158.0	160.8
North Central.........................	103.5	169.9	168.8	172.1
South.................................	102.1	139.1	127.1	154.7
West..................................	105.2	156.9	160.3	149.8

Source: Same as table 25.

Rates of retardation in age-grade school progress, derived on the basis of the total United States standards, denote that retardation occurs to a considerably greater extent among pupils living in rural areas than among those who live in urban areas. As shown in table 28, rates of retardation (both slight and definite) are highest in rural-farm areas and lowest in urban areas. Over 28 percent of the rural-farm school youths 8 to 18 years old were in retarded age-grade positions in April 1950; about 23 percent of the rural-nonfarm school children were enrolled in grades manifesting retarded levels of school performance. In contrast, only 14 percent of the urban school children were retarded in their age-grade progress.

Although these differentials may suggest that the United States standard of age-grade performance used here may be one which is chiefly urban (55 percent of the school children of these ages are urban) and perhaps not applicable to the school experience of rural youths, at the high school ages (14 to 17 years) rates of definite retardation (two or more grades) roughly equal or actually exceed rates of slight retardation (one grade) among rural pupils (table 28). In addition, at each of the age levels[16] rates of definite retardation among rural pupils are greater than the corresponding rates of slight retardation for urban children. These considerations strongly suggest that the explanation for the relatively high extent of retardation among rural pupils cannot be found in the application of the United States standards

[15] See Chapter 8.
[16] A minor exception among rural-farm pupils 8 to 13 years old is noted.

as defined in this study, although there may be some important rural-urban differences in age of school entrance, grade structures, etc.[17] Rather, it seems apparent that retardation in age-grade progress, particularly among rural pupils, is an actuality that warrants considerable remedial effort. Whether that effort lies in examining community and parental attitudes on education, in examining the effects of part-time labor on school performance; and/or in evaluating the educational practices and theories operating in these areas is not within the province of this analysis.

TABLE **28.**—PERCENT OF SCHOOL ENROLLMENT 8 TO 18 YEARS OLD IN RETARDED GRADES BY DEGREE OF RETARDATION, BY AGE AND SEX, URBAN AND RURAL: 1950

Area, degree of retardation, and sex	Total, 8 to 18 years old	8 to 13 years old	14 and 15 years old	16 and 17 years old	18 years old
URBAN					
Both sexes.....................	14.2	11.1	19.6	19.0	17.7
One grade...........................	9.3	8.2	11.6	10.3	10.5
More than one grade.................	5.0	2.9	8.0	8.7	7.2
Male...............................	17.0	13.2	23.5	23.1	21.0
One grade...........................	11.0	9.7	13.9	12.6	12.5
More than one grade.................	5.9	3.5	9.6	10.5	8.4
Female.............................	11.4	9.0	15.7	14.9	14.2
One grade...........................	7.5	6.7	9.4	8.1	8.3
More than one grade.................	3.9	2.3	6.3	6.9	6.0
RURAL NONFARM					
Both sexes.....................	22.6	19.0	30.5	27.1	29.7
One grade...........................	13.6	13.0	15.8	13.0	16.4
More than one grade.................	9.0	6.1	14.7	14.1	13.3
Male...............................	26.6	22.2	36.3	32.5	32.9
One grade...........................	15.6	14.9	18.1	15.2	17.9
More than one grade.................	10.9	7.3	18.2	17.3	15.0
Female.............................	18.4	15.7	24.4	21.6	25.8
One grade...........................	11.5	11.0	13.3	10.8	14.6
More than one grade.................	6.9	4.7	11.1	10.9	11.2
RURAL FARM					
Both sexes.....................	28.5	24.7	36.0	32.6	40.5
One grade...........................	15.2	15.0	16.2	13.5	19.6
More than one grade.................	13.3	9.7	19.9	19.1	20.9
Male...............................	32.7	28.4	41.6	37.8	43.5
One grade...........................	16.9	16.9	17.8	15.0	20.7
More than one grade.................	15.8	11.5	23.8	22.8	22.8
Female.............................	24.0	20.8	30.0	27.3	37.1
One grade...........................	13.3	13.0	14.4	11.9	18.3
More than one grade.................	10.7	7.8	15.6	15.4	18.8

Source: Appendix table E–3.

Age variations in retardation among the three residential areas shed some light on the rural-urban differentials in indicating that retarded rural pupils are more prone to leave school at those ages when compulsory attendance ceases than are their equally retarded urban cousins of the same

[17] The age-grade structure of rural-farm pupils, by single years of age, was examined in considerable detail to determine whether or not the differences between it and the total United States standard were sufficiently great to warrant the derivation of a separate rural-farm standard. The conclusion was negative. See Appendix C.

ages. However, if they are 18 years old and are only one year away from graduation (retarded one grade) rural youths are more apt to *remain* in school than are the corresponding urban youths. At age 18 and more than one grade retarded, however, urban and rural-nonfarm youths tend to drop out of school, whereas rural-farm youths persist in their school enrollment despite their overageness and the long trek to graduation (table 28).

These observations imply that at the younger teen-ages when compulsory attendance ceases, pressure upon retarded pupils to remain in school is more effective in urban areas and/or employment opportunities for retarded urban youths are less favorable than for their country age mates who are equally retarded in age-grade school progress. The data also suggests that although they may be 18 years old and retarded by two or more grades (sophomore in high school or under), rural-farm youths may be more persistent in remaining in school than are the definitely retarded 18-year-olds in urban and rural-nonfarm areas. Perhaps opportunities for combined employment and enrollment are more favorable in farm areas, particularly for the slow learners.

Regional variations in rates of retardation seem to divide the Nation into two sections: the South and the non-South. In the southern section we find: 35 percent of the Nation's school children, over 55 percent of those who are retarded in their age-grade school progress, and 65 percent of the Nation's youths who are retarded more than one grade—the definitely retarded (table 35). The remaining three major regions of the country account for 65 percent of the Nation's school children, 45 percent of total retardation in the Nation's schools, and only 35 percent of its definitely retarded youths.

Over 30 percent of the school children in the South 8 to 18 years old are in grades below those expected of them on the basis of the United States standards of age-grade progress. About half of these retarded pupils are two or more grades below their expected positions (table 29). In each of the three regions outside of the South (Northeast, North Central, and West) about 12 or 13 percent of the school children are retarded in their age-grade school progress and only about 4 percent are found two or more grades below those of the majority of their age mates.

In the South, rates of definite retardation exceed those of slight retardation in each of the older age groups: 14 and 15 years, 16 and 17 years, and 18 years of age. In addition, rates of definite retardation among southern youths of these ages exceed by far the rates of *slight* retardation for youths of corresponding ages in each of the other regions. These two considerations[18] imply that even the application of more lenient standards

---

[18] In addition, the age-grade structure of southern pupils, by single years of age, was examined to determine whether or not the differences between it and the total United States standard were sufficiently great to warrant the derivation of a separate southern standard. The conclusion was negative. See Appendix C.

of school performance in the South would not disguise the actuality of the poor school progress of its youths.

TABLE **29.**—PERCENT OF SCHOOL ENROLLMENT 8 TO 18 YEARS OLD IN RETARDED GRADES BY DEGREE OF RETARDATION, BY AGE AND SEX, FOR REGIONS: 1950

Region, degree of retardation, and sex	Total, 8 to 18 years old	8 to 13 years old	14 and 15 years old	16 and 17 years old	18 years old
NORTHEAST					
Both sexes....................	13.2	9.7	18.9	18.4	18.2
One grade.....................	8.7	7.4	11.4	9.8	11.3
More than one grade...........	4.5	2.3	7.5	8.6	6.9
Male..........................	15.9	11.7	22.7	22.2	21.1
One grade.....................	10.4	8.9	13.7	11.9	13.2
More than one grade...........	5.4	2.9	9.1	10.3	8.0
Female........................	10.4	7.6	14.9	14.5	14.8
One grade.....................	6.8	5.9	9.0	7.7	9.1
More than one grade...........	3.5	1.8	5.9	6.8	5.7
NORTH CENTRAL					
Both sexes....................	12.4	9.7	17.4	16.3	17.0
One grade.....................	8.7	7.6	11.3	9.3	11.1
More than one grade...........	3.7	2.1	6.1	6.9	5.9
Male..........................	15.4	12.0	21.8	20.2	20.3
One grade.....................	10.7	9.4	14.1	11.7	13.2
More than one grade...........	4.7	2.7	7.7	8.5	7.1
Female........................	9.4	7.4	12.9	12.3	13.3
One grade.....................	6.6	5.8	8.5	7.0	8.7
More than one grade...........	2.8	1.6	4.4	5.3	4.6
SOUTH					
Both sexes....................	30.6	26.5	39.8	36.4	35.5
One grade.....................	16.5	16.4	17.6	15.2	16.7
More than one grade...........	14.2	10.1	22.2	21.2	18.8
Male..........................	35.3	30.4	46.1	42.8	39.5
One grade.....................	18.2	18.2	19.1	17.0	18.2
More than one grade...........	17.1	12.1	27.0	25.8	21.2
Female........................	25.9	22.5	33.3	30.2	31.4
One grade.....................	14.6	14.5	16.0	13.5	15.2
More than one grade...........	11.2	8.1	17.3	16.7	16.2
WEST					
Both sexes....................	13.2	10.5	17.5	17.8	18.4
One grade.....................	9.2	8.0	11.5	10.9	11.4
More than one grade...........	4.0	2.5	6.0	6.9	7.0
Male..........................	15.7	12.4	20.9	21.6	21.6
One grade.....................	11.1	9.5	13.9	13.5	13.6
More than one grade...........	4.6	2.8	7.0	8.1	8.1
Female........................	10.5	8.5	13.9	13.7	14.3
One grade.....................	7.3	6.5	9.0	8.2	8.6
More than one grade...........	3.3	2.1	5.0	5.5	5.7

Source: Appendix table E-4.

In examining the color differentials in rates and degrees of retardation it is immediately evident that backwardness in age-grade school progress is startlingly high among nonwhite pupils. Over 40 percent of the nonwhite school children 8 to 18 years old were enrolled in grades below those expected of them on the basis of the United States standards of age-grade progress. More than half of these retarded pupils were two or more grades behind their age mates (table 30). This contrasts with only 15 percent of

76 AMERICA'S CHILDREN

the white pupils in retarded grades, about a third of whom were more than one grade below those expected of them.

TABLE **30.**—PERCENT OF SCHOOL ENROLLMENT 8 TO 18 YEARS OLD IN RETARDED GRADES BY DEGREE OF RETARDATION, COLOR, AND SEX, BY AGE: 1950

[Retardation for nonwhite measured on both U. S. standard of performance and nonwhite standard of performance]

Standard, degree of retardation, color, and sex	Total, 8 to 18 years old	8 to 13 years old	14 and 15 years old	16 and 17 years old	18 years old
BOTH SEXES					
U. S. Standard of Performance					
All classes, total retarded....	19.1	15.9	25.6	23.4	23.4
One grade............................	11.5	10.8	13.6	11.5	13.0
More than one grade.................	7.6	5.1	12.1	11.9	10.5
White, total retarded............	15.9	12.9	22.0	19.9	19.8
One grade............................	10.3	9.4	12.8	10.7	12.1
More than one grade.................	5.6	3.5	9.3	9.2	7.7
Nonwhite, total retarded........	42.2	36.6	52.4	52.3	57.1
One grade............................	20.0	20.5	19.3	18.1	21.2
More than one grade.................	22.2	16.1	33.0	34.3	35.9
Nonwhite Standard of Performance					
Nonwhite, total retarded.......	23.7	19.1	33.0	34.3	22.4
One grade............................	12.7	12.6	13.4	12.9	8.1
More than one grade.................	11.1	6.4	19.6	21.4	14.3
MALE					
U. S. Standard of Performance					
All classes, total retarded....	22.5	18.6	30.4	28.0	26.7
One grade............................	13.3	12.4	15.7	13.6	14.8
More than one grade.................	9.2	6.1	14.7	14.4	11.9
White, total retarded............	19.2	15.4	26.8	24.4	22.9
One grade............................	12.3	11.1	15.2	13.0	14.0
More than one grade.................	6.9	4.3	11.5	11.4	8.9
Nonwhite, total retarded........	47.4	41.1	58.7	59.2	64.9
One grade............................	21.2	22.1	19.5	18.7	23.0
More than one grade.................	26.2	19.0	39.2	40.6	41.9
Nonwhite Standard of Performance					
Nonwhite, total retarded.......	28.0	22.4	39.2	40.6	26.7
One grade............................	14.3	14.4	14.8	14.3	9.4
More than one grade.................	13.6	8.0	24.3	26.2	17.3
FEMALE					
U. S. Standard of Performance					
All classes, total retarded....	15.6	13.0	20.7	18.8	19.8
One grade............................	9.6	9.0	11.3	9.4	10.9
More than one grade.................	6.0	4.0	9.4	9.4	8.9
White, total retarded............	12.6	10.3	17.1	15.4	16.2
One grade............................	8.3	7.6	10.2	8.4	9.9
More than one grade.................	4.3	2.7	6.9	7.0	6.3
Nonwhite, total retarded........	37.1	32.0	46.2	45.8	49.8
One grade............................	18.8	18.9	19.1	17.5	19.6
More than one grade.................	18.3	13.1	27.1	28.3	30.2
Nonwhite Standard of Performance					
Nonwhite, total retarded.......	19.6	15.7	27.1	28.3	18.5
One grade............................	11.0	10.8	12.0	11.5	7.0
More than one grade.................	8.6	4.9	15.1	16.8	11.5

Source: Appendix tables E-2 and E-5.

At the older school ages (14 to 18 years) more than 50 percent of the nonwhite pupils were in grades signifying retarded levels of performance; more than one third of the nonwhite teen-agers were two or more grades retarded. This contrasts with about 20 percent of the white school youths of these ages enrolled in retarded grades with less than 10 percent designated as definitely retarded.

These color differentials are so great that the age-grade school experience of nonwhite pupils, by single years of age, was examined in order to determine whether standards of progress derived for the total school children of the United States were also applicable to the nonwhite group. On the basis of this examination it was concluded that the nonwhite age-grade school experiences were sufficiently different from those of the total United States to warrant the derivation of a separate standard of performance.[19]

The age pattern of grade enrollment (Appendix C, figure C–3) among nonwhite school children was found to be somewhat similar to the age-grade enrollment pattern of all school children in the United States, with one important exception: expected grade levels for each single year of age were found to comprise a three-grade span rather than a two-grade span. In effect, the redefinition of expected grades for nonwhite pupils constituted the two grades originally derived for all pupils *plus* the adjacent lower grade.

Thus it is apparent that nonwhite pupils as a group are so commonly one grade behind what may be generally expected of school children that their pattern of age-grade enrollment may be said to be different. The nonwhite standard of school performance which emerges is given below:

TABLE **31.**—NONWHITE STANDARD OF SCHOOL PERFORMANCE, BY SINGLE YEARS OF AGE: 1950

Age	Expected grades	Retarded grades		Accelerated grades
		One grade	More than one grade	
7 years old	1 and 2	...	...	3 plus
8 years old	2 and 3	1	...	4 plus
9 years old	2, 3, 4	1	...	5 plus
10 years old	3, 4, 5	2	1	6 plus
11 years old	4, 5, 6	3	1 - 2	7 plus
12 years old	5, 6, 7	4	1 - 3	8 plus
13 years old	6, 7, 8	5	1 - 4	9 plus
14 years old	7, 8, 9	6	1 - 5	10 plus
15 years old	8, 9, 10	7	1 - 6	11 plus
16 years old	9, 10, 11	8	1 - 7	12 plus
17 years old	10, 11, 12	9	1 - 8	13 plus
18 years old	10, 11, 12, 13	9	1 - 8	14 plus

Source: Appendix table C–2.

For 7- and 8-year-old pupils, the expected levels of performance are the same as those for the total United States school population of the same ages. Among pupils 9 to 17 years of age, the expected grade levels encompass

---

[19] See Appendix C.

the *three-grade* span referred to above. For 18-year-old nonwhite youths, the expected levels of school achievement leniently encompass a *four-grade* span.

As is clearly demonstrated in table 30, nonwhite school children are considerably more retarded in their school progress than are white school children, even after making some allowances for possible differences in the age-grade school experiences of the two groups. On the basis of the separate nonwhite standards of age-grade school performance about one fourth of the nonwhite school children are in grades indicating retarded performance levels, and more than 10 percent are two or more grades behind their *nonwhite* age mates. At the high school ages (14 to 17 years) more than one third of the nonwhite pupils are enrolled in retarded grades and about 20 percent may be said to be definitely retarded.

Almost three fourths of the nonwhite school children of the Nation live in the South where, in 1950, they were attending segregated schools. If we assume that the age-grade standards in these segregated schools were not different from those of other schools in the Nation, then we find that 50 percent of the southern nonwhite pupils were retarded in their school progress, and over 25 percent were definitely retarded (table 32). This contrasts with 25 percent of southern white pupils in retarded grades and only 10 percent two or more grades behind those expected of them.

TABLE **32.**—SUMMARY OF AGE-GRADE SCHOOL PERFORMANCE OF PERSONS 8 TO 18 YEARS OLD, BY AGE AND COLOR, FOR THE SOUTH: 1950

[Age-grade school performance for nonwhite measured on both U. S. standard of performance and nonwhite standard of performance]

Standard, color, and performance	Total, 8 to 18 years old	8 to 13 years old	14 and 15 years old	16 and 17 years old	18 years old
U. S. STANDARD OF PERFORMANCE					
White, total enrolled............	100.0	100.0	100.0	100.0	100.0
Expected grades....................	69.9	74.4	60.8	63.3	64.1
Retarded grades....................	24.5	20.8	33.1	29.2	28.4
One grade........................	14.6	14.0	16.8	14.2	15.8
More than one grade.............	9.9	6.8	16.3	15.0	12.6
Accelerated grades.................	3.7	2.9	4.4	5.3	7.0
Grade not reported................	1.9	1.9	1.8	2.2	0.5
Nonwhite, total enrolled.........	100.0	100.0	100.0	100.0	100.0
Expected grades....................	44.6	50.5	33.3	32.9	32.3
Retarded grades....................	49.6	43.6	61.0	60.8	62.1
One grade........................	22.2	23.6	20.2	18.6	20.2
More than one grade.............	27.3	20.1	40.8	42.2	41.8
Accelerated grades.................	4.1	4.1	4.0	4.0	5.0
Grade not reported................	1.8	1.8	1.6	2.3	0.6
NONWHITE STANDARD OF PERFORMANCE					
Nonwhite, total enrolled.........	100.0	100.0	100.0	100.0	100.0
Expected grades....................	64.8	70.3	53.5	51.5	67.1
Retarded grades....................	29.3	23.8	40.8	42.2	27.3
One grade........................	15.4	15.6	15.8	15.0	9.7
More than one grade.............	13.9	8.2	25.0	27.2	17.6
Accelerated grades.................	4.1	4.1	4.0	4.0	5.0
Grade not reported................	1.8	1.8	1.6	2.3	0.6

Source: Appendix table E–6.

Available data show that there are some important differences between the white and nonwhite school systems of the South, which may find reflection in the differential retardation rates. Statistics on white and Negro schools in the South (1949–1950)[20] show that class size in Negro schools is larger than in white schools, that teachers in Negro schools are generally paid less than in white schools, and that expenditures per pupil in Negro schools are generally less than in white schools.

If it is assumed that the standards of age-grade progress in nonwhite schools are commonly lower by about one grade, the school performance of nonwhite southern pupils then compares more favorably with that of white pupils. In applying the separate nonwhite age-grade standards to nonwhite children enrolled in school, their retardation is reduced to 29 percent, with less than 15 percent definitely retarded (table 32). Particularly at the younger ages (8 to 13 years) does the application of a separate and lower standard for nonwhite pupils in the South result in closely corresponding retardation rates between the white and nonwhite pupils. At the older ages, however, the color differences begin to widen. Among the 14- and 15-year-old white pupils, total retardation comes to about 33 percent, *declining* thereafter to less than 30 percent for those 16 and 17 years old. In both age groups slight and definite retardation are roughly equal. Among the nonwhite pupils, on the other hand, about 40 percent of the 14- and 15-year-olds are in retarded grades, *increasing* thereafter to 42 percent for those 16 and 17 years of age. In each age group definite retardation exceeds slight retardation. By age 18 years the divergence between the two color groups is less, though the degree of retardation among the nonwhite pupils is appreciably greater.

Southern nonwhite pupils 8 to 18 years of age are equally distributed between urban and rural-farm areas (39 percent each) and a smaller proportion is found in rural-nonfarm areas (22 percent). Southern white pupils of the same ages are more heavily urban (41 percent) than rural-farm (31 percent) or rural-nonfarm (28 percent). This may, in some measure, account for the color differentials in retardation. An examination of table 33[21] reveals that, on the basis of the United States standard of school performance, retardation among urban nonwhite males is considerably greater than among urban white males. The application of the lower nonwhite standard in urban areas yields lower nonwhite retardation rates at the younger ages (8 to 13 years) although higher rates at the older ages in comparison with the white males.

Both white and nonwhite retardation rates are higher in rural-farm areas than in urban areas. In the rural-farm areas, however, the color differen-

[20] U. S. Office of Education, *Biennial Survey of Education in the United States—1948–50*, Chapter 2, "Statistics of State School Systems, 1949–50," table 43.

[21] Table 33 is limited to male pupils, because their retardation is greater than that for female pupils. Similarly, the extremes of urban and rural-farm retardation rates only are considered.

tials are greater, even on the basis of the separate nonwhite standard for nonwhite pupils, particularly among those 14 to 17 years old.

It would seem, therefore, that there are motivational, economic, and other factors, in addition to those of differential school facilities and areas of residence, contributing to the comparatively high rates of retardation among nonwhite southern pupils, particularly at the later teen-ages, 14 to 17 years old.

TABLE 33.—PERCENT OF MALES 8 TO 18 YEARS OLD IN RETARDED GRADES BY DEGREE OF RETARDATION AND COLOR, BY AGE, FOR THE SOUTH, URBAN AND RURAL FARM: 1950

[Retardation for nonwhite measured on both U. S. standard of performance and nonwhite standard of performance]

Area, standard, color, and degree of retardation	Total, 8 to 18 years old	8 to 13 years old	14 and 15 years old	16 and 17 years old	18 years old
URBAN					
U. S. Standard of Performance					
White, total retarded...........	21.8	27.6	30.3	27.9	23.4
One grade........................	13.6	12.3	16.6	14.7	14.0
More than one grade..............	8.2	5.3	13.7	13.2	9.4
Nonwhite, total retarded........	41.5	34.2	53.9	55.8	55.9
One grade........................	21.1	21.0	21.4	21.0	21.1
More than one grade..............	20.4	13.2	32.5	34.8	34.8
Nonwhite Standard of Performance					
Nonwhite, total retarded........	21.4	15.6	32.4	34.8	29.1
One grade........................	12.4	11.2	15.5	14.7	7.9
More than one grade..............	9.0	4.4	16.9	20.1	11.2
RURAL FARM					
U. S. Standard of Performance					
White, total retarded...........	36.0	30.6	46.8	43.1	49.0
One grade........................	19.6	19.3	20.9	18.3	24.8
More than one grade..............	16.4	11.3	25.9	24.8	24.2
Nonwhite, total retarded........	68.0	61.8	80.3	81.9	85.3
One grade........................	24.3	28.1	17.1	14.9	17.4
More than one grade..............	43.7	33.7	63.2	67.0	67.9
Nonwhite Standard of Performance					
Nonwhite, total retarded........	47.3	39.4	63.3	67.0	51.8
One grade........................	21.6	23.6	18.0	16.7	14.9
More than one grade..............	25.7	15.8	45.3	50.3	36.9

Source: Appendix table E-7.

D. Variations in acceleration

Approximately 1 million school children, or 5 percent of the school youths 8 to 18 years old, were enrolled in grades higher than those expected for their age group in April 1950.[22]

---

[22] The proportion of school children in accelerated grades would have been higher had the enumeration been taken at the start of the school year rather than in April. At the start of the school year there are pupils who at that time would be considered underage for their grade level. During the ensuing six or seven months to the time of spring enumeration these children have birthdays which make them a whole year older to the enumerator and thus of normal age for their grade level. Thus by aging one year and still remaining in the same grade level these pupils are downgraded in their age-grade performance.

TABLE **34.**—PERCENT OF SCHOOL ENROLLMENT 8 TO 18 YEARS OLD IN ACCELERATED GRADES BY AGE AND SEX, BY COLOR, RESIDENCE, AND REGION: 1950

Area, color, and sex	Total, 8 to 18 years old	8 to 13 years old	14 and 15 years old	16 and 17 years old	18 years old
BOTH SEXES					
Total......................	4.7	4.2	5.9	4.8	5.6
White........................	4.6	4.1	5.9	4.8	5.7
Nonwhite.....................	5.0	5.1	5.2	4.4	5.0
Urban........................	5.5	4.9	7.1	5.8	7.2
Rural nonfarm................	3.3	3.1	4.1	3.4	3.3
Rural farm...................	3.7	3.7	4.3	3.2	1.2
Northeast....................	7.1	6.5	9.8	6.1	6.6
North Central...............	4.0	3.8	5.0	3.8	4.1
South........................	3.8	3.2	4.3	5.0	6.6
West.........................	4.1	3.9	4.7	3.9	4.5
MALE					
Total......................	4.0	3.7	4.9	3.8	4.8
White........................	4.0	3.6	5.1	3.9	4.9
Nonwhite.....................	3.9	4.2	3.7	2.9	3.1
Urban........................	4.8	4.3	6.2	4.7	6.2
Rural nonfarm................	2.8	2.6	3.4	2.8	2.8
Rural farm...................	3.0	3.1	3.3	2.4	1.0
Northeast....................	6.4	6.0	8.7	5.2	5.9
North Central...............	3.4	3.2	4.2	3.2	3.6
South........................	3.0	2.7	3.3	3.7	5.3
West.........................	3.5	3.4	4.1	3.1	3.8
FEMALE					
Total......................	5.4	4.8	6.8	5.8	6.5
White........................	5.3	4.6	6.8	5.8	6.5
Nonwhite.....................	6.0	5.9	6.5	5.7	6.7
Urban........................	6.3	5.4	8.1	6.9	8.4
Rural nonfarm................	3.9	3.5	4.9	4.1	3.9
Rural farm...................	4.5	4.4	5.4	3.9	1.5
Northeast....................	7.8	7.1	10.9	7.1	7.5
North Central...............	4.6	4.3	5.9	4.4	4.6
South........................	4.5	3.7	5.3	6.3	7.8
West.........................	4.7	4.4	5.4	4.8	5.5

Source: Appendix tables E-2, E-3, and E-4.

The age pattern of acceleration, like that of retardation, suggests a cumulative process, starting at about 4 percent for 8-year-old pupils and increasing gradually and slowly to about 6 percent for pupils 16 years old. At age 17 the rate of acceleration declines to 3 percent and then rises to about 5 percent for 18-year-olds (Appendix B, table B–2). The decline in the acceleration rate at age 17 denotes in large measure the discontinuation of schooling among the accelerated 17-year-olds after high school graduation, leaving a considerably diminished cohort of accelerated age mates to go on to college. The increase in the rate of acceleration at age 18 is a reflection in part of the large number of drop-outs among the 18-year-olds who have been graduated from high school in accordance with the expected pattern of school progress and also the retarded 18-year-olds

who leave before graduation.[23]   Accelerated 18-year-olds have already
been graduated from high school and are at least college sophomores who
are approaching a new goal of educational achievement.

In each age group acceleration rates are from 1 to 2 percentage points
higher for females than for males (table 34).   Urban youths are generally
more accelerated in their age-grade progress (6 percent) than are rural-
nonfarm (3 percent) or rural-farm (4 percent) youths.   Pupils residing in
the Northeast are appreciably more accelerated in their age-grade progress
(7 percent) than are school youths in other regions (4 percent).[24]

Census returns on age-grade enrollment suggest little difference between
the white and nonwhite rates of acceleration,[25] but that small difference
generally favors nonwhite pupils with a slightly higher rate.[26]   Particularly
at the younger ages does the nonwhite acceleration exceed that of white
pupils.

E. Summary and conclusions

Retardation in age-grade school progress is quite extensive in the United
States.   About 4 million or about one fifth of the Nation's school children 8 to 18 years old were retarded in their age-grade progress in April
1950.   Over 1.6 million of these pupils were two or more grades behind
the grades expected of them.   Retardation, both slight and definite, was
disproportionately high among nonwhite, rural-farm, and southern pupils
(table 35).   Nonwhite school youths comprised only 12 percent of the
total enrollment of persons 8 to 18 years old but accounted for over 20
percent of those who were retarded one grade and 35 percent of those who
were retarded more than one grade.   School children in rural-farm areas
constitute only 20 percent of the Nation's total enrollment but account for
28 percent of the slightly retarded and 36 percent of the definitely retarded.   In the South reside one third of the Nation's school youths,
more than half of the slightly retarded pupils, and almost two thirds of the
definitely retarded pupils of the country.   In the South will be found the
Nation's highest demographic dependency, lowest financial supporting capacity, lowest educational expenditures per pupil, and a long established
system of segregated schooling.

Through a myriad of well-established interconnecting pathways, the
efficacy of our schools, the progress and performance of their pupils, their
holding power, their strengths, and their shortcomings find a way into many
aspects of life.   The schools have been given the responsibility for multi-
tudinous factors relating to the care and development of children, physical,

---

[23] One of the major decision points, whether to continue or drop out of school, is generally reached
upon high school graduation.

[24] Acceleration in the South does not stand out as significantly lower than that of the other regions.

[25] Based on United States standards of age-grade progress.

[26] It is possible that some of the difference may be due to variations in the amount of upgrading in
reporting attainment.

mental, or moral. It is recognized here that the success of our educational systems is not entirely dependent upon the attitude and performance of professional teachers and other personnel and facilities; to a considerable extent the success of school systems is dependent upon the attitude of the pupils and their parents toward education and upon the cultural level of the community in which the school performs its functions.

TABLE **35.**—SCHOOL ENROLLMENT 8 TO 18 YEARS OLD BY DEGREE OF RETARDATION, BY AGE, COLOR, RESIDENCE, AND REGION: APRIL 1950

[Population figures in thousands and rounded separately]

Area, age, and color	Total enrolled		Degree of retardation					
			Total		One grade		More than one grade	
	Number	Per-cent	Number	Per-cent	Number	Per-cent	Number	Per-cent
8 TO 18 YEARS OLD								
Total...................	21,333	100.0	4,072	100.0	2,449	100.0	1,623	100.0
White...................	18,779	88.0	2,993	73.5	1,939	79.2	1,055	65.0
Nonwhite................	2,555	12.0	1,078	26.5	510	20.8	568	35.0
Urban...................	12,050	56.5	1,713	42.1	1,116	45.6	597	36.8
Rural nonfarm...........	4,828	22.6	1,091	26.8	657	26.8	433	26.7
Rural farm.............	4,455	20.9	1,268	31.1	675	27.6	593	36.5
Northeast...............	4,992	23.4	657	16.1	433	17.7	225	13.9
North Central..........	6,202	29.1	772	19.0	540	22.0	232	14.3
South..................	7,480	35.1	2,291	56.3	1,231	50.3	1,061	65.4
West...................	2,660	12.5	351	8.6	246	10.0	105	6.5
8 TO 13 YEARS OLD								
Total...................	13,385	100.0	2,122	100.0	1,439	100.0	683	100.0
White...................	11,721	87.6	1,514	71.3	1,098	76.3	415	60.8
Nonwhite................	1,664	12.4	608	28.7	341	23.7	267	39.1
Urban...................	7,417	55.4	826	38.9	607	42.2	218	31.9
Rural nonfarm...........	3,129	23.4	596	28.1	406	28.2	190	27.8
Rural farm.............	2,839	21.2	701	33.0	426	29.6	275	40.3
Northeast...............	3,050	22.8	296	13.9	224	15.6	71	10.4
North Central..........	3,863	28.9	376	17.7	294	20.4	83	12.2
South..................	4,814	36.0	1,276	60.1	788	54.8	488	71.4
West...................	1,658	12.4	174	8.2	133	9.2	41	6.0
14 TO 18 YEARS OLD								
Total...................	7,948	100.0	1,950	100.0	1,010	100.0	940	100.0
White...................	7,058	88.8	1,480	75.9	841	83.3	639	68.0
Nonwhite................	891	11.2	470	24.1	169	16.7	301	32.0
Urban...................	4,633	58.3	887	45.5	509	50.4	379	40.3
Rural nonfarm...........	1,699	21.4	495	25.4	251	24.9	243	25.9
Rural farm.............	1,616	20.3	567	29.1	249	24.7	318	33.8
Northeast...............	1,942	24.4	361	18.5	209	20.7	154	16.4
North Central..........	2,339	29.4	396	20.3	246	24.4	149	15.9
South..................	2,666	33.5	1,015	52.1	443	43.9	573	61.0
West...................	1,002	12.6	177	9.1	113	11.2	64	6.8

Source: Appendix tables E-2, E-3, and E-4.

Nonetheless, the school system, as an important agency which deals with most of the children of the country, bears the especially heavy responsibility of recognizing early the behavior difficulties and other symptoms of maladjustment of its pupils. Surely retardation in school progress is one of the more obvious of these symptoms, one generally having a spiral effect upon truancy, delinquency,[27] and a poorly trained citizenry and manpower resource.

As one approach for attacking such problems of social concern school retardation might well be minimized. The premises of the age-grade standard theory in itself require re-examination. The prescribed curriculum for given age levels may warrant more constant revisions. In addition, the effect of varying social and environmental conditions upon pupil performance may be investigated further.[28]

---

[27] Sheldon and Eleanor T. Glueck, *1,000 Juvenile Delinquents,* Harvard University Press, Cambridge, 1934. A. M. Carr-Saunders, Hermann Mannheim, and E. C. Rhodes, *Young Offenders,* Cambridge University Press, Cambridge, 1942.

[28] Some research in this area has been done. See, for example, Kenneth Eells, Allison Davis, Robert J. Havighurst, Virgil E. Herrick, and Ralph W. Tyler, *Intelligence and Cultural Differences, A study of Cultural Learning and Problem Solvency,* University of Chicago Press, Chicago, 1951, pp. 111–115.

CHAPTER 7

YOUTH AT WORK

A. Introduction

The ordinary hazards of growth to which young people are exposed—physical, mental, and moral hazards—have been found to be aggravated under some conditions of economic employment.[1] Child labor laws, enacted over a period of the last several decades, have sought to prohibit or restrict such employment by establishing a minimum age for work, by prescribing minimum standards of physical and educational fitness for employment, and by regulating the hours and conditions under which young people may work. In general it may be said that these legislative enactments have been effective in reducing the employment of young people.

That young people went to work at a later age in 1950 than at the turn of the century also reflects to a considerable extent the higher educational standards at the later date (Chapter 5, section A). Legal regulation of the employment of children and youth referred to above and its complement, compulsory school attendance laws, are two of the methods employed by society to protect children from work at early ages and to enhance the likelihood for increased educational preparation. None of the States of the Nation is now without compulsory school attendance laws; a half-century ago fourteen States had no such legislation.

Although available data on trends in the labor force participation of youths cannot be judged as accurate,[2] there is no doubt that the proportion of economically active youths declined from the turn of the century to its midpoint (table 36 and figure 20). The decade-to-decade fluctuations in the participation rates cannot reasonably be explained in terms of theories regarding the effects of economic or other conditions, but it may be concluded that the general trend has been decidedly downward, particularly for males.

---

[1] That a working environment may seriously interfere with the growth process is suggested by comparative measurements of working and school children in "Child Health in Relation to Employment," *The Social Service Review* (June 1942), pp. 317–321.

[2] Because of the large proportion of borderline cases for the younger ages, the practice of reporting gainful occupations for persons under 20 years of age was especially variable in the censuses. For further discussion, see *1950 Census of Population*, Vol. II, *Characteristics of the Population*, Part 1, U. S. Summary, Introduction, pp. 49–53.

TABLE **36.**—PERSONS IN THE LABOR FORCE, BY AGE AND SEX: 1900 AND 1920 TO 1950

[Numbers in thousands]

Age and sex	1950[1] (Apr.)	1940 (Apr.)	1930 (Apr.)	1920 (Jan.)	1900 (June)	Labor force as percent of population				
						1950 (Apr.)	1940 (Apr.)	1930 (Apr.)	1920 (Jan.)	1900 (June)
Male, 10 yrs. and over...	42,126	40,284	37,166	32,305	23,212	77.2	72.9	74.5	76.4	78.1
10 to 13 years.............	([2])	([2])	158	252	571	...	...	3.2	5.7	17.4
14 to 19 years.............	2,307	2,619	2,795	2,947	2,834	36.0	35.4	40.1	51.5	62.0
20 to 24 years.............	4,245	5,035	4,747	4,080	3,302	76.4	88.5	88.8	89.9	90.6
25 years and over.........	35,574	32,630	29,466	25,026	16,505	83.5	87.1	89.9	90.3	91.1
Female, 10 yrs. and over..	16,520	13,015	10,469	8,349	5,204	28.9	23.6	21.4	20.6	18.4
10 to 13 years.............	([2])	([2])	73	120	205	...	...	1.5	2.8	6.4
14 to 19 years.............	1,437	1,395	1,591	1,640	1,230	22.6	19.0	22.8	28.4	26.8
20 to 24 years.............	2,529	2,688	2,316	1,785	1,179	43.0	45.6	41.8	37.5	31.7
25 years and over.........	12,554	8,932	6,489	4,804	2,590	28.0	23.9	20.6	18.7	15.5

[1] Civilian labor force.
[2] Persons under 14 years old in the labor force were not enumerated in the Censuses of 1940 and 1950.

Source: *1950 Census of Population*, Vol. II, *Characteristics of the Population*, Part 1, U. S. Summary, table 118; John D. Durand, *The Labor Force in the United States: 1890-1960*, Social Science Research Council, New York, 1948, table A-6.

FIGURE **20.**—LABOR FORCE PARTICIPATION RATES OF PERSONS 14 TO 19 YEARS OLD, BY SEX: 1900 AND 1920 TO 1950

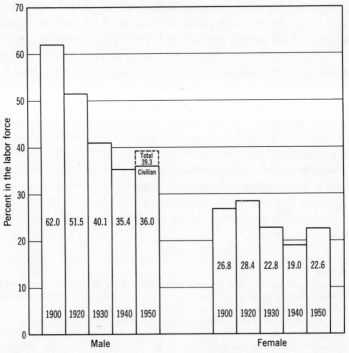

Note: Based on data in table 36.

Over one third of the Nation's youth 14 to 19 years of age were numbered among the Nation's civilian labor force in 1950 (table 37).[3]   Of a
total labor force of 62 million persons, 4.5 million or roughly 7 percent
were young people under 20 years of age.   More than 2 million of these
youths were less than 18 years old.

TABLE 37.—LABOR FORCE STATUS OF PERSONS 14 TO 24 YEARS OLD: 1940 AND 1946
TO 1950

[Data for 1946 to 1950 are derived from a sample survey and are subject to sampling variation which may be
relatively large in those cases where the estimates are based on quantities which are small]

Age and labor force status	1950	1949	1948	1947	1946	1940
14 and 15 years:						
Civilian noninstitutional population...	4,263	4,141	4,109	4,218	4,640	4,830
Civilian labor force....................	709	629	650	640	740	330
Percent in labor force..............	16.6	15.2	15.8	15.2	15.9	6.8
16 and 17 years:						
Civilian noninstitutional population...	4,083	4,146	4,279	4,318	4,580	4,890
Civilian labor force....................	1,414	1,531	1,572	1,500	1,630	1,110
Percent in labor force..............	34.6	36.9	36.7	34.7	35.6	22.7
18 and 19 years:						
Civilian noninstitutional population...	4,079	4,055	4,155	4,092	3,160	4,980
Civilian labor force....................	2,349	2,396	2,562	2,440	1,830	2,820
Percent in labor force..............	57.6	59.1	61.7	59.6	57.9	56.6
20 to 24 years:						
Civilian noninstitutional population...	11,200	11,372	11,630	11,582	10,620	11,490
Civilian labor force....................	7,276	7,121	7,261	7,230	6,300	7,800
Percent in labor force..............	65.0	62.6	62.4	62.4	59.3	67.9

Source: U. S. Bureau of the Census, Current Population Survey (unpublished data).   Data for 1940 are 1940 Census of
Population statistics revised by the Bureau of the Census for comparability with the Current Population Survey
(unpublished).

Labor force participation of young people was considerably higher in
1950 than in 1940 when approximately one quarter of the youths 14 to 19
years old were labor force members.   The increase in participation may
be explained in large part by the increase in student-workers who were
both attending school and engaging in economic activity.   The labor force
influx of teen-age boys and girls was largely a phenomenon of the war years
when, in addition to those who joined as student-workers, many left school
to take war jobs and a large number of girls transferred from the homemaker group to the labor force.[4]   This wartime expansion in the teen-age
labor force did not prove to be as temporary a development as anticipated

[3] Because of the comparatively sizable underenumeration of teen-agers in the labor force in the 1950
Census returns, the data presented here are based on U. S. Bureau of the Census, *Current Population
Reports*, Series P–57, No. 94, May 1950.   For further discussion of underenumeration of the teen-age
labor force see *1950 Census of Population*, Vol. II, *Characteristics of the Population*, Part 1, U. S.
Summary, Introduction, p. 52.

[4] Lester M. Pearlman and Leonard Eskin, "Teen-Age Youth in the Wartime Labor Force," *Monthly
Labor Review*, Vol. 60, No. 1, U. S. Department of Labor, Washington, D. C., January 1945, pp. 6–17;
John D. Durand, "The Postwar Employment of Women in the United States: A Statistical Forecast,"
International Labour Review, Vol. 48, December 1944, pp. 695–713.

by some.[5] The student-worker category alone was almost 1 million greater in 1950 than expected on the basis of 1940 trends and only 300,000 lower than could be expected on the basis of a wartime peak figure. (See appendix table E–11.)

Year-by-year fluctuations in the postwar period in the proportion of youths engaged in economic activity (table 37) cannot easily be related to views on current job opportunities or trends toward increased schooling. The fluctuations were minor although the levels of participation remained higher throughout each postwar year, 1946 to 1950, than in the prewar year of 1940.   Although more and a greater proportion of young people were labor force members in 1950 than a decade earlier, the average age of labor force entrance did not change to any notable degree.   For males 14 to 24 years old the average age of labor force entrance approximated 18 years at both dates (table 38).[6]

TABLE **38.**—AVERAGE AGE OF LABOR FORCE ENTRANCE FOR MALES 14 TO 24 YEARS OLD, BY COLOR, URBAN AND RURAL: 1950 AND 1940

Area	1950[1]			1940		
	All classes	White	Nonwhite	All classes	White	Nonwhite
United States............	17.8	17.9	16.8	18.0	18.1	17.0
Urban.....................	18.3	18.3	17.8	18.4	18.5	17.6
Rural nonfarm...............	18.2	18.3	16.8	18.1	18.2	17.2
Rural farm..................	16.5	16.6	15.8	17.2	17.3	16.4

Note: The average age of labor force entrance was estimated from the first differences in the percentage of males in the labor force for successive single years of age 14 to 24 years. These estimates were not standardized to eliminate the effects of differences in sizes of the age cohorts at birth or to eliminate the effects of irregularities in the reporting of age. The stationary population by residence was *not* available for 1950. Examination of the stationary population for 1939 by residence indicated that the variations due to residence were not sufficiently large to have much weighting effect. In addition, it may be assumed that during the course of the decade 1939 to 1949 such differences as did exist were reduced.

[1] Civilian labor force.

Source: *1950 Census of Population*, Vol. IV, *Special Reports*, Part 1, Chapter A, Employment and Personal Characteristics, table 1.

B. Variations in labor force participation and the employment status of youth, 1950

The pattern of labor force activity of young people varies in many important respects by age, sex, color, residence, and region.   Figures 21 to 25 depict these variable patterns of participation by single years of age.

---

[5] John D. Durand, *The Labor Force in the United States, 1890–1960*, Social Science Research Council, New York, 1948, p. 32, underestimated the teen-age labor force in 1950 by almost 15 percent. According to his projections based on past trends only 21 percent of persons 14 to 19 years old would be in the labor force in 1950.   Census returns for 1950 show over 35 percent of the youths of these ages in the civilian labor force.

[6] Estimates of age of labor force entrance based upon census data are not entirely accurate.   The shift from the student category to the labor force is a gradual one and it is difficult to determine when it has been completed.   It may begin with part-time work while attending school or it may begin with seasonal work during school vacations.   If the censuses had been taken during the summer, for example, the average age of labor force entrance for young men would have been much lower.   Durand, *The Labor Force in the United States, 1890–1960, op. cit.*, p. 30, gives 18 years as average age of labor force entrance in 1940 for males 14 to 24 years old.

FIGURE **21.**—LABOR FORCE PARTICIPATION RATES OF PERSONS 14 TO 24 YEARS OLD,
BY SINGLE YEARS OF AGE AND SEX: 1950

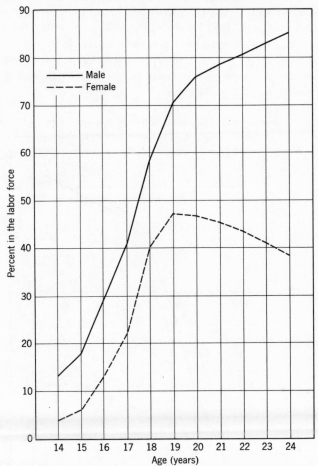

Note: Based on data in appendix table E–8.

It is apparent from figure 21 that male youths participate in the labor force to a greater degree than do female youths, at each single year of age. Only a comparatively small proportion of young teen-agers is part of the labor force; this proportion increases steadily for young males with each increase in age, slackening somewhat as a maximum is approached.   The pattern for girls is different.   Participation rates start at a very low level in the early teen-ages and rise substantially, reaching a peak at age 19. Thereafter participation declines steadily for each single year of age reflecting withdrawal from the labor market due to the responsibilities of marriage and motherhood.

Figure 22 indicates some important color differences in the pattern of labor force participation of young people.   Nonwhite youths tend to go to work at younger ages than do white youths (table 38) reflecting, in part, the relative poverty of nonwhites and, in part, their different educational standards.[7]   During the teen-ages, nonwhite males participate in economic activities to a greater extent than do white boys.   Following the age of 21 years, however, the participation of nonwhite males slackens considerably, leveling off at about 80 percent, whereas the participation of white males continues to increase with each increase in age thereby exceeding the rate for nonwhites at ages 22 to 24 years.

FIGURE **22.**—LABOR FORCE PARTICIPATION RATES OF PERSONS 14 TO 24 YEARS OLD, BY SINGLE YEARS OF AGE, COLOR, AND SEX: 1950

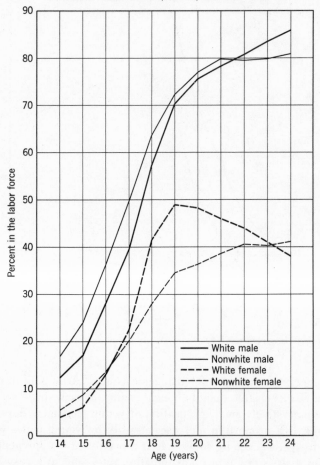

Note: Based on data in appendix table E-8.

---

[7] See Durand, *The Labor Force in the United States, 1890–1960, op. cit.,* table 18, which shows considerably lower educational attainment for nonwhite youths than for white at corresponding levels of monthly rental values of their homes.

Color differentials with respect to labor force activity of female youths are even more striking (figure 22). Although nonwhite females 14 to 16 years of age may participate in the labor force to a greater degree than white girls of the same ages, the increase in their participation with increasing age is at a substantially lower rate, with the result that between the ages of 17 and 23, white rates of participation exceed nonwhite rates, despite the declining participation rates following age 19 years for the white girls. Contrary to the experience of white females, participation among nonwhite girls continues to increase so that the maximum is reached at a later age, sometime after 24 years of age. This difference may be due in part to the fact that a large proportion of nonwhite women, though married, are employed as private household workers where opportunities for the employment of these women are favorable.

The customs, attitudes, and economic conditions governing labor force participation vary by types and sizes of communities. For example, boys living on farms generally enter the labor force about a year earlier than do nonfarm boys (table 38), because part-time employment on the family farm while also attending school is convenient and often necessary. On the other hand, employment opportunities for women in farm areas are rather limited and opportunities in urban areas are considerably greater.

Many environmental factors help to bring young people from farms into the labor force at comparatively early ages. The relatively low income of farm families[8] often makes it important or imperative for all household members to assist in the economic endeavor. Furthermore, child labor laws apply only to employment for wages thereby excluding many farm youths who often are employed as unpaid family workers. In addition, the educational standards toward which farm youth or their parents strive may be lower than the urban standard.[9] In short, rural traditions and institutions are more favorable to the employment of young people than are urban traditions and institutions.

The estimates of average age of labor force entrance for urban, rural-nonfarm, and rural-farm males given in table 38 show these differences. Furthermore, these estimates probably understate the real farm-nonfarm differences since the underreporting of student-workers is almost certainly greater in the case of farm youth. In addition, the differences are undoubtedly greater in the summer months than during the time of the census reporting. Proportionately more farm boys enter the labor force before reaching the age of 14, the effects of which are not accounted for in these estimates.

------

[8] See Herman P. Miller, *Income of the American People,* John Wiley and Sons, New York, 1955, Chapter III.

[9] The median grade of school completed by persons 25 years of age and over in 1950 was 10.2 in urban areas, 8.8 in rural-nonfarm areas, and 8.4 in rural-farm areas. Corresponding figures for 1940 were 8.8, 8.6, and 8.1.

Thus in 1950, as in earlier years, rural-farm boys participated in labor force activities to a noticeably larger extent than did rural-nonfarm or urban boys (figure 23).   On the other hand, it is the *urban* females who participate in the labor force to a greater extent than do females in the other residence groups.

FIGURE **23.**—LABOR FORCE PARTICIPATION RATES OF PERSONS 14 TO 24 YEARS OLD, BY SINGLE YEARS OF AGE AND SEX, URBAN AND RURAL: 1950

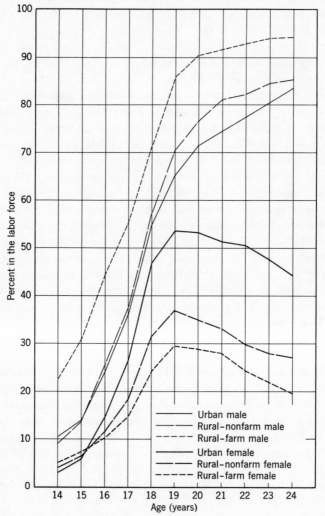

Note: Based on data in appendix table E-9.

An interesting variation in the pattern of participation among females occurs at the younger ages (14 and 15 years) where participation is highest in rural-farm areas and lowest in urban, the reversal occurring after age 15 years (figure 23).

Within urban and rural areas, the size of community often influences the presence of certain industries and, consequently, opportunities for employment. This relationship is shown, to some extent, in table 39. Employment opportunities for urban youths of high school age are less for those living in urbanized areas than for those living in smaller urban areas. Whereas 25 percent of the boys 14 to 17 years old residing in smaller urban areas are in the labor force, less than 20 percent of those living in urbanized areas are labor force members.[10] Similarly, among girls of the same ages, over 15 percent of those living in the smaller urban areas are in the labor force as compared with 12 percent of the girls living in the urbanized areas. At ages 18 and over, the reverse is true, that is, labor force participation rates are higher in urbanized areas than in the smaller urban areas for both males and females.

TABLE **39.**—PERCENT OF PERSONS 14 TO 24 YEARS OLD IN THE CIVILIAN LABOR FORCE BY AGE AND SEX, BY SIZE OF PLACE: 1950

Area and size of place	Male			Female		
	14 to 17 years	18 and 19 years	20 to 24 years	14 to 17 years	18 and 19 years	20 to 24 years
United States...............	25.0	64.1	80.8	11.4	43.7	42.9
Urban.........................	20.9	59.4	77.9	12.9	50.3	49.3
In urbanized areas...............	18.9	60.8	79.0	11.7	53.3	51.5
Places of 100,000 or more......	18.9	61.9	78.8	12.0	55.2	53.3
Places of 50,000 to 100,000....	21.7	56.8	77.7	12.8	50.7	52.0
Places of 25,000 to 50,000.....	18.9	64.4	81.7	11.6	56.6	49.1
Places of 2,500 to 25,000......	17.2	58.5	79.3	11.1	50.9	48.5
Other urban...................	17.8	59.1	80.9	10.0	45.4	42.7
Not in urbanized areas...........	25.5	56.6	75.4	15.3	44.3	43.9
Places of 25,000 or more.......	25.0	53.9	71.5	15.4	45.9	46.8
Places of less than 25,000.....	25.6	57.6	76.9	15.3	43.7	42.9
Rural nonfarm......................	21.0	63.4	82.2	10.0	34.1	30.5
Places of 1,000 to 2,500.......	22.2	64.4	86.7	12.9	38.6	36.2
Other rural nonfarm............	20.4	62.9	80.2	8.6	31.8	27.9
Rural farm........................	38.1	78.0	92.5	9.0	26.6	24.6
Places of 1,000 to 2,500.......	31.8	74.6	91.4	10.0	31.3	38.4
Other rural farm...............	38.2	78.0	92.5	9.0	26.5	24.4

Source: Derived from *1950 Census of Population*, Vol. IV, *Special Reports*, Part 1, Chapter A, Employment and Personal Characteristics, table 4.

It also appears from the data in table 39 that *within* urbanized areas, places with 50,000 to 100,000 inhabitants offer maximum work opportunities for young people of high school ages, whereas for the older teenagers highest labor force participation rates occur in urbanized places with 25,000 to 50,000 inhabitants.

The data also suggest that in rural-nonfarm areas, places with 1,000 to 2,500 inhabitants offer more employment to young people than do other rural-nonfarm areas. On the other hand, in rural-farm areas, labor force

[10] Otis Dudley Duncan and Albert J. Reiss in *Social Characteristics of Urban and Rural Communities, 1950*, John Wiley and Sons, New York, 1956, table 31, present estimates of the median age of entry into the labor force for males by size of place. Although their data are not strictly comparable with those presented here, both indicate greater labor force participation for males in smaller sized communities.

participation rates for males are less in places with 1,000 to 2,500 inhabitants than in other rural-farm areas, whereas such rates for females are
higher in the larger rural-farm areas than in the smaller ones.

Regional variations in rates of labor force participation among young
persons are shown in figures 24 and 25. Teen-age boys in the South
engage in economic activities to a greater extent than do boys in the other
regions of the Nation. Among young men in their early twenties those residing in the North Central Region participate in the labor market at
a somewhat higher rate than the young men in other regions. Male
youths 14 to 24 years of age residing in the Northeast have lowest participation rates at each single year of age. Regional differences with respect
to the labor force participation among female youths are more complex.

FIGURE 24.—LABOR FORCE PARTICIPATION RATES OF MALES 14 TO 24 YEARS OLD,
BY SINGLE YEARS OF AGE, FOR REGIONS: 1950

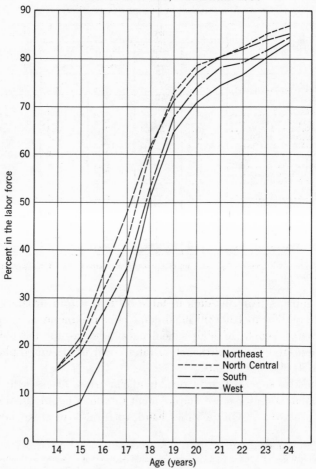

Note: Based on data in appendix table E-10.

It appears that during the early teen-ages, 14 to 17 years, girls living in the North Central Region have the highest rate of participation and that thereafter the Northeast assumes ascendency. The general pattern of participation is about the same for each of the major regions, although it should be noted that in the South, which generally possesses the lowest rates, the age of maximum participation is 21 years as compared with 19 years for the other regions. This higher age of maximum participation in the South is due in part to the concentration of nonwhite females in the South.

FIGURE **25.**—LABOR FORCE PARTICIPATION RATES OF FEMALES 14 TO 24 YEARS OLD, BY SINGLE YEARS OF AGE, FOR REGIONS: 1950

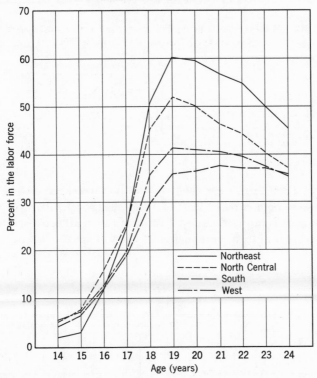

Note: Based on data in appendix table E-10.

C. Student labor force

A considerable proportion of the increase in labor force activity of young people over the past decade is due to an increase in the number of student-workers. As indicated before wartime opportunities occasioned a large influx of teen-agers into the labor force, and the postwar period did not bring a comparable reduction in teen-age workers. Between 1940 and 1950 the civilian labor force membership rates of young people increased from 7 percent to 17 percent for those 14 and 15 years old, from 23 per-

cent to 35 percent for those 16 and 17 years old, and from only 57 percent to 58 percent for those 18 and 19 years old (table 37). It is obvious
that the largest increase occurred at those ages where school attendance is
largely compulsory, reflecting gains among student-workers.

Table 40 provides further evidence of the increase in number of student-
workers in the teen-age labor force. While the total population in each of
the age groups declined by about 7 or 8 percent, the number of youths who
were both in the labor force and enrolled in school more than doubled. At
the younger teen-ages the increase amounted to 161 percent and 171 percent for the 14- and 15-year-olds and the 16- and 17-year-olds, respectively, and by almost 40 percent for the 18- and 19-year-olds.

TABLE **40.**—PERCENT CHANGE IN THE POPULATION AND THE STUDENT LABOR FORCE
14 TO 19 YEARS OLD, BY AGE: 1940 TO 1950

Age	Percent change, 1940 to 1950	
	Total population	Student labor force
Total, 14 to 19 years..........	-7.5	+111.5
14 and 15 years.....................	-8.7	+161.4
16 and 17 years.....................	-7.4	+171.0
18 and 19 years.....................	-4.1	+38.8

Source: Appendix table E–11.

In April 1950 there were about 1.3 million teen-agers (14 to 19 years
old) who were both enrolled in school and engaged in labor force activity.
These students comprised almost a third of the total teen-age labor force.
Over 70 percent of them were under 18 years of age (table 41).

TABLE **41.**—PERSONS 14 TO 19 YEARS OLD IN THE LABOR FORCE, BY SCHOOL ENROLLMENT
AND AGE: 1950

[Numbers in thousands]

Age	Total population	Total labor force		Student labor force		
		Number	Percent	Number	Percent	Percent of total labor force
Total, 14 to 19 years.....	12,783	3,962	31.0	1,269	100.0	32.0
14 and 15 years...............	4,268	445	10.4	366	28.8	82.2
16 and 17 years...............	4,173	1,124	26.9	542	42.7	48.2
18 and 19 years...............	4,342	2,393	55.1	361	28.4	15.1

Source: Derived from *1950 Census of Population*, Vol. II, *Characteristics of the Population*, Part 1, U. S. Summary,
table 122.

A teen-ager who was employed in 1950 was more apt to be enrolled in
school than was one who was looking for a job. Over a third of the employed teen-agers were enrolled in school in April 1950; only one fifth of
the unemployed teen-agers were students. Survey materials have indicated
that most unemployed persons, including young people, are seeking full-

time jobs.[11]   During the school term, unemployment among the young
seems to involve chiefly those who have left school and are available for
full-time work (table 42).

TABLE 42.—PERCENT DISTRIBUTION OF PERSONS 14 TO 19 YEARS OLD IN THE LABOR FORCE
BY EMPLOYMENT STATUS AND SEX, BY SCHOOL ENROLLMENT AND AGE: 1950

Employment status and sex	Enrolled in school				Not enrolled in school			
	Total, 14 to 19 years old	14 and 15 years old	16 and 17 years old	18 and 19 years old	Total, 14 to 19 years old	14 and 15 years old	16 and 17 years old	18 and 19 years old
Total.................	100.0	100.0	100.0	100.0	100.0	100.0	100.0	100.0
Employed....................	90.3	93.7	89.7	87.7	81.9	89.7	80.2	82.1
Unemployed..................	9.7	6.3	10.3	12.3	18.1	10.3	19.8	17.9
Male....................	100.0	100.0	100.0	100.0	100.0	100.0	100.0	100.0
Employed....................	90.2	94.6	90.3	84.8	77.1	91.7	79.0	75.8
Unemployed..................	9.8	5.4	9.7	15.2	22.9	8.3	21.0	24.2
Female.................	100.0	100.0	100.0	100.0	100.0	100.0	100.0	100.0
Employed....................	90.3	91.1	88.6	92.0	89.8	83.3	82.8	91.4
Unemployed..................	9.7	8.9	11.4	8.0	10.2	16.7	17.2	8.6

Source: Appendix table E-12.

Labor force activity on the part of young people enrolled in school varies
significantly with age, sex, color, and urban-rural residence (figures 26, 27,
28, and 29).   For young men in each age group, labor force participation
rates are higher for nonstudents than for students.   Among students, there
is some increase in labor force participation as age increases, particularly
at the late college and postgraduate levels; the rate for age 25 to 29 years
old is 20 percentage points greater than for those for 21 to 24 years old.
Among nonstudents, on the other hand, participation rates increase with
increasing age and then level off as maximum participation is approached
(over 90 percent at age 20 years and over).   Young women are less frequently in the labor force than young men of the same age and among them,
those who are students are less frequently in the labor force than those who
are not students.   This is particularly true among the teen-age groups.   At
ages 21 to 24 the labor force participation rates for students and others are
roughly equal, and at ages 25 to 29 the rates for students actually exceed
those for nonstudents.

Among both white and nonwhite youths at each age level, labor force
membership is greater for nonstudents than for students.   Among males,
both white and nonwhite, there is an increase in student participation in
the labor force with each increase in age (figure 27).   Nonwhite male
students participate in the labor force to a greater extent than do white
students at each age level up to the postcollege ages of 25 to 29 years.   For
males not enrolled in school, labor force activity for white youths 18 years
of age and over exceeds that of nonwhite youths.

---

[11] U. S. Bureau of the Census, *Current Population Reports*, Series P-50, No. 21, March 1950, table 7.

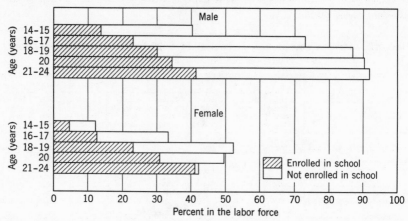

FIGURE **26.**—PERCENT OF PERSONS 14 TO 24 YEARS OLD IN THE LABOR FORCE, BY SCHOOL ENROLLMENT, AGE, AND SEX: 1950

Source: *1950 Census of Population*, Vol. II, *Characteristics of the Population*, Part 1, U. S. Summary, table 122.

Color differentials among female students participating in the labor force, as depicted in figure 27, show that participation rates increase with each increase in age level. With the exception of the youngest teen-agers (14 and 15 years old), the labor force participation of white students exceeds that of nonwhite students at each age. For females not enrolled in school the rate of labor force activity increases steadily through ages 18 and 19 years, declining persistently thereafter. For the nonwhite females who are not enrolled in school, participation increases in each successive age group.

Figures 28 and 29 show the urban-rural differentials in labor force participation on the part of young people enrolled and not enrolled in school. For males in each enrollment group, participation rates increase with age for all residence groups. At each age level, participation rates are highest in rural-farm areas, for both students and nonstudents. Urban male students under 18 and 19 years old participate in economic endeavors to a greater extent than do rural-nonfarm students, although among those not enrolled in school, rural-nonfarm boys are more apt to be in the labor force than are the urban boys. At ages 18 and 19 years, participation rates are roughly the same for both students and nonstudents in urban and rural-nonfarm areas. Male students of college age are more apt to be in the labor force if they are residing in rural-nonfarm areas than in urban areas.

The residential pattern of labor force participation among females is quite different from that for males. With the exception of the youngest teen-agers (14 and 15 years old), participation is greatest in urban areas and least in rural-farm areas for both students and nonstudents. For the youngest group, participation rates are highest in rural farm areas and lowest in urban areas. Interesting residential differences occur among the older females 21 to 24 years of age. Although in urban areas nonstudents engage in economic activities to a greater extent than do students, in the

FIGURE **27.**—PERCENT OF PERSONS 14 TO 24 YEARS OLD IN THE LABOR FORCE, BY SCHOOL
ENROLLMENT, AGE, COLOR, AND SEX: 1950

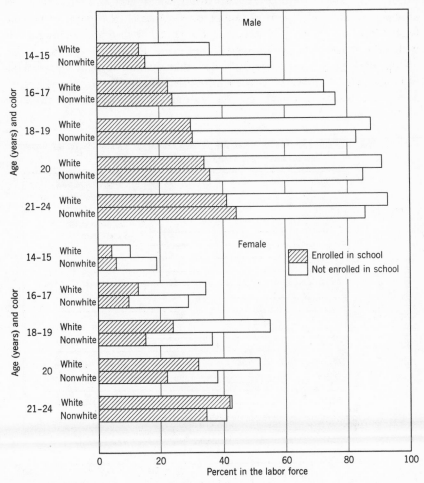

Source: Same as figure 26.

rural areas, both farm and nonfarm, student participation rates exceed those
of nonstudents.

Summary. Since 1940, the proportion of young people enrolled in
school has increased to an all-time high. Concomitantly, the employment
of school youths after school hours increased considerably during the war
years and has continued throughout the postwar years.[12] With the exception of the World War II period, the expanded opportunities of the 1940's

---

[12] More recent data on the employment of students (U. S. Bureau of the Census, *Current Population
Reports,* Series P–50, No. 51, January 1954) indicate some contraction in job openings for young people still in school between the outbreak of hostilities in Korea (about October 1950) and October 1953.
The decline occurred in both the numbers of student-workers of high school age and in their rate of
labor force participation. Similar declines occurred among college age students. Despite these declines, student-worker levels remained considerably above those before World War II.

did not bring about similar increases in the employment of out-of-school youth. In 1950, the employment of young people who had left school was roughly at the 1940 level although participation rates were somewhat higher than in 1940. The result is that in 1950 in-school teen-agers of high school ages (14 to 17 years) comprised almost 60 percent of the young work force whereas in 1940 less than a third of all young workers were students.[13] Possibly, opportunities for part-time work have helped to keep some youths in school who otherwise might drop out to seek full-time employment.

FIGURE **28.**—PERCENT OF MALES 14 TO 24 YEARS OLD IN THE LABOR FORCE, BY SCHOOL ENROLLMENT AND AGE, URBAN AND RURAL: 1950

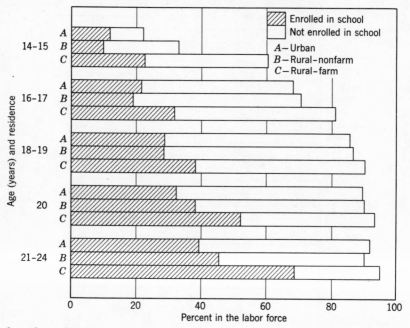

Source: Same as figure 26.

It appears that part-time employment has become a predominating pattern of work for young people. This pattern may be viewed from a twofold aspect of extreme conditions:

Under good conditions it may offer new experiences and a chance to earn money without sacrifice of schooling, and can indeed make the transition to full-time work less difficult. Under poor conditions these combined school and work activities may cost youth dearly—in diversion from interest in school, and in loss of time needed for sleep, study and play.[14]

[13] U. S. Department of Labor, Bureau of Labor Standards, *Facts About Work of School Youth 1951* (mimeographed), September 1952.
[14] *Ibid.*

FIGURE **29.**—PERCENT OF FEMALES 14 TO 24 YEARS OLD IN THE LABOR FORCE, BY SCHOOL
ENROLLMENT AND AGE, URBAN AND RURAL: 1950

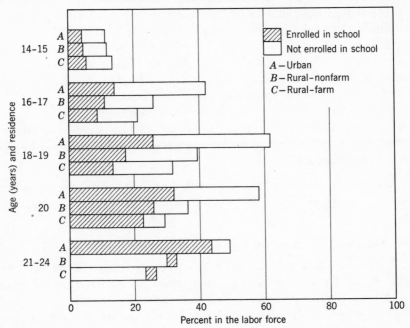

Source: Same as figure 26.

The descriptive materials presented in this section in conjunction with those on educational attainment (Chapter 5, section B) and on relative school progress (Chapter 6) indicate that there is no consistent set of demographic characteristics relating the employment of youths with school enrollment, educational attainment, and age-grade school progress. That is, it is not possible to identify a series of attributes which consistently characterize high enrollment, high attainment, high age-grade school progress, and low student employment—or vice versa. Although some of the attributes considered do occur consistently in relation to the educational measures, these same attributes do not always characterize high or low student employment. The findings may be summarized as follows:

First, with respect to sex, student employment among females is lower than that for males. Concurrently, enrollment rates, educational attainment levels, and age-grade school progress are higher for females than for males.

Second, with respect to color differentials for males, student employment is lower for whites than for nonwhites. Concurrently, enrollment rates, educational attainment levels, and age-grade school progress are higher for white males than for nonwhite males.

Third, with respect to urban-rural differentials for males, at the high school ages student employment is lowest in rural-nonfarm areas. Concurrently, enrollment rates, educational attainment levels, and age-grade school progress for these boys fall between those of urban and rural-farm youths. At the college ages, student employment is lowest in urban areas, where enrollment rates and educational attainment levels are highest.[15]

Fourth, with respect to color differentials for females, student employment is generally lower for nonwhites than for whites. Concurrently, enrollment rates, educational attainment levels, and age-grade school progress are *lower* for nonwhite females than for white females.

Fifth, with respect to urban-rural differentials for females, the *highest* student employment rates occur in urban areas. Concurrently, enrollment rates, educational attainment levels, and age-grade school progress are also highest in urban areas.

On the basis of the findings presented, then, it is not possible to say that student employment either hampers or enhances attendance or performance in school.

D. Variations in hours worked by employed youths

Employed youths not enrolled in school are typically full-time workers (that is, 35 hours or more per week); employed students, on the other hand, usually work part time during their teens and full time throughout their twenties. At the time of the 1950 Census enumeration, almost three fourths of the employed students of high school age (14 to 17 years) were part-time workers; over 70 percent of the youths of this age not enrolled in school were working at full-time jobs (table 43). For the 18- and 19-year-olds the pattern was similar; those attending school generally worked less than full time and those not enrolled in school typically worked 35 hours or more per week. Among persons 20 years of age and over, the majority of those both enrolled and not enrolled in school were employed at full-time jobs (table 44). It is important to note that about 70,000 boys and girls 14 and 15 years of age were not enrolled in school, and most of them had jobs at which they worked 35 hours or more per week. In addition, there were over 450,000 employed 16- and 17-year-olds not attending school, with about three fourths of them working at full-time jobs.

Among youths of high school ages, a higher proportion of employed girls than boys held part-time jobs outside of school hours; the boys, however, were found to be working longer hours than the girls. Over three fourths of the employed female students 14 to 17 years old were engaged in part-time work; about 45 percent held jobs at which they were working less than 15 hours per week; about a third were found to be working from 15 to 34 hours. Among the employed male students of high school age about 70 percent had part-time jobs; a third were working less than 15 hours and about 40 percent were working from 15 to 34 hours per week.

---

[15] Age-grade school progress applies to only elementary and high school ages.

TABLE **43.**—PERSONS 14 TO 17 YEARS OLD EMPLOYED AT PART-TIME AND FULL-TIME WORK,
BY SCHOOL ENROLLMENT: 1950

[Numbers in thousands]

Hours worked	Total	Enrolled in school	Not enrolled in school	Percent distribution		
				Total	Enrolled in school	Not enrolled in school
Total at work..............	1,308	793	515	100.0	100.0	100.0
Under 35 hours.................	710	580	130	54.3	73.1	25.2
35 hours or more..............	501	131	370	38.3	16.5	71.8
Hours not reported............	97	82	15	7.4	10.3	2.9

Source: Derived from *1950 Census of Population*, Vol. II, *Characteristics of the Population*, Part 1, U. S. Summary, table 122.

TABLE **44.**—HOURS WORKED DURING CENSUS WEEK BY EMPLOYED PERSONS 14 TO 29 YEARS
OLD, BY SCHOOL ENROLLMENT, AGE, AND SEX: 1950

[Population figures in thousands and rounded separately]

School enrollment, hours worked, and sex	Total, 14 to 29 years	14 and 15 years	16 and 17 years	18 and 19 years	20 years	21 to 24 years	25 to 29 years
ENROLLED IN SCHOOL							
Male, employed............	1,482	262	324	190	63	291	352
With a job but not at work....	69	11	15	11	4	15	13
At work......................	1,413	251	308	179	59	276	338
Percent at work........	100.0	100.0	100.0	100.0	100.0	100.0	100.0
1 to 14 hours.................	19.4	34.3	28.5	23.0	17.1	10.9	5.5
15 to 34 hours................	29.7	37.6	42.6	37.8	26.8	21.8	14.7
35 hours or more..............	44.4	15.6	20.1	33.6	51.3	63.3	76.9
Hours not reported............	6.5	12.5	8.8	5.5	4.8	3.9	2.9
Female, employed..........	624	82	171	138	50	108	74
With a job but not at work....	35	7	12	7	2	4	3
At work......................	588	75	160	131	47	104	71
Percent at work........	100.0	100.0	100.0	100.0	100.0	100.0	100.0
1 to 14 hours.................	26.0	47.3	40.1	24.2	17.6	9.7	4.1
15 to 34 hours................	26.1	30.4	36.8	26.7	17.4	16.8	15.8
35 hours or more..............	40.1	9.0	14.4	41.4	56.9	68.1	76.3
Hours not reported............	7.8	13.4	8.7	7.7	8.2	5.3	3.8
NOT ENROLLED IN SCHOOL							
Male, employed............	9,378	55	313	911	579	2,973	4,547
With a job but not at work....	197	1	7	20	13	65	91
At work......................	9,181	54	306	892	566	2,908	4,455
Percent at work........	100.0	100.0	100.0	100.0	100.0	100.0	100.0
1 to 14 hours.................	1.2	6.7	4.3	2.1	1.4	1.1	0.8
15 to 34 hours................	7.4	25.8	19.8	11.4	8.8	7.0	5.6
35 hours or more..............	89.2	64.4	73.4	84.0	87.5	89.6	91.5
Hours not reported............	2.2	3.1	2.6	2.5	2.4	2.3	2.1
Female, employed..........	5,010	15	144	746	451	1,785	1,870
With a job but not at work....	149	1	5	17	10	50	66
At work......................	4,861	14	139	729	441	1,734	1,803
Percent at work........	100.0	100.0	100.0	100.0	100.0	100.0	100.0
1 to 14 hours.................	2.4	13.1	5.2	2.2	1.7	1.9	2.8
15 to 34 hours................	11.1	29.5	18.5	9.4	8.6	10.1	12.7
35 hours or more..............	83.8	51.8	73.4	85.9	87.3	85.3	81.7
Hours not reported............	2.7	5.6	2.9	2.5	2.4	2.7	2.8

Source: *1950 Census of Population*, Vol. II, *Characteristics of the Population*, Part 1, U. S. Summary, table 122.

The general pattern of hours worked by students and nonstudents was similar for males and females throughout the teen-ages. Part-time employment was typical for students of both sexes, greater proportions working longer hours with increasing age. Full-time employment was typical also for nonstudents of both sexes; and again with increasing age a greater proportion of these youths joined the ranks of those who worked longer hours. After age 20, the pattern of employment for those not enrolled in school differed between males and females. Whereas among males a larger proportion became full-time workers, among employed females increasing age was coupled with a declining proportion engaged in full-time work.

A similar pattern of hours worked by students and nonstudents was found for the three residence groups: urban, rural-nonfarm, and rural-farm. Part-time employment was typical for teen-age students in all three residence groups; in each, increasing age brought with it a larger proportion of persons working longer hours, full-time employment becoming typical for students at about age 20 (table 45). The majority of employed youths not in school held full-time jobs in all three areas.

Among male youths of high school ages, a higher proportion of urban boys compared to nonurban boys held part-time jobs outside of school hours; rural-farm boys, however, were found to be working longer hours than those living in nonfarm areas. Over three fourths of the employed urban male students of high school ages were engaged in part-time work as compared with about 70 percent of the employed students in rural-nonfarm areas and 65 percent in rural-farm areas. Among the employed male students in urban areas, however, about 45 percent held jobs at which they were working less than 15 hours per week, in contrast to the rural-farm employed male students where only 6 percent were working less than 15 hours and well over half were working from 15 to 34 hours per week, as well as attending school. While less than 15 percent of the nonfarm employed male students 14 to 17 years old were working at full-time jobs, almost a third of those in rural-farm areas held full-time jobs while still enrolled in school. As indicated in section C of this chapter, most of the rural-farm student-workers were employed in agriculture as unpaid workers on family-operated farms. This kind of work may readily be performed outside of school hours.

Employed boys of high school ages not enrolled in school generally held full-time jobs.[16] The proportion of boys not in school who were working 35 hours or more per week was greater among rural farm boys than among those living in nonfarm areas.

Among the 18- and 19-year-old males, student employment was still typically on a part-time basis. By age 20 the majority of employed male students enrolled in school were working 35 hours or more per week: 67

---

[16] Urban males 14 and 15 years old are a noted exception.

TABLE 45.—HOURS WORKED DURING CENSUS WEEK BY EMPLOYED MALES 14 TO 29 YEARS OLD, BY SCHOOL ENROLLMENT AND AGE, URBAN AND RURAL: 1950

[Population figures in thousands and rounded separately]

Area, school enrollment, and hours worked	Total, 14 to 29 years	14 and 15 years	16 and 17 years	18 and 19 years	20 years	21 to 24 years	25 to 29 years
ENROLLED IN SCHOOL							
Urban							
Employed.................	971	121	173	126	49	231	270
With a job but not at work....	51	7	10	8	3	13	11
At work......................	920	114	163	119	46	219	259
Percent at work........	100.0	100.0	100.0	100.0	100.0	100.0	100.0
1 to 14 hours................	22.8	55.3	38.9	27.1	19.2	12.1	6.1
15 to 34 hours...............	25.0	20.5	37.4	36.2	27.4	23.1	15.4
35 hours or more.............	45.2	6.1	12.8	30.9	48.7	60.9	75.7
Hours not reported...........	6.9	18.0	10.9	5.9	4.7	4.0	2.9
Rural Nonfarm							
Employed.................	210	41	54	28	7	35	46
With a job but not at work....	12	2	3	2	(1)	2	2
At work......................	198	39	51	26	7	33	44
Percent at work........	100.0	100.0	100.0	100.0	100.0	100.0	100.0
1 to 14 hours................	24.7	45.1	35.9	27.7	15.3	9.0	5.2
15 to 34 hours...............	26.6	27.3	36.2	36.1	24.5	19.1	15.5
35 hours or more.............	40.6	12.4	18.0	30.0	54.3	67.6	75.7
Hours not reported...........	8.0	15.3	10.0	6.2	6.0	4.3	3.5
Rural Farm							
Employed.................	301	100	97	36	7	25	36
With a job but not at work....	6	2	2	1	(1)	1	1
At work......................	295	98	95	35	6	24	36
Percent at work........	100.0	100.0	100.0	100.0	100.0	100.0	100.0
1 to 14 hours................	5.2	5.7	6.6	6.0	4.1	2.1	1.4
15 to 34 hours...............	46.3	61.4	54.9	44.7	24.6	14.4	9.3
35 hours or more.............	44.3	28.0	33.9	45.3	67.0	80.4	87.1
Hours not reported...........	4.2	4.9	4.5	4.0	4.3	3.1	2.3
NOT ENROLLED IN SCHOOL							
Urban							
Employed.................	5,789	10	107	461	323	1,849	3,040
With a job but not at work....	129	1	3	11	8	43	63
At work......................	5,660	9	104	449	315	1,806	2,977
Percent at work........	100.0	100.0	100.0	100.0	100.0	100.0	100.0
1 to 14 hours................	1.0	21.6	6.5	2.1	1.2	0.9	0.7
15 to 34 hours...............	5.6	21.4	18.4	9.2	6.8	5.5	4.5
35 hours or more.............	91.2	49.1	72.0	86.1	89.8	91.3	92.9
Hours not reported...........	2.2	7.9	3.1	2.6	2.2	2.2	2.0
Rural Nonfarm							
Employed.................	1,912	10	66	185	119	617	913
With a job but not at work....	45	(1)	2	5	3	15	21
At work......................	1,866	10	64	181	116	603	893
Percent at work........	100.0	100.0	100.0	100.0	100.0	100.0	100.0
1 to 14 hours................	1.8	10.5	6.0	3.2	2.0	1.5	1.2
15 to 34 hours...............	10.0	29.1	23.4	14.3	11.6	9.7	8.0
35 hours or more.............	85.7	55.8	67.1	79.5	83.5	86.3	88.6
Hours not reported...........	2.5	4.6	3.5	3.0	2.9	2.5	2.2
Rural Farm							
Employed.................	1,677	36	140	265	136	506	593
With a job but not at work....	22	(1)	2	3	2	7	8
At work......................	1,654	35	138	262	134	499	585
Percent at work........	100.0	100.0	100.0	100.0	100.0	100.0	100.0
1 to 14 hours................	1.2	1.7	1.8	1.3	1.1	1.1	1.0
15 to 34 hours...............	10.8	26.0	19.1	13.2	10.9	9.3	7.9
35 hours or more.............	86.0	70.7	77.3	83.5	85.7	87.4	88.9
Hours not reported...........	2.1	1.5	1.8	2.0	2.2	2.1	2.1

[1] Less than 1,000.

Source: Same as table 44.

percent in rural-farm areas, 54 percent in rural-nonfarm areas, and almost 50 percent of the male students in urban areas were so engaged.

Among the employed male students aged 21 years and over, a smaller proportion in rural areas participated in full-time work activity. In contrast, among the nonstudents a larger proportion of the urban employed than the rural employed males had jobs at which they worked 35 hours or more per week.

Similar residential variations occurred among the females. For females of high school ages, a higher proportion of urban than nonurban girls held part-time jobs outside of school hours; however, rural-farm girls were found to be working longer hours than the other girls (table 46). Almost 80 percent of the employed urban female students of high school ages had part-time jobs as contrasted with about 70 percent of the rural-farm employed students. Among the urban girls, however, about half had jobs at which they were working less than 15 hours per week, as contrasted with about 15 percent of the rural-farm employed students.

In contrast to the males, employed urban female students 18 and 19 years old generally worked longer hours than did girls from other areas. Over 45 percent of the urban student-workers worked 35 hours or more per week as compared with about 30 percent of girls from rural-non-farm and rural-farm areas. Also notably different from the experience of the males, among the females a greater proportion of urban student-workers age 20 years and over held full-time jobs than did the student-workers in other areas. Similarly, among the nonstudent females, greater proportions at each age level of those residing in urban areas were employed at full-time jobs.

E. Industrial and occupational affiliations of employed youths

Young workers in 1950, as in previous years, were employed predominantly in industries and occupations which require relatively little skill or previous work experience. Agriculture was the largest employer of young boys, and personal services the largest employer of young girls in 1950. Young male workers were primarily engaged as farm laborers, newsboys, and delivery boys; young female workers were employed largely as private household workers and retail salesgirls.[17]

Although most industries, except agriculture and personal services, had

---

[17] This conforms with the work patterns described in the book by Delbert C. Miller and William H. Form, *Industrial Sociology; An Introduction to the Sociology of Work Relations*, Harper and Brothers, New York, 1951, pp. 556 ff., which elaborates the picture of young workers entering the labor market in the lower rungs of the occupational ladder. See also, A. J. Jaffe and R. O. Carleton, *Occupational Mobility in the United States, 1930–1960*, King's Crown Press, Columbia University, New York, 1954, Chapter 4. Along these same lines Philip M. Hauser in "Mobility in Labor Force Participation" in E. W. Bakke (Ed.), *Labor Mobility and Economic Opportunity*, The Technology Press of Massachusetts Institute of Technology and John Wiley and Sons, New York, 1954, table 8, shows that the greatest mobility in labor force participation occurs among persons under 20 years old.

TABLE **46.**—HOURS WORKED DURING CENSUS WEEK BY EMPLOYED FEMALES 14 TO 29 YEARS OLD, BY SCHOOL ENROLLMENT AND AGE, URBAN AND RURAL: 1950

[Population figures in thousands and rounded separately]

Area, school enrollment, and hours worked	Total, 14 to 29 years	14 and 15 years	16 and 17 years	18 and 19 years	20 years	21 to 24 years	25 to 29 years
ENROLLED IN SCHOOL							
Urban							
Employed..................	467	42	115	111	43	94	63
With a job but not at work....	25	4	8	6	2	4	2
At work......................	442	38	107	106	41	90	60
Percent at work.........	100.0	100.0	100.0	100.0	100.0	100.0	100.0
1 to 14 hours................	25.7	62.6	43.1	23.9	17.5	9.9	4.0
15 to 34 hours..............	22.7	18.0	34.3	24.8	16.7	16.2	15.0
35 hours or more.............	44.2	4.5	14.1	43.8	57.6	68.9	77.4
Hours not reported...........	7.4	15.0	8.5	7.5	8.1	5.0	3.6
Rural Nonfarm							
Employed..................	89	18	32	16	5	11	8
With a job but not at work....	6	2	2	1	(1)	(1)	(1)
At work......................	83	16	29	16	5	10	7
Percent at work.........	100.0	100.0	100.0	100.0	100.0	100.0	100.0
1 to 14 hours................	35.2	55.7	43.9	31.1	22.8	9.6	6.0
15 to 34 hours..............	27.2	23.7	34.1	29.8	19.0	19.3	17.9
35 hours or more.............	28.5	8.2	12.9	30.8	49.7	62.9	71.6
Hours not reported...........	9.1	12.4	9.1	8.3	8.5	8.2	4.5
Rural Farm							
Employed..................	67	23	25	10	2	4	3
With a job but not at work....	4	2	2	1	(1)	(1)	(1)
At work......................	63	21	23	10	2	4	3
Percent at work.........	100.0	100.0	100.0	100.0	100.0	100.0	100.0
1 to 14 hours................	15.4	13.4	21.1	16.6	7.4	5.3	2.5
15 to 34 hours..............	48.5	57.7	51.8	43.1	26.9	23.3	24.7
35 hours or more.............	26.6	17.6	17.8	32.0	57.3	64.8	66.7
Hours not reported...........	9.4	11.3	9.3	8.3	8.4	6.7	6.1
NOT ENROLLED IN SCHOOL							
Urban							
Employed..................	3,910	5	94	559	348	1,419	1,485
With a job but not at work....	107	(1)	3	11	7	37	49
At work......................	3,803	5	91	548	341	1,382	1,436
Percent at work.........	100.0	100.0	100.0	100.0	100.0	100.0	100.0
1 to 14 hours................	2.0	17.0	4.5	1.8	1.4	1.6	2.4
15 to 34 hours..............	9.2	19.9	14.9	7.5	6.8	8.4	10.7
35 hours or more.............	86.3	58.1	78.1	88.4	89.6	87.4	84.2
Hours not reported...........	2.5	4.9	2.6	2.3	2.2	2.5	2.7
Rural Nonfarm							
Employed..................	743	4	28	117	68	256	270
With a job but not at work....	27	(1)	1	3	2	9	12
At work......................	716	3	27	114	66	247	259
Percent at work.........	100.0	100.0	100.0	100.0	100.0	100.0	100.0
1 to 14 hours................	3.9	16.8	7.9	3.4	3.0	3.2	4.7
15 to 34 hours..............	14.8	26.0	19.3	12.7	12.2	13.9	16.4
35 hours or more.............	78.2	51.2	69.2	81.0	81.7	80.0	75.6
Hours not reported...........	3.1	6.0	3.5	2.8	3.0	2.9	3.2
Rural Farm							
Employed..................	358	6	23	69	36	110	115
With a job but not at work....	16	(1)	1	2	1	5	6
At work......................	342	5	22	67	34	106	109
Percent at work.........	100.0	100.0	100.0	100.0	100.0	100.0	100.0
1 to 14 hours................	3.4	6.8	4.8	3.0	2.5	2.9	3.9
15 to 34 hours..............	25.0	41.4	32.8	19.5	19.7	22.9	29.9
35 hours or more.............	67.8	45.7	58.7	73.9	74.2	70.4	62.5
Hours not reported...........	3.8	6.0	3.7	3.6	3.6	3.8	3.8

[1] Less than 1,000.

Source: Same as table 44.

a substantial increase in young workers between 1940 and 1950, the gains were very uneven, resulting in a considerably changed industrial pattern for employed youths (table 47). Agriculture, although still the largest employer of youths of high school age (14 to 17 years old), lost considerably in relative importance during the 1940 decade. Among the 14- and 15-year-olds the proportion of those employed in agriculture declined from 68 percent to 42 percent. A corresponding decrease occurred among the 16- and 17-year-olds, where agriculture employed 48 percent in 1940 and only 29 percent in 1950. Manufacturing and trade have gained in relative importance as employers of young teen-agers whereas the service industries have lost.

TABLE 47.—PERCENT DISTRIBUTION OF EMPLOYED PERSONS 14 to 24 YEARS OLD, BY MAJOR INDUSTRY GROUP AND AGE: 1950 AND 1940

Year and major industry group	Total, 14 to 24 years	14 and 15 years	16 and 17 years	18 and 19 years	20 to 24 years
1950					
Total	100.0	100.0	100.0	100.0	100.0
Agriculture, forestry, and fisheries	14.3	42.3	29.4	15.0	10.2
Mining	1.2	0.3	0.3	0.9	1.6
Construction	4.5	0.8	2.6	3.9	5.2
Manufacturing	25.7	16.8	14.6	24.4	28.2
Transportation, communication, and other public utilities	7.0	1.0	2.3	5.8	8.4
Wholesale and retail trade	21.3	15.5	28.4	24.2	19.7
Finance, insurance, and real estate	4.2	0.3	1.4	5.6	4.4
Business and repair services	2.3	0.5	1.4	2.0	2.7
Personal services	5.6	11.5	8.3	5.6	4.8
Entertainment and recreation services	1.6	3.1	4.0	1.7	1.1
Professional and related services	7.8	1.8	3.5	7.5	8.8
Public administration	2.7	0.3	0.3	1.6	3.5
Industry not reported	2.0	5.8	3.4	1.9	1.6
1940					
Total	100.0	100.0	100.0	100.0	100.0
Agriculture, forestry, and fisheries	21.6	68.1	47.7	24.2	16.5
Mining	1.4	(1)	0.3	1.0	1.8
Construction	2.7	0.5	1.4	2.3	3.1
Manufacturing	25.1	9.0	13.0	22.4	27.7
Transportation, communication, and other public utilities	4.0	0.5	1.7	3.0	4.7
Wholesale and retail trade	18.1	8.1	14.0	18.9	18.6
Finance, insurance, and real estate	2.5	(1)	0.6	2.2	2.8
Business and repair services	1.6	0.5	1.0	1.5	1.8
Personal services	10.4	8.1	14.0	12.4	9.5
Entertainment and recreation services	1.2	1.0	1.7	1.4	1.1
Professional and related services	6.2	1.0	1.7	5.0	7.2
Public administration	3.1	(1)	0.2	3.2	3.4
Industry not reported	2.2	3.3	2.9	2.5	2.0

[1] Less than 0.1 percent.

Source: Appendix table E-13.

Similar changes occurred in the industrial employment pattern of the 18- and 19-year-olds. Manufacturing and trade actually replaced agriculture as the largest employer and the service industries lost in relative importance.

The gains in teen-age workers in the trade occurred chiefly in retail trade and the losses in the service industries occurred primarily in the personal services.

In general, changes in the industrial affiliations of young workers were similar to changes in the affiliations of all employed persons. To that extent they may be said to reflect changes in the economic structure of the Nation, but the differences in the changes which occurred between young workers and total workers may be said to reflect more variations in the employment opportunities offered to youthful and to mature workers.

In examining table 48 we find that in the four most important industrial affiliations of young workers (agriculture, manufacturing, retail trade, and personal services), the changes which occurred among the teen-age affiliations do reflect changes in the total industrial employment pattern. The exodus from agriculture and personal services was more abrupt for teen-age employment than for total employment, however, as was the gain in retail trade. Increases in manufacturing industries, on the other hand, were somewhat greater for the total employed than among the teen-agers.

TABLE **48.**—PERCENT DISTRIBUTION OF TOTAL EMPLOYED AND TEEN-AGE EMPLOYED PERSONS, BY SELECTED INDUSTRIES: 1950 AND 1940

Industry	Total employed		Teen-age employed	
	1950	1940	1950	1940
Total..........................	100.0	100.0	100.0	100.0
Agriculture.......................	12.4	18.8	22.2	33.5
Manufacturing......................	25.9	23.4	20.7	19.0
Retail trade.......................	15.2	14.0	22.0	17.5
Personal service...................	6.2	8.9	7.0	12.5
Other..............................	40.3	34.9	28.1	17.5

Source: See appendix table E–13.

Age variations in the industrial affiliations of young workers show the declining relative importance of agriculture with increasing age and the concomitant gain in manufacturing and trade. In contrast with personal services, which decline in importance with increasing age, the professional and related services experience consistent gains.[18]

Agriculture was the largest employer of young boys of high school ages, accounting for almost 45 percent of their total employment (table 49). Manufacturing (chiefly the printing and publishing industries) provided employment for about one sixth of employed boys 14 to 17 years of age. Among the young females, personal services (mostly in private households) employed almost 40 percent of girls 14 and 15 years old and the trade industries (chiefly retail trade in general merchandise and in restaurants) accounted for about 40 percent of those 16 and 17 years old.

For the older teen-age youths (18 and 19 years) employment of males was concentrated in agriculture, manufacturing, and trade (chiefly retail trade in food stores and gasoline service stations) with each comprising about one quarter of the total employment. Manufacturing and trade

---

[18] See footnote 17.

(mostly in general merchandise stores and restaurants) provided the most important bases of employment for females of these ages, with professional services and finance sharing the secondary orders of importance. Among the professional services, it was the medical and health services which contributed to most of the employment of girls 18 and 19 years old.

TABLE 49.—INDUSTRIAL DISTRIBUTION OF EMPLOYED PERSONS 14 YEARS OLD AND OVER, AND 14 TO 24 YEARS OLD BY AGE, BY SEX: 1950

Major industry group and sex	14 years old and over	14 to 24 years old			
		14 and 15 years old	16 and 17 years old	18 and 19 years old	20 to 24 years old
Male, employed......................	100.0	100.0	100.0	100.0	100.0
Agriculture, forestry, and fisheries......	15.8	47.8	39.8	24.6	15.0
Mining................................	2.2	0.2	0.5	1.5	2.4
Construction..........................	8.2	1.1	3.7	6.6	8.0
Manufacturing.........................	27.0	21.1	15.2	26.3	29.9
Transportation, communication, and other public utilities........................	9.1	0.9	2.4	5.0	8.8
Wholesale and retail trade.............	17.3	14.9	23.7	22.0	18.8
Finance, insurance, and real estate.......	2.8	0.3	0.5	1.6	2.0
Business and repair services.............	3.0	0.8	1.8	2.6	3.4
Personal services.....................	2.9	3.1	3.0	2.7	2.4
Entertainment and recreation services.....	1.0	3.6	4.4	1.9	1.2
Professional and related services........	4.8	1.2	1.6	2.5	3.4
Public administration..................	4.5	0.3	0.3	1.0	3.3
Industry not reported..................	1.3	4.7	3.1	1.8	1.4
Female, employed.....................	100.0	100.0	100.0	100.0	100.0
Agriculture, forestry, and fisheries......	3.8	24.3	9.0	3.0	2.2
Mining................................	0.1	(1)	(1)	0.1	0.2
Construction..........................	0.6	0.2	0.3	0.5	0.7
Manufacturing.........................	23.2	2.8	13.5	22.0	25.4
Transportation, communication, and other public utilities........................	4.3	0.5	2.1	6.9	7.7
Wholesale and retail trade.............	22.6	17.0	37.6	26.9	21.2
Finance, insurance, and real estate.......	5.0	0.3	3.1	10.7	8.3
Business and repair services.............	1.2	0.2	0.6	1.3	1.4
Personal services.....................	14.8	38.8	18.9	9.2	8.7
Entertainment and recreation services.....	0.9	2.3	3.4	1.3	1.0
Professional and related services........	17.3	4.1	7.1	13.8	17.6
Public administration..................	4.1	0.2	0.5	2.2	3.8
Industry not reported..................	2.1	9.3	3.8	2.0	1.8

[1] Less than 0.1 percent.

Source: *1950 Census of Population*, Vol. II, *Characteristics of the Population*, Part 1, U. S. Summary, table 132.

Among older youths 20 to 24 years old, manufacturing and trade again provided the chief bases of employment for both males and females.

The occupational affiliations of young workers in 1950, in contrast to those of employed persons of all ages, indicate that young people are more generally employed in those occupations where skill and training requirements are among the lowest and where remuneration is correspondingly low. About a third of the employed young boys 14 and 15 years old were farm laborers employed as unpaid family workers; in contrast only 1 percent of the employed males of all ages were unpaid family workers on farms. A fifth of the young boys were sales workers (largely as newsboys in printing and publishing industries). Over a third of the employed girls 14 and 15 years of age were working as private household workers, and about a fifth as farm laborers, unpaid family workers (table 50).

TABLE **50.**—Occupational Distribution of Employed Persons 14 Years Old and Over, and 14 to 24 Years Old by Age, by Sex: 1950

Major occupation group and sex	14 years old and over	14 to 24 years old			
		14 and 15 years old	16 and 17 years old	18 and 19 years old	20 to 24 years old
Male, employed.............................	100.0	100.0	100.0	100.0	100.0
Professional, technical, and kindred workers.....	7.3	0.6	0.5	1.9	5.5
Farmers and farm managers.......................	10.3	2.4	2.7	3.5	5.6
Managers, officials, and proprietors, exc. farm..	10.7	0.7	0.5	1.2	3.5
Clerical and kindred workers.....................	6.4	1.8	4.8	9.4	9.4
Sales workers....................................	6.4	22.2	10.8	7.3	6.9
Craftsmen, foremen, and kindred workers..........	18.6	1.3	3.3	8.1	14.8
Operatives and kindred workers...................	20.1	6.9	15.8	25.9	28.1
Private household workers........................	0.2	0.6	0.3	0.2	0.1
Service workers, except private household........	5.9	7.2	9.4	6.1	4.6
Farm laborers and foremen........................	4.8	44.9	35.9	20.1	8.7
Farm laborers, unpaid family workers...........	1.4	33.7	21.9	9.9	2.8
Farm laborers, exc. unpaid, and farm foremen...	3.4	11.2	14.0	10.3	5.9
Laborers, except farm and mine...................	8.1	7.1	13.0	14.5	11.4
Occupation not reported..........................	1.1	4.3	2.9	1.8	1.4
Female, employed.............................	100.0	100.0	100.0	100.0	100.0
Professional, technical, and kindred workers.....	12.3	1.7	1.6	6.6	12.5
Farmers and farm managers.......................	0.7	0.7	0.2	0.1	0.1
Managers, officials, and proprietors, exc. farm..	4.3	0.3	0.3	0.5	1.2
Clerical and kindred workers.....................	27.3	3.2	17.2	44.7	44.4
Sales workers....................................	8.5	10.1	21.7	11.1	6.7
Craftsmen, foremen, and kindred workers..........	1.5	0.2	0.5	0.7	1.0
Operatives and kindred workers...................	19.2	2.3	12.9	14.9	16.5
Private household workers........................	8.5	36.9	15.4	5.7	4.6
Service workers, except private household........	12.2	11.4	16.7	10.6	9.0
Farm laborers and foremen........................	2.9	23.6	8.7	2.7	2.0
Farm laborers, unpaid family workers...........	2.0	17.5	6.0	1.7	1.2
Farm laborers, exc. unpaid, and farm foremen...	0.8	6.1	2.6	1.0	0.7
Laborers, except farm and mine...................	0.8	0.8	0.9	0.7	0.7
Occupation not reported..........................	1.8	8.8	3.8	1.6	1.3

Source: *1950 Census of Population*, Vol. II, *Characteristics of the Population*, Part 1, U. S. Summary, table 127.

Employed boys 16 and 17 years of age also work largely as farm laborers; one fifth were employed as unpaid family workers and one seventh as paid farm laborers and foremen. Operatives and kindred workers (largely in manufacturing and as truck drivers, delivery men, and auto service attendants) accounted for 15 percent of the total employment of boys 16 and 17 years old, and laborers (in trade, manufacturing, and construction) accounted for 13 percent. Among the employed females of these ages, sales workers (in retail trade) were most heavily represented (one fifth of the total) with clerical and kindred workers and service workers not in private households (primarily waitresses) accounting for about one sixth of the total employment.

One in every four employed boys 18 and 19 years old was an operative or kindred worker, and one in every five, a farm laborer; an additional 15 percent were employed as laborers not in farms and mines. Almost half of the employed girls of these ages were clerical workers, and an additional 15 percent were operatives.

F. Summary

Labor force participation on the part of young people in the United States has declined considerably between the beginning of the century and the present, largely reflecting the efficacy of child labor laws and the rising educational standards of the Nation. Although the proportion of economically active youths declined from 1900 to 1950, labor force participation of young people was higher in 1950 than in 1940. This labor force increase of teen-agers is due largely to the influx of student-workers which was occasioned by the onset of World War II and which continued thereafter.

The younger student-workers (of teen-ages) generally work at part-time jobs (less than 35 hours a week), while youngsters who have left school are typically employed in full-time work. From the data at hand one cannot infer that student employment hampers school performance.

The employment of young males is perceptibly higher in rural-farm areas than in other residence areas. Agriculture is the largest single employer of teen-age boys, and employment is generally in farm labor, especially unpaid family work. Many youths, primarily urban, are employed as salesworkers (generally newsboys and delivery boys) for the printing and publishing industries.

Young females are more typically employed in urban areas as private household workers or salesworkers for the retail industries.

· It is apparent that young workers are employed in those industries and occupations which require little skill and experience and which pay low wages. Often early entrance into the labor force is at the expense of further schooling and future potential earnings.[19]

---

[19] Paul C. Glick, "Educational Attainment and Occupational Advancement," *Transactions of the Second World Congress of Sociology*, held in Liége, Belgium, from August 24 to September 1, 1953, International Sociological Association, London, 1954; Paul C. Glick and Herman P. Miller, "Educational Level and Potential Income," *American Sociological Review*, Vol. 21, No. 3, June 1956, pp. 307–312.

CHAPTER 8

VARIATIONS IN THE LABOR FORCE
PARTICIPATION OF YOUTH

A. Introduction

Labor force participation of youths is dependent upon a variety of factors; included among them are current economic circumstances, existing social controls and customs, certain characteristics of youth, and the relationship of these characteristics to the propensity to work. In contrast to the relative stability of labor force participation in the adult male population, labor force membership among youths is comparatively sensitive to general economic conditions. The instability of the youthful labor force may be explained in large part by so-called "marginal" workers who comprise a significant proportion of the total youth labor force and whose entrance into the labor force or engagement in other activities (like schooling) depends to a considerable extent upon current job opportunities.

The precise nature of the relationship between current opportunities and participation has not been determined. Economic theorists have held diverse views on the relationship between the price of labor, for example, and its supply, particularly with reference to "additional workers." There is the theory of an inverse relationship between the size of the labor force and wages which is based on the contention that during economic depressions those not normally in the labor force seek employment. Some exponents of the "additional worker" theory also hold that the labor force expands during a boom period, because women and school-age youths are attracted to the market by high wages and available jobs. This view seems to be in conflict with the theory of the inverse relationship between the wage level and labor supply.[1]

Social controls, such as legislative programs and employment practices, also exert an influence upon the participation of youths in economic activity and the degree of this participation. Such controls are usually of a restrictive nature, designed to keep young people from leaving school and entering the labor force. Each State in the Nation, with one possible exception, has enacted minimum age requirements for employment during

---

[1] For a concise summary of the various economic views see John D. Durand, *The Labor Force in the United States, 1890–1960*, Social Science Research Council, New York, 1948, Chapter 4.

school hours. These State requirements vary somewhat but generally they comprise the following:[2]

At age 18 youths are no longer affected by legislative acts concerning employment and they can work at any type of employment they are offered.

At age 16 most occupations are open to youths provided they are not listed as "hazardous." Also at age 16 youths are not restricted to jobs *outside* of school hours.

At ages 14 and 15 youths are eligible to work, but only at certain restricted types of employment and only outside of school hours.

Although nondemographic factors, such as the character of employment opportunities and practices, wage levels, legal restrictions, and personal aspirations may exercise a more immediate and direct influence upon labor force participation, particularly among a marginal group, it has been found that demographic factors are important determinants of labor market membership.[3] In addition, variations in demographic characteristics may reflect, in part, variations in other factors comprising that complex of interrelationships affecting participation.

In this chapter we attempt to assess the extent to which variations in the demographic characteristics of youths are associated with, and tend to promote, their labor force membership. In contrast to the studies referred to in footnote 3 (Durand and Wolfbein and Jaffe) which viewed the effects of demographic factors upon *changes* in labor force membership, this analysis examines the *static* relationship between demographic characteristics and the propensity to work. That is, it attempts to examine the association between given characteristics of youth and their labor force membership as of April 1950. It also attempts to assess the relative impact or importance of these characteristics upon the total youth labor force. Among the characteristics which are considered in this connection are sex, age, color, residence, geographical location, school enrollment, educational attainment, marital status, household relationship, and previous work experience.

Association is examined with respect to degree and direction. The association of any one characteristic with labor force membership is measured by the labor force participation rate of youths possessing that characteristic: the higher the rate of participation, the higher the degree of association. Those characteristics for which the participation rate is above the average rate for the age-sex cohort being examined are said to be *positively* associated with labor force membership. Those characteristics whose rates fall below the average rate are said to be *negatively* associated with participation.

---

[2] U. S. Department of Labor, *A Guide to Child-Labor Provisions of the Fair Labor Standards Act,* Child Labor Bulletin No. 101, 1953.

[3] Durand, *op. cit.;* and S. L. Wolfbein and A. J. Jaffe, "Demographic Factors in Labor Force Growth," *American Sociological Review,* Vol. XI, No. 4, August 1946, pp. 392–396.

Furthermore, insofar as many of the variables being considered are not independent of each other, this investigation attempts to measure *net* association as well as *gross* association. A *net* measure is differentiated from a *gross* measure in that it holds constant the effects of one or more additional variables.

The necessity for attempting to assess the relative importance or impact of a given characteristic upon the propensity to work emerges from two considerations:

(1) Many characteristics which are highly associated with participation pertain to only a small number of youths (heads of households), and

(2) the range of differential rates within some characteristic categories is considerably greater than the range within other categories (household relationship as compared with regional location).

These considerations (size and homogeneity) add an aspect to the relationship between demographic characteristics and the labor force participation supplemental to that of association, the aspect of the relative impact of a given characteristic upon labor force membership. The measure derived to assess this impact will be discussed later.

In the analysis which follows younger teen-agers (under 18 years of age) are differentiated from older youths (18 and 19 years of age) for both males and females.

B. Gross association and impact[4]

Table 51 gives the labor force participation rates for each of the sex-age cohorts by each of the characteristics under consideration. In general it may be noted that these rates are higher for males than for females and higher for older youths than for younger ones. Also, there is considerable variation in the degree and direction of association of the various characteristics, although the same characteristic (head of household) ranks highest for each age-sex group. Among males in both age classes, labor force participation is higher for nonwhites than for whites. In contrast, among females it is higher for nonwhites only for those of high school ages. Among the older females, labor force participation is higher for whites than for nonwhites.

Interesting differences between the two sexes arise with respect to the residential distribution of youths in the labor force. Here it may be observed that for both age groups of males, labor force participation is greatest in rural-farm areas. Among females, on the other hand, for both age groups participation is greatest in urban areas, perhaps reflecting the urban-rural differential employment opportunities for the two sexes.

Among urban youths, residence in the fringe areas seems more favorable to labor force participation for males of both age groups and the younger

---

[4] Some portions of the descriptive materials presented here are necessarily repetitious of those presented in Chapter 7.

females. The older females, on the other hand, are more prone to economic activity if they are residing within the urbanized areas (central cities). Central cities of 50,000 to 100,000 population appear to offer greater employment opportunities to young teen-agers of both sexes than do places of other sizes. For the older teen-agers, residence in places of 25,000 to 50,000 population seems to be the most favorable for labor force participation.

TABLE 51.—LABOR FORCE PARTICIPATION RATES OF PERSONS 14 TO 19 YEARS OLD BY SELECTED DEMOGRAPHIC CHARACTERISTICS, BY AGE AND SEX: 1950

[Rates are based on civilian labor force unless otherwise designated]

Characteristic	Percent in the labor force			
	Male		Female	
	14 to 17 years	18 and 19 years	14 to 17 years	18 and 19 years
Total..............................	25.0	64.1	11.4	43.7
White.............................	24.1	63.6	11.4	45.3
Nonwhite..........................	31.6	67.7	11.9	31.2
Urban.............................	20.9	59.4	12.9	50.3
In urbanized areas...............	18.9	60.8	11.7	53.3
Places of 100,000 or more.....	18.9	61.9	12.0	55.2
Places of 50,000 to 100,000...	21.7	56.8	12.8	50.7
Places of 25,000 to 50,000....	18.9	64.4	11.6	56.6
Places of 2,500 to 25,000.....	17.2	58.5	11.1	50.9
Other urban...................	17.8	59.1	10.0	45.4
Not in urbanized areas...........	25.5	56.6	15.3	44.3
Rural nonfarm.....................	21.0	63.4	10.0	34.1
Rural farm........................	38.1	78.0	9.0	26.6
Northeast.........................	15.7	57.7	10.5	55.5
North Central.....................	27.1	66.9	13.5	48.8
South............................	29.8	66.3	10.4	32.8
West..............................	24.0	60.2	11.3	38.4
Enrolled in school................	17.5	28.5	8.1	23.0
Not enrolled in school............	65.3	85.5	29.1	52.3
Retarded in school performance....	34.2	...	14.1	...
Not retarded in school performance........	20.3	...	10.7	...
Completed 8 grades or less........	...	82.3	...	31.5
Completed more than 8 grades......	...	58.6	...	46.4
Completed less than high school...	...	67.8	...	32.4
Completed high school or more.....	...	60.0	...	55.0
Worked in 1949....................	57.0	80.2	41.9	68.3
Did not work in 1949..............	11.0	34.9	5.2	16.3
Married, spouse present...........	70.3	93.0	12.0	21.7
Single............................	24.6	62.2	11.3	52.6
Other.............................	59.1	74.0	26.0	42.6
Head of household[1]..............	76.7	93.4	44.7	72.2
Spouse of head[1].................	} 24.8	} 67.5	{ 11.5	{ 20.5
Other relative of head[1].........			11.1	51.2
Not relative of head[1]...........	35.8	61.0	19.3	42.5

[1] Total labor force.

Source: *1950 Census of Population*, Vol. IV, *Special Reports*, Part 1, Chapter A, Employment and Personal Characteristics, tables 1, 4 to 7, 12, and 14; Part 5, Chapter B, Education, table 9.

With respect to regional differentials in labor force participation, younger males aged 14 to 17 years residing in the South have the highest rate, closely followed by those in the North Central Region. Among the older males these two regions rank about equally.[5]   The regional distribution of labor force participation rates for females is somewhat different.   Among the younger females 14 to 17 years of age, the highest rate occurs in the North Central Region, and among the older females, the highest rate occurs in the Northeast.

Similar patterns of participation among the sex-age groups are observed in examining school enrollment variations.   Namely, higher participation rates occur among youths who are not enrolled in school, as might be expected.   An interesting pattern arises with respect to the educational attainment of youths in the labor force.   Among males of high school ages, those who are retarded in school, or at least retarded in the grade of school completed for their age group, are more apt to be in the labor force than those who have experienced the normal pattern of school progress.   Over a third of young boys who are backward in their age-grade progress engage in labor force activities whereas only a fifth of those who are not retarded are in the labor force.   Among females of high school ages, the differences in participation for the retarded and nonretarded groups are smaller, 14 and 11 percent, respectively.   Among the older males 18 and 19 years of age, those who have not gone beyond elementary school participate in the labor force to a greater extent than those who have completed more than eight grades, 82 percent as compared with 59 percent.   In contrast, among the older females the better educated are more apt to be in the labor force than are those who have not completed elementary school.   These same sex differences are repeated at the high school level of achievement; namely, males who have *not* completed high school are more apt to be in the labor force (68 percent) than those who have completed high school (60 percent), and among females, high school graduates participate in the labor force to a greater extent (55 percent) than those who did not finish their secondary education (32 percent).

In an attempt to assess the relationship between previous work experience and labor force participation of youths, data on number of weeks worked in 1949 were examined.   From these data it was assumed that all those who had experienced any weeks of work in 1949 were experienced workers.   Those who did not have work experience in 1949 were assumed to be new workers in 1950.   Labor force participation of experienced youths is, of course, considerably higher for all sex-age groups than for new workers, 57 and 11 percent, respectively, for the younger males, 42 and 5 percent for the younger females, 80 and 35 percent for older males, and 68 and 16 percent for older females.

With respect to marital status we find that boys of both age groups are more apt to participate in the labor force if they are married, with spouse present.   Among females, on the other hand, the younger females are more

---

[5] There is probably greater underenumeration of the teen-age labor force in the South.

apt to be in the labor force if they are either widowed or divorced and older females are more apt to be in the labor force if they are single.

With respect to household relationship, the pattern is similar for all age-sex groups, namely, heads of household have considerably higher labor force participation rates than any of the other relationships.

In re-examining these characteristics by rank order association, we find that among the characteristics most highly and positively associated with labor force participation for each sex-age group are *head of household, non-enrollment in school,* and *previous work experience.* Considerable differences in degree and direction of association occur among many of the variables. Although rural-farm residence is relatively highly and positively associated with labor force participation of males of both age groups, it is negatively associated with participation among females. Although retardation in school performance is positively associated with labor force participation among the younger males and females, notable sex differences occur in the relationship of educational attainment and labor force membership of older youths. Specifically, for the males the completion of eight grades or *less* and the completion of *less* than high school is positively associated with participation, whereas for females the *completion* of elementary and high school is positively associated with labor force activity. Being married is positively and highly associated with the labor force activity of males in both age classes, positively though slightly associated with the participation of females of high school ages, and negatively associated with the participation of older females.

Relating these observations to data on the numbers of youths possessing the various characteristics and to the extent of differential participation within a characteristic category made it apparent that the relative impact or importance of the various characteristics also warrants consideration. To this end a measure of *relative importance* was derived.

The measure represents a combined function of (1) the numbers of youths possessing a given characteristic and (2) the extent of the differential rates of participation within the characteristic category being scrutinized. Let us examine each of these separately:

(1) It is conceivable that a characteristic, which is highly associated with participation, is shared by so few youths that it does not "contribute" many to the total active group. An example of this is found in examining participation by household relationship where it was noted that the highest participation rate for youths occurred among those who were "heads of households." However, the number of youths who are heads of households is very small; thus the importance of this characteristic to the total participation cannot be large, despite its high rate of association.

(2) The measure of "impact" or "importance" is also a function of the degree of differential participation among the components of a characteristic category. In this respect it provides an indication of the heterogeneity

of the characteristic groups with regard to participation or the impact of a given characteristic upon labor force activity. It is conceivable, for example, and more so for older participants, that rates of labor force activity within one characteristic category could be about equal, thereby vitiating the importance or impact of any one component characteristic upon the propensity to be in the labor force. Particularly among male adults, for example, it is possible that participation rates would not differ much by the various household relationships. Although association would be high in each case, the importance (with respect to labor force activity) of being identified by one relationship or another would be negligible. Among youths, the relative homogeneity of behavior with respect to labor force activity differs markedly for the various characteristic categories. Thus being identified by some characteristics is of more (or less) importance (with respect to participation) than is identification by other characteristics.

The measure of importance or impact as a combined function of both size and differentiation is a crude measure; it does not distinguish between each of its aspects and represents *only* the joint functionings of both.

In deriving this measure a method of expected cases was used.[6] An expected labor force was computed on the assumption that participation in the labor force took place at a rate complementary to that of the particular characteristic being examined. For example, to measure the relative importance of being "head of household" it was assumed that *all* youths participated in the labor force at the rate of those who were *not* heads of households, or at a rate complementary to those who were heads of households. The resultant expected labor force, that is, a labor force assuming that all youths were *not* heads of households, was compared with the observed total labor force for the particular sex-age group. The difference between the expected labor force and the observed labor force was computed. The size of this difference is the basic indicator of the size of relative importance—the greater the difference, the greater the impact or importance.[7]

In order to derive a relative measure of importance from among the factors being considered, the difference between the expected and observed labor force is expressed as a percentage of the observed labor force. These figures appear in table 52 for those characteristics which are positively associated with labor force participation.

---

[6] For fuller statement see Appendix D.

[7] Arithmetically, if a positively associated characteristic is shared by a small number of youths, the complement rate will be close to the rate of total average participation. If we use this rate to determine an expected labor force, the expected figure will then be close to the observed figure and the difference will be small. Similarly, if there is very little difference between the rates in one category of characteristics, again the complement rate will be close to the observed rate, and the differences between the expected and the observed labor force will be small. The smallest impact will result where both size and differentiation are small; the largest impact will result where both aspects are large. However, if one aspect is relatively large and the other small, the effect of one tends to balance the effect of the other.

TABLE 52.—GROSS IMPACT OF SELECTED DEMOGRAPHIC CHARACTERISTICS IN LABOR FORCE PARTICIPATION OF PERSONS 14 TO 19 YEARS OLD, BY AGE AND SEX: 1950

[Difference between expected and observed labor force expressed as a percent of the observed labor force. Based on civilian labor force unless otherwise designated]

Characteristic	Male		Female	
	14 to 17 years	18 and 19 years	14 to 17 years	18 and 19 years
White	(1)	(1)	(1)	28.5
Nonwhite	3.5	0.7	0.2	(1)
Urban	(1)	(1)	16.0	29.0
In urbanized areas	(1)	4.8	(1)	11.9
Places of 100,000 or more	(1)	3.2	(1)	6.4
Places of 50,000 to 100,000	1.6	(1)	(1)	(1)
Places of 25,000 to 50,000	(1)	0.3	(1)	4.4
Places of 2,500 to 25,000	(1)	(1)	(1)	(1)
Other urban	(1)	(1)	(1)	(1)
Not in urbanized areas	9.8	(1)	9.8	(1)
Rural nonfarm	(1)	(1)	(1)	(1)
Rural farm	15.9	5.7	(1)	(1)
Northeast	(1)	(1)	(1)	8.8
North Central	2.7	2.8	7.2	4.5
South	10.7	2.8	(1)	(1)
West	(1)	(1)	(1)	(1)
Enrolled in school	(1)	(1)	(1)	(1)
Not enrolled in school	30.0	53.1	29.1	47.1
Retarded in school performance	18.7	...	6.4	...
Not retarded in school performance	(1)	...	(1)	...
Completed 8 grades or less	...	8.5	...	(1)
Completed more than 8 grades	...	(1)	...	27.9
Completed less than high school	...	6.4	...	(1)
Completed high school or more	...	(1)	...	25.8
Worked in 1949	56.0	45.5	54.5	62.7
Did not work in 1949	(1)	(1)	(1)	(1)
Married, spouse present	0.7	0.9	0.2	(1)
Single	(1)	(1)	(1)	45.3
Other	0.7	0.1	1.2	(1)
Head of household[2]	1.2	2.6	0.4	0.5
Spouse of head[2]				
Other relative of head[2]	(1)	0.9	0.4	(1)
Not relative of head[2]	1.6	(1)	2.2	30.8

[1] Characteristic is negatively associated with labor force participation.
[2] Total labor force.

Source: Derived from table 51 and method discussed in Appendix D.

An examination of table 52 indicates that there is considerable variation in the degree of importance among the factors for the different sex-age cohorts. It may also be noted that the impact of the characteristics being examined is generally greater for females than for males. Particularly, the importance of these characteristics is relatively high for older females.

Specific variations in the relative importance of these demographic characteristics are striking. For example, among the younger males and females of both age groups, previous work experience (work in 1949) is the most important factor conducive to labor force participation, amounting to about 56 percent for males 14 to 17 years of age, 55 percent for the younger females, and 63 percent for the older females 18 and 19 years of age. For the older males, however, not being enrolled in school appears to be of greater importance (53 percent) than does previous work experience (45 percent), which ranks second in the relative impact of factors affecting labor force activity.

With respect to school performance of youths of high school age, the retarded ones of both sexes are more apt to be in the labor force than are those who have experienced the expected pattern of school performance or have exceeded the expected performance levels. However, the impact of this factor upon labor force participation is considerably greater for young males (19 percent) than for females (6 percent).

Marked differences between the two sexes are observed in examining the importance of educational attainment on labor force participation. As indicated previously, and again in table 52, the completion of more than an elementary education and a secondary education is *negatively* associated with labor force participation of older male youths (18 and 19 years) whereas among the females there is a high *positive* association between educational achievement at both levels and membership in the labor force. In addition, the *completion* of primary and secondary education contributes importantly, 28 percent and 26 percent, respectively, to the labor force participation of older females. Among males, on the other hand, the importance of an *incomplete* secondary education amounts to 6 percent, and the importance of *no* secondary education comes to 8 percent.

There are also notable sex differences in residential variations of labor force participation among youths. Whereas rural-farm residence is positively associated with the participation of males, among females urban residence is associated positively with labor force membership. In addition, the importance of residential location is relatively high among the younger males and females of both age groups. The importance of rural-farm residence amounts to 16 percent for the younger males, while among the females urban residence contributes 16 percent and 29 percent to the labor force participation of the younger and older groups, respectively. The importance of rural-farm residence among the older males amounts to only 6 percent. Thus, although the association of rural-farm residence and participation is higher for older males, its relative impact is considerably greater for younger males.

For urban youths of high school ages, residence outside the central cities is positively associated with labor force participation, contributing about 10 percent to both the males and females. Among the older urban youths, on the other hand, residence within the urbanized area is positively associated with participation, although it is a more important characteristic for females than for males (12 percent and 5 percent, respectively). Places of 100,000 inhabitants or more appear to be of greatest importance, succeeded by places of 25,000 to 50,000 inhabitants.

With respect to the effect of marital status upon the labor force participation of youth, we find that despite some high associations with participation, the relative importance of differences in status to participation is negligible for all youths except for females 18 and 19 years of age. Among the latter group, being "single" is a highly important factor (45 percent).   Similarly, with respect to household relationship, we find that for males of both age classes and for the younger females, differences in household relationships do not play an important role in labor force participation although some relationships are highly associated with participation.   However, among the older females, being related to head of household other than as spouse is not only highly associated with labor force participation but is an important factor relative to the importance of other demographic factors.

The same pattern of importance occurs with respect to color.   Among males in both age groups and the younger females, color is not a particularly important characteristic, but for the older females we find that being white is an impotant characteristic (28 percent).

With respect to the regional variations in labor force participation, residing in the South is of some importance for younger males (11 percent), whereas for the older males residence in the North Central Region and the South shares a small relative impact (3 percent each).   Among the younger females, residence in the North Central Region exercises greater influence (7 percent) than residence in any of the other regions.   For the older females, residence in the Northeast and North Central Regions contributes to labor force participation at the rates of 9 percent and 5 percent, respectively.

In summary, it might be stressed again that the impact of factors being considered is greater for labor force participation of older female youths than for either the younger females or males of both age groups.   In addition, there are striking age-sex variations both in the factors which are important to the propensity of youths to work and in the *degree* of their importance.

Among younger males 14 to 17 years of age, the rank order of characteristics important to participation in the labor force is as follows: experience in 1949, nonenrollment in school, retardation in grade completed, rural-farm residence, residence in the South, and other factors of negligible importance.

Among the older males 18 and 19 years of age, the rank order is different: nonenrollment in school, experience in 1949, no school beyond elementary school, noncompletion of high school, rural-farm residence, residence in the North Central Region and the South, and others of negligible importance.

In addition to the differences in these factors and their rank order, it may be observed that the degree of importance for each factor is generally less for the older males than for the younger ones.

Among the younger females 14 to 17 years of age, the rank order of the relative importance of the various characteristics to participation is as follows: experience in 1949, nonenrollment in school, urban residence, residence in the North Central Region, retardation in school performance, and other factors of negligible importance.

Among the older females 18 and 19 years of age, the rank order is different: experience in 1949, nonenrollment in school; single marital status, urban residence, white, completion of elementary school, completion of high school, relation to head of household other than spouse, residence in Northeast and North Central Regions.

It appears from the analysis of these measures that the relationship between demographic characteristics and the labor force participation of youths varies by the age and sex of the participating youths. The variations in themselves suggest differential employment opportunities available to youths and also the differential social roles and responsibilities of youths which exercise a push or pull toward labor force activity. It is obvious that being the head of a household, whether a youth or an adult, whether male or female, entails certain economic responsibilities which would lead to labor force participation. However, such a role is not common among youths, and thus it does not add heavily to the labor force participation of young people. On the other hand, the availability of full-time jobs[8] to youths, including those of high school ages, is an important single factor affecting drop-outs from school and entrance into the labor force. These opportunities appear to be more prevalent in farm areas for males and more prevalent in urban areas for females. In addition, work opportunities for males, particularly the younger ones, are greater in the South, whereas the greater opportunities for females occur in the North.

Being backward in school progress exercises a considerable influence upon minors to enter labor force activity. This influence is greater among males than among females, as might be expected, because males leaving school have little alternative but to enter the labor market, whereas their retarded sisters may avoid the alternative of self-support via the path of matrimony. Actually, data for older youths imply that it is the poorly educated boys and the better-educated girls who are contributing to the Nation's economic endeavors.

At least single variable analysis of the data would lead to these conclusions. However, they may be misleading, for the effect of any one characteristic upon labor force participation may be but a reflection of the influence of other characteristics.

C. Net association[9]

For the purposes of this investigation, net association is defined as the association of any given characteristic with labor force participation while holding constant the effects of another specific characteristic. "Holding

---

[8] Characterized by those "not enrolled in school."

[9] A measure of importance or impact is not easily applicable on a net basis, because the weighting process involved in the standardization tends to vitiate the original intent of the measure, that is to assess the importance of a characteristic with respect to the numbers of youths possessing it and with respect to its differentiating capacity.

constant" involves standardizing the given rates of participation (that is, those positively associated with participation) by the experience of the population complementary to the one under scrutiny.[10] For example, in examining the net association of rural-farm residence and labor force participation of males of high school ages while holding constant school enrollment, the net rate is derived on the assumption that the enrollment pattern in rural-farm areas is the same as the enrollment pattern of boys in nonfarm areas.

Tables 53 and 54 show the gross and net association rates of the positively associated characteristics.

It was pointed out earlier that rural-farm boys of high school ages participate in the labor force to a greater extent than do young boys in either of the other two residential groups. It appears from table 53 that this higher rate in rural-farm areas is, to some extent, a function of previous work experience available to young boys in rural-farm areas. If we were to assume that young boys in rural-farm areas had the same rate of previous work experience as did boys who lived outside of rural-farm areas, then the labor force participation rate of rural-farm boys would be reduced from 38 percent to 32 percent. Also a factor in the high participation rate in rural-farm areas is the school enrollment pattern of youngsters in these areas. If we were to assume that rural-farm boys were enrolled in school to the same extent as were boys residing outside of rural-farm areas, their participation rate would again be reduced from 38 to 32 percent. Reductions in the participation of the younger rural-farm males also occur in holding constant color and region although to a rather negligible extent.

TABLE 53.—GROSS AND NET ASSOCIATION OF SELECTED DEMOGRAPHIC CHARACTERISTICS TO LABOR FORCE PARTICIPATION OF PERSONS 14 TO 17 YEARS OLD, BY SEX: 1950

Characteristic	Association rate[1]		Characteristic	Association rate[1]	
	Male	Female		Male	Female
Worked in 1949..................	57.0	41.9	Color (nonwhite)................	31.6	11.9
Color constant[2]..............	56.8	42.4	Residence constant[3]..........	28.9	11.5
Residence constant[3]..........	56.7	43.1	Region constant[4]..............	22.0	9.4
Not enrolled in school..........	65.3	29.1	Experience constant...........	31.1	10.9
Color constant[2]..............	64.8	29.2	School performance constant[5]...	24.6	9.8
Region constant[4].............	63.2	30.1	Enrollment constant...........	26.8	10.3
Residence constant[3]..........	62.7	30.2			
Retarded in grade completed......	34.2	14.1	Region........................	29.8	13.5
Color constant[2]..............	33.1	13.8	Color constant[2]..............	27.9	12.8
Region constant[4].............	31.7	14.7	Residence constant[3]..........	26.9	13.4
			School performance constant[5]...	24.8	12.8
Residence (rural farm, urban)[3]...	38.1	12.9	Enrollment constant...........	24.7	14.4
Color constant[2]..............	37.1	12.8			
Region constant[4].............	35.7	12.9			
Experience constant...........	31.9	15.1			
Enrollment constant...........	32.4	13.9			

[1] Labor force participation rate.
[2] Nonwhite for males and females.
[3] Rural farm for males; urban for females.
[4] South for males; North Central for females.
[5] Data available for only South and non-South classification; figures refer to South for males and non-South for females.

Source: Same as table 52.

[10] See Appendix D for methodological statement.

Among the characteristics being considered, the most important single factor related to the high rate of participation among nonwhite males of high school ages is their regional distribution (72 percent in the South). If we were to assume that nonwhite boys were distributed throughout the regions of the United States in the same pattern as were white boys, then their rate of participation in the labor force would be reduced from 32 to 22 percent.   A sizable reduction in nonwhite labor force participation of these young boys also takes place in holding constant school performance. That is, if nonwhites were retarded in their school performance to the same extent as white boys, their labor force participation would be reduced to 25 percent.   Furthermore, if they were enrolled in school to the same extent as white boys, their participation rate would be reduced to 27 percent. Were nonwhite boys distributed in the same manner among the residential groups as white boys, nonwhite youngsters would be participating in labor force activity at the rate of 29 percent instead of 32 percent.   If they had the previous work experience of white youths, however, reduction in their participation would be negligible.   Thus it appears that color differentials in labor force activity of males 14 to 17 years old are to a considerable extent a function of the high concentration of nonwhites in the South and in rural-farm areas, their higher rates of nonenrollment, and their greater retardation in school performance.

Sizable reductions in labor force participation of young boys would also occur in the South if their rates of school enrollment and school performance levels were the same as those experienced by boys outside the South. Actually, participation rates would then be reduced from 30 percent to 25 percent in each case.   However, in the South retardation is more prevalent than is nonenrollment.   The factor of retardation exposes to possible labor force activity more than twice the number of boys as does the characteristic of nonenrollment (50 percent of the southern schoolboys are retarded as compared with 22 percent of the southern boys not enrolled in school).

The effects of holding other variables constant, one at a time, upon previous work experience, retardation in school, and not being enrolled in school are relatively small, reductions varying from 0 to 2 percent.

Net effects of the variables considered in table 53 are less marked for young females than for males.   In no instance does a net change due to holding another characteristic constant exceed 3 percent and in most cases it amounts to only 1 or 2 percent.   The largest reductions in participation occur in removing the effects of region and school performance upon the membership rate of nonwhite girls.   The largest increase in rate of participation occurs in assuming that urban girls were exposed to the same previous work experience as were nonurban girls.[11]   Insofar as the urban labor force is comprised of a smaller proportion of experienced workers, controlling for experience results in an increase of participation (3 percent).

---

[11] For the urban population by size of place, only a color control is possible.   In each applicable instance, "holding color constant" does not affect the gross rate of association.

The interrelationships of demographic characteristics affecting labor force participation among older youths 18 and 19 years of age are given in table 54. Again, they are more marked among the males, where the effects of the various educational factors upon labor force participation for the non-white, rural-farm, and southern youths are especially perceptible. For example, nonwhite labor force participation would be reduced by almost 10 percent if we were to assume that nonwhite male youths completed their elementary schooling to the same extent as did white male youths. In addition a considerable though smaller reduction would also occur if we were to assume that the educational achievement of nonwhites at the high school level were the same as for white youths. At the elementary school level the rates would be reduced from 68 percent to 59 percent and at the high school level to 62 percent. Thus it appears that the higher participation of nonwhite male youths is to a decided extent a function of their lower educational attainment.

TABLE 54.—GROSS AND NET ASSOCIATION OF SELECTED DEMOGRAPHIC CHARACTERISTICS TO LABOR FORCE PARTICIPATION OF PERSONS 18 AND 19 YEARS OLD, BY SEX: 1950

Characteristic	Association rate[1]		Characteristic	Association rate[1]	
	Male	Female		Male	Female
Worked in 1949.....................	80.2	68.3	Region (South, Northeast)[4].......	66.3	55.5
Color constant[2]..............	80.3	67.3	Color constant[2].............	64.7	54.3
Residence constant[3]..........	79.4	66.0	Elementary school constant[5]..	59.8	47.5
Not enrolled in school...........	85.5	52.3	High school constant[5]........	63.2	45.1
Color constant[2]..............	85.7	52.7	Enrollment constant..........	62.5	55.8
Region constant[4].............	84.8	52.8	Residence constant[3]..........	62.9	52.2
Residence constant[3]..........	84.9	54.1			
Educational attainment:			Residence (rural farm, urban)[3]...	78.0	50.3
Elementary school[5].............	82.3	46.4	Color constant[2]..............	77.7	49.7
Color constant[2]..............	82.6	43.6	Region constant[4].............	77.0	46.9
Region constant[6].............	81.2	42.1	Experience constant..........	76.8	43.1
High school[5]....................	67.8	55.0	Enrollment constant..........	68.8	52.8
Color constant[2]..............	67.2	52.6	Marital status constant[7]......	78.0	46.4
Region constant[6].............	66.3	52.2			
			Marital status (married, spouse		
Color (nonwhite, white)[2]........	67.7	45.3	present; single)[7]..............	93.0	52.6
Residence constant[3]..........	65.7	43.0	Color constant[2].............	93.0	52.0
Region constant[4].............	59.8	38.9	Residence constant[3].........	93.1	50.7
Experience constant..........	72.5	38.8			
Elementary school constant[5]..	59.0	41.5			
High school constant[5].......	61.9	38.4			
Enrollment constant..........	61.7	46.9			
Marital status constant[7].....	67.6	44.2			

[1] Labor force participation rate.

[2] Nonwhite for males; white for females.

[3] Rural farm for males; urban for females.

[4] South for males; Northeast for females.

[5] For males: Completed elementary school or less; completed less than high school. For females: Completed more than elementary school; completed high school or more.

[6] Data available for only South and non-South classification; figures refer to South for males and non-South for females.

[7] For males: Married with spouse present. For females: Single.

Source: Same as table 52.

In addition, had nonwhite males 18 and 19 years of age been enrolled in the schools of the Nation to the same extent as white males in 1950, their labor force participation rate would be reduced from 68 percent to 62 percent.

On the other hand, in holding constant previous work experience, labor force membership of nonwhite youths is increased to 72 percent, reflecting a larger proportion of an available population without previous work experience among the nonwhites (44 percent as compared with 36 percent for white youths). It appears that there are proportionately more inexperienced nonwhite youths in the population not being absorbed in the labor force than white youths in the same category. The schools of the Nation are not absorbing these young men and many are left in the wasteland between school and labor force activity.

Obviously, the concentration of nonwhites in the South considerably affects their labor force participation rate. If we were to assume that nonwhite youths were distributed throughout the regions of the United States in accordance with the pattern of white youths, their labor force participation would be reduced to about 60 percent.

White–nonwhite differentials with respect to marital status and urban-rural residence do not significantly affect the differentials in labor force participation.

Regional variations in educational attainment of male youths account to a considerable extent for the high rate of labor force participation in the South. About two thirds of the male youths in the South were in the labor force in 1950. However, if we were to assume that southern youths went beyond elementary schooling to the same extent as youths did in other regions of the Nation, their labor force participation would be reduced to less than 60 percent. The reduction at the high school level (that is, completing high school or more) is, of course, not as great, from 66 to 63 percent.

Regional variations in school enrollment and in rural-urban residence also account for some of the differential in labor force participation. Color differentials at this age level are not particularly significant in affecting the southern rate.

Among the characteristics being examined, the most important single factor affecting the high rate of participation among rural-farm youths is school enrollment. That is, if rural-farm youths in 1950 were enrolled in school to the same extent as youths outside of rural-farm areas, their labor force participation would be reduced by about 10 percent, from 78 percent to 69 percent. The effects of color, region, experience, and marital status, taken one at a time, upon the labor force participation of rural-farm youths are insignificant.

The effects of color and residential differentials upon the labor force participation of male youths who are married (with wife present) are negligible or nonexistent. In holding each of these variables constant, one at a time, the participation rate of 93 percent does not change.

The interrelationships of the selected characteristics upon differential labor force participation by work experience, school enrollment, and educational achievement are also negligible.

Labor force participation of older female youths 18 and 19 years of age appears to be of a nature different from that of other youths. As discussed earlier, females of this age are more apt to be in the labor force if they are white, urban, relatively well-educated, residing in the Northeast, and single. Younger females, on the other hand, were more likely to be in the labor force if they were nonwhite, urban, residing in the North Central Region, retarded in school performance, and widowed, separated, or divorced. Males of both age groups participated in the labor force to a greater degree if they were nonwhite, from rural-farm areas, residing in the South, retarded in school, and married.

The older females 18 and 19 years of age have reached the peak of their activity in the labor force. Before this age they are prone to remain in school to a greater extent than males, and after this age they are exposed to the possibilities of marriage and motherhood and retirement from the labor force, at least for the time being.[12]

With young females, as with young males, the educational characteristics are the most highly interrelated with others affecting labor force participation. In contrast to the experience of the males, however, the interrelationships seem to be in the opposite direction. For example, the high rate of participation in the Northeast would be reduced from 55 percent to 45 percent by holding educational achievement at the high school level constant. That is, if these young women in the Northeast completed their secondary education or more only to the extent experienced by women in the other regions of the Nation, their participation rate would be reduced by 10 percentage points. A similar reduction of about 8 percent would occur if young women in the Northeast had not gone beyond elementary school in accordance with the pattern of women in the other regions of the country. The effect of the residential distribution of these girls is relatively small and the effects of color and school enrollment are minimal. Thus, in viewing these characteristics one at a time, it appears that the high educational standards of the Northeast may account, in part, for its high rate of labor force participation among females 18 and 19 years of age.

The high rate among white females is attributable to some extent to their high educational achievement, their regional distribution, and their previous work experience. If white females were to complete their secondary or higher education at the rate that nonwhite females did, their labor force participation would be reduced from 45 to 38 percent. Assuming that the regional distribution of white females were the same as that of nonwhite females, the labor force participation rate for the white girls would be reduced to 39 percent. Similarly, if the white girls had the previous work experience of the nonwhite girls, their labor force activity would again be reduced to 39 percent. The effects of marital status, rural-urban distribu-

---

[12] See figure 21.

tion, and school enrollment upon the participation of these young females are negligible.

Among all the characteristics being considered, the availability of previous work experience is the most significant single factor affecting the high rate of labor force activity of urban females. On the assumption that these young women were exposed to the experience pattern of their age cohorts outside of urban areas, their rate would be reduced from 50 percent to 43 percent. In assuming that they were distributed among the marital status categories as were nonurban females of the same age, their labor force participation would be reduced to 46 percent. In holding region constant, the rate is reduced to 47 percent, and in holding enrollment constant, the rate is raised to 53 percent. The effect of color is minimal.

Insofar as it is the better educated young women who are more apt to be in the labor force, it is not surprising that their rates of participation are reduced in holding constant both color and region. The effects of these factors upon the association of previous work experience and not being enrolled in school are small, as the effect of residence upon school enrollment is small.

D. Summary

This analysis has attempted to examine the nature and degree of the relationship between the demographic characteristics of youths and the propensity of youths to work. It was found that among males of high school ages, 14 to 17 years old, previous work experience, nonenrollment in school, retardation in school performance, rural-farm residence, and residence in the South were characteristics which were highly associated with labor force membership and also important with respect to the numbers of youths possessing them and their differentiating capacities with respect to participation. Of high association and importance for females of high school ages are previous work experience, nonenrollment in school, urban residence, residence in the North Central Region, and retardation in school performance.

The high rates of association and importance of rural-farm and residence in the South among the boys are to some extent a function of the work experience available in these areas and the comparatively lower school enrollment rates. In addition, the high participation rate in the South is to an important extent a function of the high rate of retardation in school performance.

The interrelationships of factors are less perceptible for the younger females. Perhaps the most revealing of those examined is that of previous work experience upon urban residence. Here it was found that if the opportunity for previous work experience found in *non*urban areas were available to urban girls, their participation would be increased markedly, reflecting the "new worker" nature of the urban labor force of young girls in contrast to the "experienced" nature of the young male labor force in farm areas.

Among the older males 18 and 19 years of age, high rates of association and importance were found for previous work experience, the lack of a high school education, rural-farm residence, and residence in the North Central Region and in the South.

For the older females, the following characteristics were found to be both highly associated and important with respect to participation: previous work experience, single status, urban residence, white, completion of elementary and high school, and residence in the Northeast and North Central Regions.

The most startling interrelationships of factors were found in examining the effects of the various educational factors upon labor force participation. Among the nonwhite, farm, and southern boys, high rates of participation were, in each case, a partial function of low educational attainment. The reverse was found to be true for the older female youths where the highest rates of participation were due, in part, to high levels of educational achievement.

Thus, as found in the single variable analysis, a multivariable examination further buttresses the conclusion that backwardness in school performance leads to early drop-outs from school and entrance into the labor force. Furthermore, insofar as retardation is higher among males than for females, and boys have no alternative but to enter the labor market, it is not surprising to find that it is the poorly educated male youths and the better-educated girls who contribute to the economic activities of the young people of the Nation.

CHAPTER 9

SUMMARY AND CONCLUSIONS

The child and youth group is composed of those members of the population who are in the various stages of transition from the complete dependency of the very young to the functioning as responsible individuals of the adult community. The significance of a particular age depends on the social environment. The behavior expected of persons and the areas of activity considered appropriate for them are governed in large part by the prevailing culture patterns. The equipment with which a child or youth enters the several stages of the transition to adulthood and the institutions designed to help him make these changes depend in large measure upon the social climate in which he grew up. In this study two major distinctions are considered: residence in rural and urban areas and residence in the different regions of the Nation. The differences between boys and girls and between white and colored are considered in relation to the background of type of residence.

The largest concentration of children and young people is in the South. Here the proportion living in rural areas is especially high. This region is characterized by the highest fertility rates in the Nation and by the lowest per capita incomes. It is an area from which large numbers of migrants go to the North and the West. The fact that white and Negro children grow up in different social environments has significant effects on the adequacy of the training for adulthood which is provided. More than 35 percent of all the young people under 14 years of age and also of those 14 to 19 years old live in the South. Less than 30 percent of the Nation's children live in the North Central States, less than 25 percent live in the Northeast, and only about 12 percent are in the West.

Almost two thirds (64 percent) of the Nation's population is urban but only 58 percent of children under 14 live in urban areas. About 20 percent of the total population live in rural-nonfarm areas as do 23 percent of the children. Almost 20 percent of the Nation's children, but 15 percent of the total population, live in rural-farm areas.

Size of family is often considered in relation to the economic capacity to provide for all family members. In somewhat similar fashion, the relation of the number of children to the number of adults in an area is related to the ability of that area to support the services education, health, etc., re-

quired by the youthful population. Relative to the number of children and
youth, the South has fewer adults than other regions. Dependency ratios
are higher in rural-farm areas than in either urban or rural-nonfarm areas,
and they are higher among the nonwhite than among the white population.

Generally those States which are characterized by a high ratio of children and youth to adults of productive ages may also be characterized by
low family income, poor housing conditions, low expenditures for schooling, and poor educational performance (Chapter 3). Children who grow
up in some States have inferior educational and welfare facilities and thus
are disadvantaged by relative State poverty just as they may reflect family
poverty. The continuing streams of migration from farm to city and from
areas of comparative disadvantage to areas of superior opportunity make
the differences in the training of youth a matter of national interest. These
differences seem likely to persist so long as the public support of programs
and institutions for children rests primarily on the resources of the States.

Projected changes in the population structure of the Nation between
1950 and 1970 are shown in figure 30. Particularly striking are the heavy
losses of population in each of the age groups between 25 and 50 and the
large increases among the young. Changes in the total population structure
will be reflected in the Nation's family composition. The effects of the
high birth rates of the 1921–1924 period have resulted in the high rate of
new family formation by young couples 20 to 30 years later. When the
relatively small number of children born between 1932 to 1937 reach ma-
turity there may be a decided decrease in family formation, followed by an
upswing after the babies born during the war reach the age of marriage.

The expanding population of the Nation has brought with it great
increases in school enrollment. The expansion in the school enrollment of
children and youth, however, has far outpaced the increase in their total
numbers. Since the turn of the century, increases in both the numbers of
children and youth and in the proportion of those enrolled in school occurred in all age groups, although more markedly at the high school and
college levels. Recent population projections by the Bureau of the Census
suggests that the number of persons 18 to 24 years old, representing
roughly the college age groups, will increase rapidly after 1960 and may
reach almost 25 million by 1970, or 10 million more than in July 1955.[1]
Elementary school enrollments will probably reach 30 million by 1959 as
compared with 26 million in 1956. During the same period high school
enrollments will increase from about 8.5 to 9.1 million. The large elementary school population of the current decade will advance to the high
school grades during the next decade so that for every three pupils now enrolled in high school there will be between four and five in 1965.

The other side of the problem of providing educational facilities for the

---

[1] U. S. Bureau of the Census, *Current Population Reports*, Series P–25, No. 123, table 1.

additional millions who may want them is that of the holding power of our secondary schools and the ability of many pupils to make normal progress in school.

Over 4 million persons between the ages of 8 and 18 who were in school in 1950 were retarded in their progress in school which fell below the norms for their respective ages. Retardation is strikingly high among the nonwhite, rural-farm, and southern pupils.

FIGURE 30.—AGE-SEX DISTRIBUTION OF THE POPULATION, 1950, AND PROJECTED FOR 1970

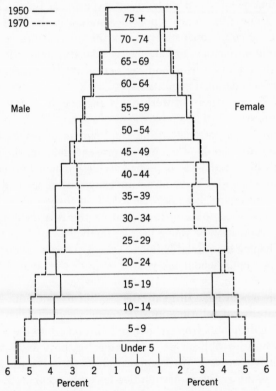

Source: U. S. Bureau of the Census, *Current Population Reports*, Series P-25, No. 123, table 1.

Retardation in school is closely related to relatively low school enrollment rates and relatively high rates of participation in the labor force for young men 14 to 17 years old. In relation to these the nonwhite, rural, and southern pupils are markedly different from their white, urban, and nonsouthern counterparts. However, despite these relationships and despite the concentration of nonwhite and rural-farm pupils in the South, the data presented have not explained many of the differences in retardation. A full explanation would need to recognize individual factors, particularly motivational, economic, and other factors as contributing to high rates of retardation.

Two different points of view are emphasized in relation to youth at work: (1) work provides young people with added equipment for entering the adult world, and (2) early entrance into the labor force is often at the expense of further schooling and future earnings.

Work has many values aside from the purely economic. It is generally important that young people be introduced gradually into the work responsibilities and attitudes of adulthood. Early entrance into the labor force provides young people with a learning experience in the handling and spending of money; for many it provides status, in the eyes of both their peers and of the community elders. On the other hand, education has a definite bearing on income, and the better educated generally have a wider range of work to choose from and are better able to approach the fulfillment of their occupational aspirations.

The predominant pattern of work for young people over the past several years has been the part-time employment of students. There is no consistent set of characteristics relating the employment of youths to attendance or performance in school. The findings presented do not show that student employment either hampers or enhances attendance or performance in school. It appears that more direct investigation is needed to secure an answer to the questions that might be asked on this point.

The materials shed some further light on the relationship between the labor force participation of young people, their place of residence and their schooling (Chapter 8). Retardation in school progress exercises a considerable influence upon school age youths to enter the labor force. This influence is greater among males than females, as might be expected, for males leaving school have little alternative but to enter the labor market.

The availability of full-time jobs to young people is also an important factor affecting drop-outs from school and entrance into the working force. These opportunities appear to be greater for boys in farm areas and for girls in urban areas. Work opportunities for boys are greater in the South, whereas the greater opportunities for girls occur in the North.

In a multivariate analysis it was found that among nonwhite, farm, and southern boys high rates of labor force participation were, in each case, a partial function of low educational attainment. The reverse was found to be true for the girls where the highest rates of labor force participation were due, in part, to high levels of educational attainment. The multivariate examination further fortifies the conclusion that backwardness in school performance leads to early drop-outs from school. The early entrants into the labor force include a disproportionately large number of poorly educated boys.

The facts that poorly educated boys enter the working force in disproportionately large numbers and that higher income among mature workers is closely related to high educational achievement suggest that from both the individual and social viewpoints there are advantages to keeping young people in school. The inadequacy of physical facilities and personnel shortages in schooling may further increase both retardation and drop-outs, the effects of which will be reflected in our future manpower resources. Additional provisions for part-time work for students, with the major emphasis of both time and effort on the school, may aid in offsetting the effects of poorly educated young men joining the full-time labor market.

The data presented in this study have only partial and indirect bearing on the problems of dependency, retardation in schooling, and the labor force participation of young people. Further research in these areas may be concentrated more beneficially with a direct approach to some of the following questions:

What are the effects of varying social, economic, and other environmental conditions upon drop-out from and poor performance in school? Hollingshead[2] suggests that class position is associated very strongly with whether an adolescent is in or out of school—that the social class to which a child belongs is a really significant factor in his relation to the school. On the one hand, the class and family cultures furnish the child with certain beliefs about schooling and the perception of what it may offer him. On the other hand, professional administrators, teachers, etc., provide pupils in the several classes with differential attitudes toward the school system. The child who is susceptible to early withdrawal from school generally associates with boys and girls who are also exposed to the same class and social pressures which motivate him to leave school.

What differences occur in the work patterns of early entrants (whether or not they are retarded in school) and later entrants into the labor force? What, if any, are the differences in their occupational aspirations and achievements?

What is the effect of student employment upon attendance and performance in school? What is the relationship between school performance and the reasons for part-time work? Are the retarded pupils more likely to seek and accept part-time employment and/or does part-time employment contribute to retardation? What is the relationship between school performance and the reasons for remaining in school while working? Are the motivations for remaining in school while working conducive to expected or retarded performance in school?

What, if any, are the differences in the migratory patterns of the retarded pupils and early drop-outs from school as compared with those who complete their secondary education in the expected age-grade positions? How do their work patterns differ from those in both the areas of origin and destination?

---

[2] August B. Hollingshead, *Elmtown's Youth—The Impact of Social Classes on Adolescents*, John Wiley and Sons, New York, 1949.

The data reviewed in these pages give rise to these and other broad questions representing gaps in our knowledge and understanding of some differences among children and youth coming from varying social milieux in the Nation. The study has identified some selected demographic characteristics which bear upon these differences, but only a more direct approach and specifically oriented and designed research can answer the questions and fill the gaps in our knowledge.

BIBLIOGRAPHY

Abrams, R. H. (Ed.), "The American Family in World War II," *The Annals of the American Academy of Political and Social Science*, Vol. 229, September 1943.

Anonymous, "Child Health in Relation to Employment," *The Social Service Review*, Vol. XVI, No. 2, June 1942.

Ayres, L. P., *Laggards in Our Schools*, A Study of Retardation and Elimination in City School Systems, Russell Sage Foundation, New York, 1909.

Bernert, E. H., *Volume and Composition of Net Migration from Rural-farm Populations, 1930–40, for the United States, Major Geographic Divisions and States*, U. S. Department of Agriculture, Bureau of Agricultural Economics (mimeographed), January 1944.

——— and G. K. Bowles, *Farm Migration, 1940–45, An Annotated Bibliography*, U. S. Department of Agriculture, Bureau of Agricultural Economics (mimeographed), September 1947.

Bossard, J. H. S., *The Sociology of Child Development*, Harper and Brothers, New York, 1948 and 1954.

Bowles, G. K., *Farm Population . . . Net Migration from the Rural Farm Population, 1940–50*, U. S. Department of Agriculture, Agricultural Marketing Service, Statistical Bulletin 176, Washington, D. C., June, 1956.

Carlisle, J. C., and L. A. Williams, "What Pupils Are Being Eliminated?" *Clearing House*, Vol. XIII, No. 4, December 1938.

Carr-Saunders, A. M., H. Mannheim, and E. C. Rhodes, *Young Offenders*, Cambridge University Press, Cambridge, 1942.

City Superintendent of Schools of the City of New York, *Annual Report of the City Superintendent of Schools*, Board of Education, City of New York, New York, 1904–1913 (issued annually).

Cottrell, L. S., "The Adjustment of the Individual to His Age and Sex Roles," *American Sociological Review*, Vol. 7, No. 5, October 1942.

Dillon, H. J., *Early School Leavers, A Major Educational Problem*, National Child Labor Committee, New York, 1949.

Duncan, O. D., and A. J. Reiss, *Social Characteristics of Urban and Rural Communities, 1950*, John Wiley and Sons, New York, 1956.

Durand, J. D., *The Labor Force in the United States: 1890–1960*, Social Science Research Council, New York, 1948.

———, "The Postwar Employment of Women in the United States: A Statistical Forecast," *International Labor Review*, Vol. 48, No. 12, December 1944.

Eckert, R. E., and T. D. Marshall, *Why Youth Leave School*, The Regents Inquiry, McGraw-Hill Book Company, New York, 1938.

Eells K., A. Davis, R. J. Havighurst, V. E. Herrick, and R. W. Tyler, *Intelligence and Cultural Differences:* A Study of Cultural Learning and Problem Solving, University of Chicago Press, Chicago, 1951.

Elliott, M. A., "The Scope and Meaning of Divorce," in H. Becker and R. Hill (Eds.), *Family, Marriage, and Parenthood*, D. C. Heath and Company, Boston, 1955.

Elsbree, W. S., *Pupil Progress in Elementary School*, Teachers College, Columbia University, New York, 1943.

Faris, R. E. L., "Interaction of Generations and Family Stability," *American Sociological Review*, Vol. XII, No. 2, April 1947.

Fine, B., "Education in Review," *New York Times*, October 17, 1954.

Frazier, E. F., *The Negro Family in The United States*, University of Chicago Press, Chicago, 1939.

Glick, P. C., "Population Changes: Their Effect on Children and Youth," Paper presented at the Midcentury White House Conference on Children and Youth (mimeographed), Washington, D. C., December 4, 1950.

————, "Educational Attainment and Occupational Advancement," *Transactions of the Second World Congress of Sociology*, held in Liége, Belgium from August 24–31, 1953, International Sociological Association, London, 1954.

————, "The Family Cycle," *American Sociological Review*, Vol. XII, No. 2, April 1947.

————, *American Families*, John Wiley and Sons, New York, 1957.

———— and H. P. Miller, "Educational Level and Potential Income," *American Sociological Review*, Vol. XXI, No. 2, June 1956.

Glueck, S. and E., *1,000 Juvenile Delinquents*, Harvard University Press, Cambridge, 1934.

Gragg, W. L., "Survey of Drop-Outs," *Clearing House*, Vol. XXVI, No. 7, March 1952.

———— "Some Factors Which Distinguish Drop-Outs From High School Graduates," *Occupations*, Vol. XXVIII, No. 7, April 1949.

Harris, S. E., *The Market for College Graduates*, Harvard University Press, Cambridge, 1949.

Hauser, P. M., "Mobility in Labor Force Participation, in E. W. Bakke (Ed.), *Labor Mobility and Economic Opportunity*, The Technology Press of the Massachusetts Institute of Technology and John Wiley and Sons, New York, 1954.

Hecker, S. E., "Early School Leavers in Kentucky," *Bulletin of the Bureau of School Service*, Vol. XXV, No. 4, June 1953.

Hollingshead, A. S., *Elmtown's Youth—The Impact of Social Classes on Adolescents*, John Wiley and Sons, New York, 1949.

Jaffe, A. J., and R. O. Carleton, *Occupational Mobility in the United States, 1930–1960*, King's Crown Press, Columbia University, New York, 1954.

Lambert, S. M., "Increasing Education's Holding Power," *Journal of the National Educational Association*, Vol. XXXIX, No. 9, December 1950.

Landis, P., *Adolescence and Youth, The Process of Maturing*, McGraw-Hill Book Company, New York, 1952.

———— *The Adolescent in the Family*, D. Appleton-Century Company, New York, 1934.

———— *Population Problems—A Cultural Interpretation* (2nd Ed.), prepared by P. Hatt, American Book Company, New York, 1954.

Linton, R., "Age and Sex Categories," *American Sociological Review*, Vol. 7, No. 5, October 1942.

Liveley, C. E., and C. Taeuber, *Rural Migration in the United States*, U. S. Government Printing Office, Washington, D. C., 1939.

Mangus, A. R., "Personality Adjustment of Rural and Urban Children," *American Sociological Review*, Vol. 13, No. 5, October 1948.

Metropolitan Life Insurance Company, "Children in Broken Families," *Statistical Bulletin*, Vol. 36, No. 2, February 1955.

Miller, D. C., and W. H. Form, *Industrial Sociology: An Introduction to the Sociology of Work Relations*, Harper and Brothers, New York, 1951.

Miller, H. P., *Income of the American People*, John Wiley and Sons, New York, 1955.

Mowrer, E., *Family Disorganization*, University of Chicago Press, Chicago, 1927.

National Education Association, "Not a Moment To Lose," A Symposium in *Journal of the National Education Association*, Vol. 43, No. 8, November 1954.

New York State Education Department, *Improvement of Holding Power Through a Continuous Study of Youth in School*, University of the State of New York Press, Albany, 1952.

Odum, H. W., and H. E. Moore, *American Regionalism: A Cultural-Historical Approach to National Integration*, Henry Holt and Company, New York, 1938.

Parsons, T., "Age and Sex in the Social Structure of the United States," *American Socio-logical Review*, Vol. 7, No. 5, October 1942.

Pearlman, L. M., and L. Eskin, "Teen-Age Youth in the Wartime Labor Force," *Monthly Labor Review*, Vol. 60, No. 1, U. S. Department of Labor, Washington, D. C., January 1945.

President's Commission on Higher Education, *Higher Education for American Democracy*, Washington D. C., Government Printing Office, 1947.

Segel, D., *Handbook for Compiling Age-Grade-Progress Statistics*, U. S. Department of In-terior, Office of Education, Pamphlet No. 83, Government Printing Office, Washington, D. C., 1938.

Snepp, D. W., "Why They Drop Out," *Journal of the National Association of Secondary Principals*, Vol. XXXV, No. 180, October 1951.

Spiegelman, M., "The Broken Family—Widowhood and Orphanhood," *The Annals of the American Academy of Political and Social Science*, Vol. 188, November 1936.

Stinebaugh, V., "Why Pupils Leave School," *American School Board Journal*, Vol. LXXII, No. 3, September 1951.

Sullenger, T. E., *Social Determinants in Juvenile Delinquency*, John Wiley and Sons, New York, 1936.

United Nations, Department of Social Affairs, *The Determinants and Consequences of Popu-lation Trends*, A Summary of the Findings of Studies on the Relationships between Popu-lation Changes and Economic and Social Conditions, Population Studies, No. 17, United Nations, New York, 1953.

U. S. Department of Commerce, Bureau of the Census, *Current Population Reports—Con-sumer Income*, Series P–60, No. 7, Income of Families and Persons in the United States: 1949, Washington, D. C., February 1951.

————, *Current Population Reports—Consumer Income*, Series P–60, No. 15, Family In-come in the United States: 1952, Washington, D. C., April 1954.

————, *Current Population Reports—Population Characteristics*, Series P–20, No. 3, School Enrollment of the Civilian Population: October 1949, Washington, D. C., April 1950.

————, *Current Population Reports—Population Characteristics*, Series P–20, No. 32, Children and Youth: 1950, Washington, D. C., December 1950.

————, *Current Population Reports—Population Characteristics*, Series P–20, No. 46, Fer-tility of the Population: April 1952, Washington, D. C., December 1953.

————, *Current Population Reports—Population Characteristics*, Series P–20, No. 54, School Enrollment: October 1954, Washington, D. C., January 1955.

————, *Current Population Reports—Population Estimates*, Series P–25, No. 85, Projec-tion of School Enrollment in the United States: 1953 to 1965, Washington, D. C., De-cember 1953.

————, *Current Population Reports—Population Estimates*, Series P–25, No. 123, Revised Projections of the Population of the United States, By Age and Sex: 1960 to 1975, Wash-ington, D. C., October 1955.

————, *Current Population Reports—Labor Force*, Series P–50, No. 51, Employment of Students: October 1953, Washington, D. C., January 1954.

————, *Current Population Reports—Labor Force*, Series P–50, No. 21, Full-Time and Part-Time Workers: November 1949, Washington, D. C., March 1950.

————, *Current Population Reports—Labor Force*, Series P–50, No. 29, Marital and Family Characteristics of the Labor Force in the United States: March 1950, Washington, D. C., May 1951.

————, *Current Population Reports—Labor Force*, Series P–50, No. 62, Marital and Family Characteristics of the Labor Force in the United States: April 1955 and 1954, Washington, D. C., December 1955.

————, *Current Population Reports—Labor Force*, Series P–50, No. 23, School Enroll-ment of Workers in the United States: October 1949, Washington, D. C., May 1950.

————, *Current Population Reports—Labor Force,* Series P-57, No. 94, Monthly Report on the Labor Force, April 1950, Washington, D. C., May 1950.

————, *U. S. Census of Population: 1950,* Vol. II, Characteristics of the Population, Part 1, U. S. Summary, Government Printing Office, Washington, D. C., 1953.

————, *U. S. Census of Population: 1950,* Vol. IV, *Special Reports,* Part 1, Chapter A, Employment and Personal Characteristics, Government Printing Office, Washington, D. C., 1953.

————, *U. S. Census of Population: 1950,* Vol. IV, *Special Reports,* Part 2, Chapter A, General Characteristics of Families, U. S. Government Printing Office, Washington, D. C., 1955.

————, *U. S. Census of Population: 1950,* Vol. IV, *Special Reports,* Part 2, Chapter C, Institutional Population, Government Printing Office, Washington, D. C., 1953.

————, *U. S. Census of Population: 1950,* Vol. IV, *Special Reports,* Part 5, Chapter A, Characteristics By Size of Place, Government Printing Office, Washington, D. C., 1953.

————, *U. S. Census of Population: 1950,* Vol. IV, *Special Reports,* Part 5, Chapter B, Education, Government Printing Office, Washington, D. C. 1953.

————, *Sixteenth Census of the United States: 1940, Population,* Vol. IV, *Characteristics by Age,* Part 1, U. S. Summary, Government Printing Office, Washington, D. C., 1943.

U. S. Department of Health, Education, and Welfare, Social Security Administration, "Age of Population and Per Capita Income, by State, 1953," *Social Security Bulletin,* Vol. 17, No. 12, December 1954.

U. S. Department of Labor, Bureau of Labor Standards, *Facts About Work of School Youth 1951,* Washington, D. C., September 1952 (mimeographed).

U. S. Department of Labor, Bureau of Labor Statistics, *Family Budget of City Worker, October 1950,* Bulletin No. 1021, Government Printing Office, Washington, D. C., 1951.

U. S. Department of Labor, Wage and Hour and Public Contracts Division, *A Guide to Child-Labor Provisions of The Fair Labor Standards Act,* Child Labor Bulletin No. 101, Government Printing Office, Washington, D. C., September 1953.

U. S. Office of Education, *Biennial Survey of Education in the United States—1948–50,* Chapter 2, "Statistics of State School Systems, 1949–50," Government Printing Office, Washington, D. C., 1952.

Vance, R. B., *Human Geography of the South; A Study in Regional Resources and Human Adequacy,* University of North Carolina Press, Chapel Hill, 1932.

———— and N. Danielevsky, *All These People, The Nation's Human Resources in the South,* University of North Carolina Press, Chapel Hill, 1945.

Waller, W., *The Family—A Dynamic Interpretation* (Revised by R. Hill), Dryden Press, New York, 1951.

White House Conference on Child Health and Protection, *The Adolescent in the Family,* D. Appleton-Century Company, New York, 1934.

White House Conference on Children in a Democracy, *Final Report,* U. S. Government Printing Office, Washington, D. C., 1942.

Wirth, L., *Urban and Rural Living, Planning Post-War Ways of Life for American Youth,* National Council for the Social Studies and the National Association of Secondary School Principals, Washington, D. C., 1944.

————, "Urbanism as a Way of Life," *American Journal of Sociology,* Vol. XLIV, No. 1, July 1938.

Wolfle, D., *America's Resources of Specialized Talent: A Current Appraisal and A Look Ahead,* The Report of the Commission on Human Resources and Advanced Training, Harper and Brothers, New York, 1954.

Wolfbein, S. L., and A. J. Jaffe, "Demographic Factors in Labor Force Growth," *American Sociological Review,* Vol. XI, No. 4, August 1946.

Woofter, T. J., "Larger or Smaller Families for America?", in H. Becker and R. Hill (Eds.), *Family, Marriage and Parenthood,* D. C. Heath and Company, Boston, 1955.

A P P E N D I X   A*

THE NONSCHOOL POPULATION[1]

Over 18.3 million, or 40 percent, of the Nation's children and youth 5 to 24 years of age were *not* enrolled in regular schools at the time of the last census enumeration (table A–1).

As discussed in Chapter 5 and summarized in table A–1, enrollment rates are highest for persons of compulsory school age. Table A–1 shows that the peak enrollment occurs among persons 7 to 13 years old, and that enrollment rates are lower for the younger and older age groups. Only about 4 percent of the 7- to 13-year-olds are *not* enrolled in school, whereas one third of the 14- to 19-year-olds, about three fifths of the 5- and 6-year-olds, and almost nine tenths of the 20- to 24-year-olds are not enrolled in school. Numerically we find that of the total 18.3 million persons not enrolled in school, over one half, or about 10 million persons, are between the ages of 20 and 24 years. The distribution of the remaining 8.3 million is as follows: 4.3 million, 14 to 19 years old; 3.3 million, 5 and 6 years old; and 0.7 million, 7 to 13 years old.

TABLE **A–1.**—Persons 5 to 24 Years Old, by School Enrollment and Age: 1950

[Numbers in thousands]

Enrollment status	Total, 5 to 24 years	5 and 6 years	7 to 13 years	14 to 19 years	20 to 24 years	Percent distribution				
						Total, 5 to 24 years	5 and 6 years	7 to 13 years	14 to 19 years	20 to 24 years
Total....................	46,493	5,495	16,778	12,783	11,437	100.0	100.0	100.0	100.0	100.0
Enrolled in regular schools..	28,176	2,159	16,055	8,481	1,480	60.6	39.3	95.7	66.3	12.9
Not enrolled in regular schools....................	18,316	3,336	723	4,301	9,957	39.4	60.7	4.3	33.6	87.1

Source: *1950 Census of Population*, Vol. II, *Characteristics of the Population*, Part 1, U. S. Summary, table 110.

---

* Prepared by James N. Ypsilantis.

[1] The nonschool population includes all persons 5 to 24 years of age who were *not* enrolled in *regular schools* for the period February 1, 1950 to the time the census was taken, April 1950.

Regular schools include all public, private, and parochial schools, colleges and universities, or professional schools where enrollment may lead to an elementary or high school diploma or a college, university, or professional school degree. Enrollment could be during the day or evening, either full-time or part-time. Also, if a person were receiving regular instruction at home from a tutor and if the instruction were considered comparable to that of a regular school or college, the person was counted as enrolled. Enrollment in a correspondence course was counted only if the course was given by a reg-

141

As shown in table A–2, the nonschool population at the younger ages (5 and 6 and 7 to 13 years) is more male than female. At the older ages (14 to 19 and 20 to 24 years) there are more females than males in the nonschool population.

In summarizing tables A–1 and A–2 it may be said that the nonschool population is comprised mainly of persons too young to attend school[2] or those over 14 years of age, who in many States are not required to attend school.[3]

Table A–3 indicates that the majority of youths not enrolled in school are in the civilian labor force: 2.7 million youths aged 14 to 19 years and 6.5 million youths 20 to 24 years old are not enrolled in school but are in the labor force. The majority of nonschool youths in the labor force are males. There are 5.8 million males 14 to 24 years of age who are not enrolled in school and are in the labor force as compared to the 3.4 million females.

---

ular school (for example, a university) and if the person received credit for it in a regular school system. Persons enrolled in correspondence courses other than these were *not* counted as enrolled.

Excluded from regular school enrollment were children enrolled in kindergarten and in nursery schools. Also excluded were persons enrolled in vocational, trade, or business schools, unless such schools were graded and considered a part of the regular school system. Persons receiving on–the–job training in connection with their work were not counted as enrolled in school. Source: *1950 Census of Population*, Vol. II, *Characteristics of the Population*, Part 1, U. S. Summary, Introduction, pp. 44–45.

[2] According to State laws of *all but four* States (Illinois, Michigan, New Mexico, and Ohio), ages 5 and 6 years are below the compulsory school age; however, many countries and/or cities require children to enter school in the fall if they are 6 years old or will reach that age before a specified date, such as January 1.

Thirteen States do not require a student to attend school until he is 8 years old. These States are: Arizona, California, Colorado, Georgia, Idaho, Minnesota, Montana, New Hampshire, Oregon, Pennsylvania, Utah, Vermont, and Washington. The remaining 31 States all set age 7 as the minimum age for compulsory attendance. See Maris M. Proffitt and David Segel (Eds.), *School Census, Compulsory Education, Child-Labor—State Laws and Regulations*, U. S. Office of Education, 1945, table II, p. 15.

[3] In four States (Georgia, Louisiana, Missouri, and North Carolina) compulsory school attendance legally ceases at age 14.

In twelve States (Arizona, Arkansas, Kansas, Michigan, Oregon, South Dakota, Tennessee, Texas, Utah, Virginia, West Virginia, and Wyoming) completion of the eighth grade exempts a pupil from further attendance.

Eight States (Alabama, Connecticut, Illinois, Iowa, Kentucky, Massachusetts, New Mexico, and Wisconsin) exempts pupils aged 14 who are working.

Eight States, including four mentioned above, exempts pupils who have completed the eighth grade and are 14 years of age (Alabama, Colorado, Delaware, Iowa, Massachusetts, Nevada, New Hampshire, and New Jersey).

Four States require that a pupil be 14 years old, working, and have completed the eighth grade (Indiana, Maryland, Nebraska, and Oklahoma).

Vermont exempts 15-year-olds who have completed the sixth grade, and Idaho, Maine, North Dakota, and Washington exempts 15-year-olds if they have completed the eighth grade.

Six States (Florida, Minnesota, Mississippi, Montana, Rhode Island, and South Carolina) exempts pupils aged 16 and over, and four States (California, New York, Ohio, and Pennsylvania) exempts 16-year-old pupils if they are employed.

Proffitt and Segel, *op. cit.*, pp. 80–164.

TABLE **A-2.**—PERSONS 5 TO 24 YEARS OLD NOT ENROLLED IN SCHOOL, BY AGE
AND SEX: 1950

[Numbers in thousands]

Sex	Total, 5 to 24 years	5 and 6 years	7 to 13 years	14 to 19 years	20 to 24 years	Percent distribution				
						Total, 5 to 24 years	5 and 6 years	7 to 13 years	14 to 19 years	20 to 24 years
Total................	18,316	3,336	723	4,301	9,957	100.0	100.0	100.0	100.0	100.0
Male....................	8,696	1,711	379	2,078	4,528	47.5	51.3	52.4	48.3	45.5
Female..................	9,620	1,625	344	2,223	5,429	52.5	48.7	47.6	51.7	54.5

Source: Derived from *1950 Census of Population*, Vol. II, *Characteristics of the Population*, Part 1, U. S. Summary, table 110.

TABLE **A-3.**—PERSONS 5 TO 24 YEARS OLD NOT ENROLLED IN SCHOOL, BY CENSUS CATEGORY, AGE, AND SEX: 1950

[Numbers in thousands]

Age and sex	Total not enrolled in school		Civilian labor force	Keeping house	Kinder-garten	Armed Forces	Institu-tional popu-lation	Other
	Number	Percent						
Total, 5 to 24 yrs. old...	18,316	100.0	9,177	3,775	904	533	196	3,731
Male..........................	8,696	47.5	5,801	42	461	522	139	1,731
Female........................	9,620	52.5	3,377	3,733	443	11	56	2,000
5 and 6 years old..............	3,336	18.2	...	...	904	...	9	2,423
7 to 13 years old..............	723	3.9	...	...	...	...	24	699
14 to 19 years old.............	4,301	23.5	2,667	932	...	217	162	610
20 to 24 years old.............	9,957	54.4	6,511	2,843	...	316		

Source: *1950 Census of Population*, Vol. II, *Characteristics of the Population*, Part 1, U. S. Summary, tables 109, 110, 118, and 122; Vol. IV, *Special Reports*, Part 2, Chapter C, Institutional Population, table 14.

Table A–4 affords a closer inspection of nonschool youths who are in the civilian labor force. This table shows a more detailed age classification of the 2.7 million teen-age youths who are in the labor force. About 65 percent of the nonenrolled youths of high school ages[4] in the labor force are males. Among males of high school ages participating in the labor force, a higher proportion are not enrolled in school (55 percent) as compared with those who are student-workers (45 percent). There are proportionately more males among the nonenrolled 14- to 15- and 16- to 17-year-olds in the labor force than male student-workers for these same age groups. Among females in the same age groups we find that the enrolled females participate in the labor force as student-workers to a slightly higher degree than do the out-of-school workers.

Male youths 14 to 17 years old participate in the labor force as out-of-school workers to a greater degree than as student-workers. A higher proportion of female students are participating in labor force activity than nonschool females of the same ages. For youths 18 and 19 years of age,

---

[4] Assumption is that one half of the 14-year-olds, one half of the 18-year-olds, and all the 15-, 16-, and 17-year-old youths are of high school ages.

approximately 60 percent of the males and 40 percent of the females are participating in labor force activity regardless of whether or not they are enrolled in school. Among the enrolled males aged 20 to 24 years we find that approximately 71 percent are engaged in some labor force activity, whereas among their nonschool age mates only 64 percent are in the labor force. This is to be expected, for at these ages the nonschool youths are likely to be called into the armed services.

TABLE **A-4.**—PERSONS 14 TO 24 YEARS OLD IN THE CIVILIAN LABOR FORCE, BY SCHOOL ENROLLMENT, AGE, AND SEX: 1950

[Numbers in thousands]

Enrollment status and sex	Total, 14 to 24 years old	14 and 15 years old	16 and 17 years old	18 and 19 years old	20 to 24 years old	Percent distribution				
						Total, 14 to 24 years old	14 and 15 years old	16 and 17 years old	18 and 19 years old	20 to 24 years old
Enrolled, total......	1,873	367	553	375	578	100.0	100.0	100.0	100.0	100.0
Male.....................	1,273	277	360	225	411	68.0	75.5	65.1	60.0	71.1
Female...................	600	90	193	150	167	32.0	24.5	34.9	40.0	28.9
Not enrolled, total..	9,178	78	571	2,018	6,511	100.0	100.0	100.0	100.0	100.0
Male.....................	5,801	60	397	1,202	4,142	63.2	77.0	69.5	59.6	63.6
Female...................	3,377	18	174	816	2,369	36.8	23.1	30.5	40.4	36.4

Source: *1950 Census of Population*, Vol. II, *Characteristics of the Population*, Part 1, U. S. Summary, table 122.

On the other hand, among the females in this age group of 20 to 24 years of age we find that 29 percent of the school youths are in the labor force as compared to 36 percent of the nonschool females in this age group who are in the labor force. Although many of the 20- to 24-year-old females are married, they participate to a greater degree in the labor force than their student sisters.

The second largest category of youths who were presumably not enrolled in school is the group of 3.8 million 14- to 24-year-old youths who are "keeping house."[5] Youths in this category are by and large those persons who are primarily occupied with their own housework as young homemakers. All but 42,000 of these youths are females and in this category we find approximately 900,000 14- to 19-year-olds and 2.8 million 20- to 24-year-olds (table A–3).

The third largest category of young persons who are not enrolled in school is that of the 5- and 6-year-olds who were enrolled in kindergarten (900,000).

The fourth largest category of youths presumably not enrolled in regular schools was composed of the 533,000 persons 14 to 24 years old who were in the Armed Forces.[6] The minimum age of acceptance into all

---

[5] Figures for "keeping house" are total figures and may include some persons who were enrolled in school.

[6] Figures for Armed Forces are total figures and may include some persons who were enrolled in school.

branches of the Armed Forces is age 17 for the male and age 18 for the female youths. Thus this figure of 533,000 youths in the Armed Forces within the continental United States represents some 522,000 males aged 17 to 24 years and 11,000 females aged 18 to 24 years.

The last group which could be accounted for in the census tabulations is the *institutional population,* comprising, by and large, the inmates of correctional institutions, hospitals for mental diseases, tuberculosis hospitals, homes for neglected and dependent children, homes for the physically and mentally handicapped, homes for unwed mothers, detention homes, and training schools for juvenile delinquents. Resident staff members and their children are not included in the institutional population. This definition excludes general hospitals and also Armed Forces institutional population.[7] In the category of institutional population we find approximately 200,000 youths between the ages of 5 and 24 years. Of this total group about 140,000, or 70 percent, are male. About 25,000, or less than 15 percent of the institutional population, are of compulsory school ages (7 to 13 years).[8] Actually, the institutional population accounts for only 1 percent of persons 5 to 24 years old not enrolled in school.

The five census categories mentioned above (civilian labor force, keeping house, kindergarten, Armed Forces, and institutional population) account for approximately 80 percent of the youths between the ages of 5 and 24 years who were not enrolled in school. As shown in table A–5, these five categories total 14.6 million of the original 18.3 million nonschool population. In the remaining category of "others" we find 3.7 million youths not yet accounted for, the majority of whom are between the ages of 5 and 6 years. Among the "others," 2.4 million are 5 and 6 years old, about 700,000 are 7 to 13 years old, and some 600,000 are between the ages of 14 and 24 years.

From tables A–1, A–4, and A–5 we find that among the 5.5 million 5- and 6-year-olds there were 2.2 million children attending regular schools at the time of the enumeration and an additional 900,000 enrolled in kindergarten. About 2.4 million children were neither enrolled in regular schools nor in kindergarten.[9] Although some 5- and 6-year-old children enrolled in school at the fall opening there are many who dropped out prior to the enumeration in the spring. Then, too, probably an additional unknown but smaller number had been enrolled in school *after* Feb-

---

[7] For detailed definition of institutional population see *1950 Census of Population,* Vol. IV, *Special Reports,* Part 2, Chapter C, Institutional Population, p. 4.

[8] *Ibid.,* table 14.

[9] There are no laws compelling 5-year-olds to attend school. Only in Illinois, Michigan, New Mexico, and Ohio are 6-year-olds required to attend school. See Proffitt and Segel, *op. cit.*

There is reason to believe that the proportion of 5- and 6-year-olds not enrolled in school in 1950 should have been still larger. There were approximately 300,000 5- and 6-year-olds enumerated as enrolled in school but with year of school not reported. It is likely that most of these children were not enrolled in school but were edited as enrolled in school because no report on school enrollment was made for them. *1950 Census of Population,* Vol. II, *Characteristics of the Population,* Part 1, U. S. Summary, p. 45.

ruary 1, 1950, but had been erroneously returned as not enrolled in school because their school had closed before the time of enumeration or for other reasons, such as fire, floods, or similar catastrophes.

TABLE **A-5**.—PERSONS 5 TO 24 YEARS OLD NOT ENROLLED IN SCHOOL ACCOUNTED FOR
BY CENSUS CATEGORIES: 1950

[Numbers in thousands]

Census category	Number	Percent
Total not enrolled.........................	18,316	100.0
Total accounted for.............................	14,585	79.6
Civilian labor force........................	9,177	50.1
Keeping house..............................	3,775	20.6
Kindergarten...............................	904	4.9
Armed Forces...............................	533	2.9
Institutional population...................	196	1.1
Other...	3,732	20.4
5 and 6 years old..........................	2,423	13.2
7 to 13 years old..........................	699	3.8
14 to 24 years old.........................	610	3.3

Source: Derived from table A-3.

Table A–5 also shows that approximately 700,000 children 7 to 13 years old in 1950 were neither enrolled in school nor accounted for in any other census categories. The number of these children who were at home because of physical or mental handicaps or because the very young ones were below the compulsory school age in October of 1949 is unknown.

As noted earlier, there are thirteen States that do not require 7-year-olds to attend school and forty-four States that do not require 6-year-olds to attend school. It is probable that many of the 7-year-old children who were not enrolled in school in April 1950 may have been 6 years old at the start of the school term and thus in many States were not required to attend school. There is also reason to believe that a substantial minority of persons 10 to 13 years old were in the labor force, although not so enumerated in 1950.[10] In addition, it is conceivable that at the time of the enumeration a small portion of these 7- to 13-year-olds were not enrolled in school because of the termination of the school year, flood, fire, or disruption of school for other reasons, and they were thus erroneously returned as not enrolled in school.

The last and smallest category of "others" among the youths unaccounted for is the group of 600,000 persons 14 to 24 years old. Many of this last group undoubtedly had completed their schooling and were voluntarily idle. Some, having been graduated from one school system (high school graduates of January 1950), may have been awaiting the commencement of college in the fall of 1950 while others were voluntarily idle.

---

[10] U. S. Department of Labor, Bureau of Labor Standards, "Caution: Children Under 14 at Work," January 24, 1951. Also census returns show that 260,000 children 15 years old and 185,000 children 14 years old were in the labor force in 1950 (*1950 Census of Population*, Vol. II, *Characteristics of the Population*, Part 1, U. S. Summary, table 119).

Included among the 14- to 24-year-olds were also some who were enrolled in business, vocational, and trade schools or similar schools that are not graded and not considered part of the regular school system.

In summary, census categories account for almost 80 percent of the young people 5 to 24 years old who were not enrolled in school. They accounted for 5 percent of the 5- and 6-year-old children, 75 percent of the youths 14 to 24 years old who were not enrolled in school, and only one tenth of 1 percent of those of compulsory school ages (table A–6). Of those not accounted for by census classification (20 percent), over 13 percent were 5- and 6-year-old children who were not required to attend school, or who had dropped out between fall and spring enrollments: 3 percent were 14- to 24-year-olds, many of whom had completed their education and were voluntarily idle or enrolled in other types of schools. The remaining 4 percent were 7- to 13-year-old children not enrolled in school, some of whom were too young to enter school at the beginning of the term and some of whom may have been at work.

Also to be considered are the almost inescapable errors that occur in census enumerations.

TABLE **A–6.**—SUMMARY OF PERSONS 5 TO 24 YEARS OLD NOT ENROLLED IN SCHOOL,
BY AGE: 1950

[Numbers in thousands]

Age	Total not enrolled	Total accounted for	Other	Percent distribution		
				Total not enrolled	Total accounted for	Other
Total, 5 to 24 years old.....	18,316	14,585	3,732	100.0	79.6	20.4
5 and 6 years old...............	3,336	913	2,423	18.2	5.0	13.2
7 to 13 years old...............	723	24	699	3.9	0.1	3.8
14 to 24 years old...............	14,258	13,648	610	77.8	74.5	3.3

Source: Derived from table A-3.

A P P E N D I X   B

A MEASURE OF RELATIVE PROGRESSION OF THE SCHOOL POPULATION OF THE UNITED STATES: APRIL 1950 *

The school experience of children and youth in the United States is basically one in which the pupil enters a school system at a certain minimum age level and from then on is expected to proceed within the system from grade to grade at a regular pace of achievement. It is generally accepted that the pupil is to spend one year in each grade, that in eight years he shall have progressed through eight grade levels, and by the end of a twelve-year period he shall have completed his elementary and high school training. But this is not always the result. Although the *general* pattern of achievement and experience may be one of yearly promotion to the next grade, there are pupils who move faster and "skip" grades, and there are pupils who are held back and have to repeat grades.[1]

The problem at hand is to define the normal pattern of progression and to single out those portions of the school population which are deviant (retarded or accelerated in their school progression). Retardation is defined as a slowness of progress through school as a result of nonpromotion—a lagging behind from the expected pattern of progress through the school system. Correspondingly, acceleration is defined as progression more rapid than the expected pattern. Both retardation and acceleration are deviations from a norm that we would expect each child to have achieved or experienced at each specified age level.

In most earlier studies retardation was measured in terms of pupils too old to be in the grade in which they were enrolled. That is, retardation was a deviation below an expected age spread for each grade or school level.[2] The designation of retarded pupils was derived from a table of

---

* Prepared in collaboration with James N. Ypsilantis. Except for minor revisions, the material presented here appeared originally in the paper by Eleanor H. Bernert and James N. Ypsilantis, "A Measure of the Relative Progression of the School Population of the United States: April 1950," *Journal of Educational Research*, Vol. XLIX, No. 4, December 1955, pp. 251–262.

[1] In some areas of the United States a policy of "social promotion" is practiced. Under this system the pupil is promoted along with his age-grade cohort and generally is not allowed to fall behind or proceed ahead although his actual performance might be below or above that of the cohort. The extent of this promotional practice is not known.

[2] David Segel, *Handbook for Compiling Age-Grade-Progress Statistics*, U. S. Office of Education, Washington, D. C., 1938, Pamphlet No. 83.

"normal ages" from each grade. These ages were arbitrarily assigned. Generally, they were "accepted by common consent as the normal ages for these grades by nearly all the schoolmen who have interested themselves in the problem." [3]

Since this study is focused on *youth* and their characteristics rather than on the *schools*, retardation is expressed in the reverse order of terms used by the earlier investigators. Whereas their basic measure was one of "expected ages" for each grade level, this study's emphasis is on the "expected grade level" for each age category. [4] In addition, empirically derived norms replace those arbitrarily designated.

Before a child can be enrolled in the school system, he must have reached a certain age. This minimum age requirement may vary somewhat but there is always a lower limit placed on the age of entrance for prospective pupils. Many pupils do not attain this minimum age level until a few months *after* the school term has begun and they therefore have to wait until the next starting date; this wait is often for a year. In addition, many parents, whatever their motives may be, are content to have their child wait a full year before they enroll him in the school system, even though he may already have reached the minimum age level just prior to the start of school.

These children who are waiting for the next term to begin enter school at the grade level just below that of their age mates who did not wait. This results at the outset in a two-grade span of participation for each succeeding age group. That is, pupils in specific age groups are not to be found in one grade but usually spread out over two adjacent grades. [5]

Thus, at the very outset of initial enrollment into the school system there is some "lagging behind." This lagging behind persists usually throughout the pupil's school experience because of his late entrance. If a child enters school before he is 8 years of age and continues to progress each year according to the expected pattern, he is not designated as a retarded pupil. If, on the other hand, he enters school at age 8 or over, he is designated as retarded, although his school experience may follow the expected pattern after entrance. [6]

Assuming that usually a child may begin elementary school (postkindergarten) some time during the ages of 6 or 7 and that he must have experienced at least a year or two of schooling before he can begin to deviate

[3] Leonard P. Ayres, *Laggards in Our Schools*, Russell Sage Foundation, New York, 1909. See also, City Superintendent of Schools of the City of New York, *Annual Report of the City Superintendent of Schools*, 1904–1913, Board of Education, City of New York, 1904–1913. Issued annually.

[4] The single-year-of-age distribution for each grade of enrollment was also examined. It was found that total enrollment at each year of age was concentrated in two adjacent grades. These grades corresponded with the expected grades for each year of age derived here.

[5] This pattern of a two-grade span of participation for each single year of age, 7 to 17 years, is shown in *1950 Census of Population*, Vol. II, *Characteristics of the Population*, Part 1, U. S. Summary, table 112.

[6] Thirty-five States require a child to attend school by the age of 7 years. Thirteen States do not require a child to attend school until age 8 is reached.

from the expected promotional pattern, we cannot begin to measure relative progress until he has reached at least the age of 8 years. Thus those under 8 years old are excluded from consideration.[7]

FIGURE **B-1.**—POPULATION 7 TO 18 YEARS OLD, BY GRADE OF SCHOOL IN WHICH ENROLLED, BY SINGLE YEARS OF AGE: 1950

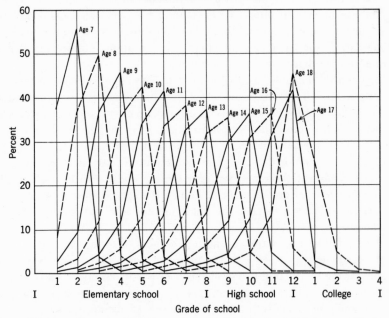

Source: *1950 Census of Population*, Vol. II, *Characteristics of the Population*, Part 1, U. S. Summary, table 112.

Figure B-1 shows the school enrollment of persons by single years of age, 7 to 18 years, by the proportion enrolled in each grade level of elementary and secondary schools. Age 18 was selected as the upper age limit of the group to be analyzed, for several reasons. First, on the bases of the twelve grade levels generally found in the elementary and secondary school systems in the United States and of our premise of an expected stay of one year in each grade level, we would expect each pupil to spend twelve years to complete the total passage. Therefore the twelve successive ages from 7 years (assumed to be the latest entrance age) to 18 years were selected. Second, with each age increase from 19 to 24 years the distribution becomes increasingly more skewed and even bimodal so that the range between the mean, median, and modal grades for each single year of age becomes far too great to attempt to define a norm for the group. That is, "going to school" in itself is not the norm for these age groups as compared to the earlier age groups (see figure B-2).

---

[7] October is generally a more favorable month than April for studying school enrollment and age-grade variations, for October data are less affected by "drop-outs," midyear promotions, or graduations. However, the necessary detailed data are available only for April.

FIGURE **B-2.**—POPULATION 19 TO 24 YEARS OLD, BY GRADE OF SCHOOL IN WHICH ENROLLED, BY SINGLE YEARS OF AGE: 1950

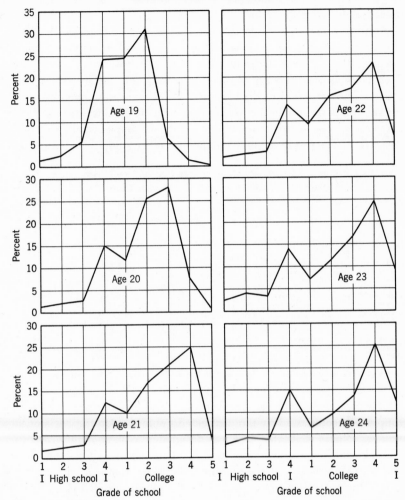

Source: Same as figure B-1.

The similarity of the pattern of grade enrollment with each age, with the notable exception of age 18, is striking, as shown in figure B–1. At each age the majority of pupils are in the modal class and in the *lower adjacent grade*. Also at each age there is a very rapid drop in the percentage of pupils in the grades immediately above and below the *two-grade span* of the modal class and its largest adjacent group. With each increase in age of one year there is a concurrent increase of one grade in the upper and lower limits of the two-year span. Also with each increase of age there is generally a declining peak in the modal class and a concomitant widening of the base.

The curve of grade enrollment for the 18-year-olds differs markedly from the other age curves. Among youth aged 18 years the second largest group is found in the grade *above* the modal grade rather than in the grade immediately *below* the mode.

Assuming a two-grade participation span, tentative grade "norms" or "expected grades" were designated for each age. The "norms" established for ages 8 to 17 were the modal grade and its lower adjacent grade; the "norm" established for age 18 was the modal grade and its higher adjacent grade. The mean and median grade of enrollment was computed for each age for comparison with the modal grade in determining whether the "tentative norm" (two-grade span per age group) encompassed all three of these measures. The results of these computations are summarized in table B–1.

TABLE **B–1.**—MODAL, MEDIAN, AND MEAN YEAR OF SCHOOL ENROLLMENT AND THE EXPECTED, RETARDED, AND ACCELERATED GRADES, BY SINGLE YEARS OF AGE: 1950

Age	Grade in which enrolled			Expected grades	Retarded grades	Accelerated grades
	Mode	Median	Mean			
	(1)	(2)	(3)	(4)	(5)	(6)
7 years old............................	2	2.2	2.2	1 and 2	0	3 plus
8 years old............................	3	3.1	3.0	2 and 3	1	4 plus
9 years old............................	4	4.0	3.9	3 and 4	1 - 2	5 plus
10 years old............................	5	4.9	4.8	4 and 5	1 - 3	6 plus
11 years old............................	6	5.9	5.7	5 and 6	1 - 4	7 plus
12 years old............................	7	6.8	6.6	6 and 7	1 - 5	8 plus
13 years old............................	8	7.8	7.6	7 and 8	1 - 6	9 plus
14 years old............................	9	8.8	8.5	8 and 9	1 - 7	10 plus
15 years old............................	10	9.8	9.4	9 and 10	1 - 8	11 plus
16 years old............................	11	10.8	10.6	10 and 11	1 - 9	12 plus
17 years old............................	12	12.0	11.9	11 and 12	1 - 10	13 plus
18 years old............................	12	12.6	12.4	12 and 13	1 - 11	14 plus

Source: *1950 Census of Population*, Vol. II, *Characteristics of the Population*, Part 1, U. S. Summary, table 112.

Table B–1 shows that the mean, median, and modal grades for each age group are encompassed by the "expected grades." On the basis of these findings, column 4 of table B–1 was designated as the *normal achievement level* for each respective age category. This column shows the "norm" from which deviations of retardation and acceleration can be determined.

Once the norms are so designated, all the pupils enrolled in grade levels below the norm, for each age, are considered *retarded*. Likewise all the pupils enrolled in grades above their expected norms are designated as *accelerated*. Columns 5 and 6 of table B–1 show the retarded and accelerated grades for each single year of age. In essence, then, the school population is divided into three main groups, namely, (1) *retarded*, (2) *accelerated*, and (3) *expected*. Groups 1 and 2 are based on deviations from group 3. In addition, those designated as retarded are classified into two groups: (*a*) one grade retarded and (*b*) more than one grade retarded. It is possible that included among those who are just one grade below the "expected" are those who entered school at age 8 or later, and those whose birthdays occur between October and April; had they been enumerated in the fall month, these late entrants would not have been in a retarded age-grade group. Others in this category include those who have fallen behind the norm due to nonpromotion, but with the data available at present, it is not possible to further identify this group. On the other hand, the group comprising the category of more than one grade retarded may generally be considered as backward in age-grade progress.

In summary, then, the expected grades of performance for each age group are based on the following considerations: (1) because of the initial pattern of school enrollment and the waiting period involved for the pupils who come of age after the school term starts, expected grades encompass at least two adjacent grades, (2) expected grades for each age group encompass a majority of that age group, (3) expected grades encompass all three measures of central tendency (mean, median, and mode), (4) no one of the deviant grades has more pupils enrolled in it than any of the expected grades, and (5) the expected grades conform to a pattern of *progression*, namely, that with each increase in age of the pupil there is an increase in the expected grade of performance.

Table B–2 shows the distribution of the 1950 school population of the United States among the three major categories, expected, retarded, and accelerated, and the two subcategories of retarded. Whereas acceleration among all the age groups remains near a relative constant of 4 to 6 percent, the range of total retardation varies from a relative low of 6.6 percent for the 8-year-olds to a high of 26.3 percent among the 15-year-olds. Total retardation appears to be cumulative from ages 8 through 15 years.[8] Although at each year of age, except 16, those retarded one grade comprise a large proportion of the total than those retarded more than one grade, the proportionate contribution of the latter group increases at a faster pace, from ages 8 through 16, than does the former. At age 16 the group retarded more than one grade actually comprises a larger proportion of the total than the group retarded one grade.

In the total age group (8 to 18 years), *3 out of 4* pupils are in expected grades, *1 out of 20* is in an accelerated grade, *1 out of 8* is retarded one grade, and *1 out of 12* is retarded more than one grade.

Because of errors in reporting age[9] and because of the cumbersomeness of handling single-year-of-age data in comparative analyses, it was necessary to define some significant broad age groupings of the school population.

---

[8] The decline after age 15 may be accounted for, in large part, by the greater likelihood of retarded pupils of dropping out of school upon reaching the legal age limit.

[9] It has been noted that the number of 14-year-old pupils returned as being enrolled in the first grade is unexpectedly large, in many instances exceeding the number of 13-year-olds returned as enrolled in the first grade. Although the size of this group is too small to affect the derived standards of age-grade school progress, it is interesting to note that it has occurred chiefly in those areas where retardation is least.

In the North Central and Northeast Regions and the West, among urban white, pupils there are 2 to 8 times as many 14-year-olds in the first grade as 13-year-olds. In the South, among rural nonwhite pupils, on the other hand, the number of 14-year-olds returned as enrolled in the first grade is generally within the size limits expected on the basis of a statistically normal age distribution in each age.

TABLE **B-2.**—RELATIVE PERFORMANCE OF SCHOOL ENROLLMENT 8 TO 18 YEARS OLD,
BY SINGLE YEARS OF AGE: 1950

[Numbers in thousands]

Age	Total enrolled	Expected grades	Retarded grades			Accelerated grades	Grade not reported
			Total	One grade	More than one grade		
Total, 8 to 18 years.....	21,333	15,798	4,072	2,449	1,623	993	471
8 years old..................	2,448	2,126	162	162	...	95	66
9 years old..................	2,258	1,865	252	205	47	88	54
10 years old.................	2,229	1,734	351	257	95	94	49
11 years old.................	2,146	1,622	388	258	130	88	48
12 years old.................	2,205	1,585	475	281	193	99	47
13 years old.................	2,099	1,460	495	277	218	99	44
14 years old.................	2,026	1,358	506	273	232	118	43
15 years old.................	1,946	1,278	513	265	247	114	41
16 years old.................	1,682	1,126	415	200	215	104	37
17 years old.................	1,427	1,032	313	159	154	45	37
18 years old.................	868	611	203	113	91	48	5
PERCENT DISTRIBUTION							
Total, 8 to 18 years.....	100.0	74.1	19.1	11.5	7.6	4.7	2.2
8 years old..................	100.0	86.8	6.6	6.6	...	3.9	2.7
9 years old..................	100.0	82.6	11.2	9.1	2.1	3.9	2.4
10 years old.................	100.0	77.8	15.7	11.5	4.3	4.2	2.2
11 years old.................	100.0	75.6	18.1	12.0	6.1	4.1	2.2
12 years old.................	100.0	71.9	21.5	12.7	8.8	4.5	2.1
13 years old.................	100.0	69.6	23.6	13.2	10.4	4.7	2.1
14 years old.................	100.0	67.0	25.0	13.5	11.5	5.8	2.1
15 years old.................	100.0	65.7	26.4	13.6	12.7	5.9	2.1
16 years old.................	100.0	66.9	24.7	11.9	12.8	6.2	2.2
17 years old.................	100.0	72.3	21.9	11.1	10.8	3.2	2.6
18 years old.................	100.0	70.4	23.4	13.0	10.5	5.5	0.6

Source: Same as table B-1.

An examination of enrollment by single years of age for three grade classes (elementary school, high school, and college) indicates some reasonable cut-off points in the age data (table B–3). Single year enrollment rates for each grade level show breaking points between the ages of 13 and 14 years, 17 and 18 years, and between 18 and 19 years of age. Between each break in the age classification there is a difference of about 30 to 40 percent in the proportions enrolled in the various grade levels. For example, among the proportion of 13-year-olds enrolled in grades 1 through 8, as compared to the 14-year-olds enrolled in the same grade span, we find a drop from 93.1 percent to 56.8 percent. A similar change seems to occur between the 17- and 18-year-olds, and the 18- and 19-year-olds at the higher levels of schooling. From these data, therefore, it appears that the most significant age groups for school enrollment, excluding the 7-year-olds, are: 8 to 13 years, 14 to 17 years, and 18 years of age.

In relating these age groups to data available from census reports and also to the various age levels at which school youths become eligible to enter the labor force under child labor laws,[10] some readjustment of the above age groups seemed to be in order, especially since participation in

---

[10] U. S. Department of Labor, *A Guide to Child Labor Provisions of the Fair Labor Standards Act* 1953, Child Labor Bulletin No. 101.

the labor force often means conflict or competition with the regular attendance in school.

At age 18, youths are no longer affected by the child labor legislation and they can work at any type of employment they are offered. No occupation is closed to them provided that they can meet the requirements of the job. At age 16 most occupations are also open to youths provided that they are not occupations listed as "hazardous" under the child labor laws. Also at age 16, youths are not restricted to jobs only after school hours, so that in many cases working is in direct conflict with the school program. At ages 14 and 15, youths are eligible to work, but *only at certain restricted* types of employment and only after school hours. Thus it seems from the child labor legislation that the crucial ages of entrance into the labor force at varying degrees of participation are ages 14, 16, and 18.

TABLE **B–3.**—PERCENT OF POPULATION 8 TO 19 YEARS OLD ENROLLED IN ELEMENTARY SCHOOL, HIGH SCHOOL, AND COLLEGE, BY SINGLE YEARS OF AGE: 1950

Age	Elementary school (grades 1 to 8)	High school (grades 9 to 12)	College	Not reported
8 years old..................	97.2	...	...	2.7
9 years old..................	97.6	...	...	2.4
10 years old.................	97.7	...	...	2.2
11 years old.................	97.5	0.2	...	2.2
12 years old.................	97.2	0.7	...	2.1
13 years old.................	93.1	4.7	...	2.1
14 years old.................	56.8	41.2	...	2.1
15 years old.................	26.4	71.4	0.1	2.1
16 years old.................	12.7	84.8	0.3	2.2
17 years old.................	6.4	87.9	3.2	2.6
18 years old.................	3.5	65.1	30.7	0.1
19 years old.................	3.4	33.5	62.6	0.4

Source: Same as table B–1.

Taking into consideration this information and the findings of table B–3, the following age breaks emerge as the most significant ones: ages 8 through 13 years, 14 through 15 years, 16 through 17 years, and 18 years of age.[11] The 8- to 13-year age group covers, roughly, youths at the elementary school level, prior to any influence on their attendance because of competition from the labor force. From age 14 and up, the groupings would take into account the various age levels at which the pupil became more subject to pulls from the labor force sphere in terms of both part-time and full-time employment.

Using these age groupings, the data by single years of age were regrouped to form table B–4 showing the school enrollment of the school population

[11] Table B–3 is based upon a school system of 8 elementary and 4 high school grades. If we regroup grades of school in accordance with another system commonly in operation in the United States (grades 1 through 6, 7 through 9, and 10 through 12), the data yield the following age groups: 8 through 11 years, 12 through 14 years, 15 through 17 years, and 18 years. However, since this age classification tends to conceal significant age groupings in accordance with legal requirements of labor force participation, it was judged less meaningful for the purposes at hand.

according to the three classes of expected, retarded, and accelerated grades and the two subcategories of retarded.

This table provides a base, or a standard, for determining *relative* retardation or acceleration for the various color, ethnic, regional, and residential groups in the United States. Or, if more appropriate, the same procedures may be used to derive a comparable standard of performance for each regional group, residential group, etc.

TABLE **B–4.**—SCHOOL ENROLLMENT 8 TO 18 YEARS OLD IN EXPECTED, RETARDED, AND ACCELERATED GRADE LEVELS: 1950

[Numbers in thousands]

Grade level	Total, 8 to 18 years old	8 to 13 years old	14 and 15 years old	16 and 17 years old	18 years old
Total enrolled................	21,333	13,385	3,972	3,109	868
Expected grades....................	15,798	10,392	2,637	2,158	610
Retarded grades....................	4,072	2,122	1,018	728	203
One grade.....................	2,449	1,439	539	358	113
More than one grade...........	1,623	683	480	370	91
Accelerated grades................	993	563	232	149	48
Grade not reported...............	471	307	84	74	5
PERCENT DISTRIBUTION					
Total enrolled................	100.0	100.0	100.0	100.0	100.0
Expected grades....................	74.1	77.6	66.4	69.4	70.4
Retarded grades....................	19.1	15.9	25.6	23.4	23.4
One grade.....................	11.5	10.8	13.6	11.5	13.0
More than one grade...........	7.6	5.1	12.1	11.9	10.5
Accelerated grades................	4.7	4.2	5.9	4.8	5.6
Grade not reported...............	2.2	2.3	2.1	2.4	0.6

Source: Same as table B-1.

A P P E N D I X   C

STANDARDS OF AGE-GRADE SCHOOL PROGRESS FOR THE SOUTHERN, RURAL-FARM, AND NONWHITE SCHOOL POPULATIONS *

In applying the standard of age-grade school progress to the various population subgroups (color, residence, and region), it was found that there were some subgroups that had relatively large proportions of their youths enrolled in grades denoting retardation. In many cases the number of youths in these retarded groups was so large that further scrutiny of their patterns of school progress was warranted.

On the basis of the United States standards of performance for 8- to 18-year-old pupils, approximately 40 percent of the nonwhite, 31 percent of the southern pupils, and 29 percent of the rural-farm pupils were retarded in their age-grade progress.[1] Among the older pupils 14 to 18 years of age, over 50 percent of the nonwhite and approximately 35 to 40 percent of the rural-farm and southern pupils were in retarded grade levels. These large proportions of youths retarded in their school performance raised the question of whether the pattern of school progression for these groups was sufficiently different from that of the total United States to warrant the specification of other age-grade standards.

One of the first criteria used in the selection of standards of age-grade progress was to ensure that the grades initially selected as expected levels of performance for each age did encompass the measures of mean, modal, and median grade of attainment for pupils at each single year of age. Therefore the mean, modal and median grades of attainment for the nonwhite, rural-farm, and southern pupils were computed to see whether these measures continued to fall within the expected grade span.

Table C–1 summarizes these findings. For the total United States school population 8 to 18 years old, these three measures fall within the two-grade span of expected performance at each single year of age. This table further indicates that for the total United States the modal grade for each single year of age corresponds with the *upper* grade of achievement of the two-grade span of expected levels and that the mean and median grades of attainment generally fall in the *upper* portion of the two-grade span.

---

* Prepared by James N. Ypsilantis.
[1] See Chapter 6, tables 28, 29, and 30.

TABLE **C-1.**—COMPARISON OF U. S. STANDARD OF EXPECTED GRADES WITH CENTRAL TENDENCY
MEASURES OF GRADE OF SCHOOL ENROLLMENT, FOR THE POPULATION 8 TO 18 YEARS OLD,
BY SINGLE YEARS OF AGE, FOR THE UNITED STATES, FOR THE SOUTH, FOR RURAL FARM, AND
FOR NONWHITE: 1950

Age (years)	Expected grades (U. S. standard)	United States			South			Rural farm			Nonwhite		
		Mode	Me-dian	Mean	Mode	Me-dian	Mean	Mode	Me-dian	Mean	Mode	Me-dian	Mean
8	2 - 3	3.0	3.1	3.0	2.0	2.9	2.8	2.0	2.9	2.9	2.0	2.8	2.8
9	3 - 4	4.0	4.0	3.9	3.0	3.7	3.7	3.0	3.8	3.7	3.0	3.6	3.6
10	4 - 5	5.0	4.9	4.8	4.0	4.6	4.5	4.0	4.7	4.5	4.0	4.3	4.3
11	5 - 6	6.0	5.9	5.7	5.0	5.6	5.2	5.0	5.7	5.5	5.0	5.2	5.1
12	6 - 7	7.0	6.8	6.6	6.0	6.4	6.2	6.0	6.6	6.3	6.0	6.1	5.9
13	7 - 8	8.0	7.8	7.6	7.0	7.4	7.1	7.0	7.5	7.2	7.0	6.9	6.7
14	8 - 9	9.0	8.8	8.5	8.0	8.3	8.0	8.0	8.5	8.1	8.0	7.8	7.6
15	9 - 10	10.0	9.8	9.4	9.0	9.3	8.9	9.0	9.4	9.0	9.0	8.8	8.5
16	10 - 11	11.0	10.8	10.6	10.0	10.4	9.9	10.0	10.5	9.8	10.0	9.8	9.4
17	11 - 12	12.0	12.0	11.9	12.0	11.5	11.0	12.0	11.6	11.1	11.0	10.8	10.3
18	12 - 13	12.0	12.6	12.4	12.0	12.4	12.0	12.0	12.1	11.6	12.0	11.7	11.2

Source: Derived from *1950 Census of Population*, Vol. II, *Characteristics of the Population*, Part 1, U. S. Summary, tables 112 and 152.

Among the southern pupils, with the exception of the mean grade of attainment for the 15- and 16-year-old pupils, all three measures fall within the two-grade span of expected achievement, as measured by the United States standards of performance. The mean grade of achievement for the 15- and 16-year-old pupils is just one tenth of a grade below that of the expected level of performance. Among the southern pupils, generally the modal grade of attainment per age specific corresponds with the *lower* grade of the two-grade span, and in general the other two measures (mean and median) fall within the *lower* portion of the two-grade span of achievement.

In comparing the three measures of attainment at each single year of age for the rural-farm pupils, the two-grade span of expected performance emerges. With the exception of the mean grade of attainment for 16- and 18-year-old pupils, all three measures of central tendency for each age fall within the two-grade span of expected grades, as designated by the United States standards. Rural-farm pupils, as the southern pupils, exhibit a similar pattern in their performance, namely, that the modal grade of attainment at each age level generally corresponds to the *lower* grade of the two-grade span and that in general the other two measures (mean and median) tend to fall within the *lower* portion of the two-grade span of achievement.

At the time of this initial inspection of the data it was found that, although some of the central tendency measures for the rural-farm and southern pupils were lower than those derived for the total United States age-grade school experience, the deviations were not sufficient to warrant separate standards of performance. Among the nonwhite pupils, however, in many cases the mean and median grades of attainment *did not fall* within the expected two-grade span of achievement. The modal grade of attainment for the nonwhites, as with the rural-farm and southern pupils, tended to correspond with the *lower* grade of the two-grade span, but the other two measures often did not fall within this span.   At the older ages, the two-grade span of achievement was not sufficiently large to encompass all of the measures, indicating that especially at these ages the nonwhite pattern of performance deviates considerably from that of the United States standards and that a closer inspection of the distribution of nonwhite pupils in the various age-grade levels may be warranted.

Following methods similar to those used in Appendix B, we found that the school performance of the southern, rural-farm, and nonwhite pupils was plotted, as shown in figures C–1, C–2, and C–3.   From figures C–1 and C–2 it is apparent that the distribution of southern and rural-farm pupils in the various grades is fairly similar to that of the total United States school population, with these variations: The peak of each distribution (mode) is in the lower portion of the two-grade span.   Each of the two grades selected contains at least 25 percent of the total age enrollment, and the grade immediately below this span has less than 20 percent of the total enrollment for each age group (10 to 20 percent).   The general United States distributions differ only in that the modal grade is in the upper level of the two-grade span, that each grade in this span contains at least 30 percent of the total age enrollment, and that the grade immediately below the two-grade span has from 5 to 15 percent of the total age enrollment. Furthermore, the proportion of pupils enrolled in the grade levels above the expected span indicates that there is little difference between the total United States, the South, the rural-farm, and the nonwhite rates of acceleration.   All four have the same grades designated as "accelerated" per age specific.

FIGURE **C–1.**—POPULATION 7 TO 18 YEARS OLD, BY GRADE OF SCHOOL IN WHICH ENROLLED, BY SINGLE YEARS OF AGE, FOR THE SOUTH: 1950

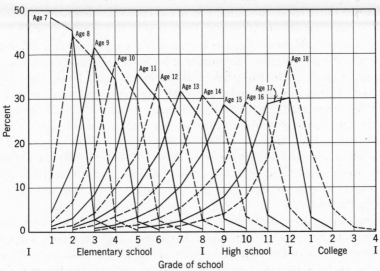

Source: Derived from *1950 Census of Population*, Vol. II, *Characteristics of the Population*, Part 1, U. S. Summary, table 152.

FIGURE **C-2.**—RURAL-FARM POPULATION 7 TO 18 YEARS OLD, BY GRADE OF SCHOOL IN WHICH ENROLLED, BY SINGLE YEARS OF AGE: 1950

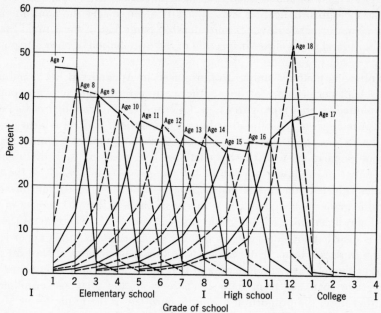

Source: Derived from *1950 Census of Population,* Vol. II, *Characteristics of the Population,* Part 1, U. S. Summary, table 112.

On the basis of the findings in table C–1 and of the comparisons made above of the distribution and performance of the pupils in the southern states and rural-farm areas, it was concluded that the differences were not sufficiently large to warrant a respecification of a standard of progression.

On the other hand, the pattern of performance for the nonwhite pupils shows some important differences from that of the general United States pattern of performance. For the United States pattern we have found that generally the modal grade of attainment for each age group coincides with the upper grade of the two-grade span in the expected level, whereas for the nonwhite pupils the modal grade of attainment coincides in general with the lower grade of the two-grade span. For the United States as a whole, each grade within the expected span contains more pupils per age specific than any grade not in the expected span. However, among the nonwhite pupils we find that for some ages (11 to 16 and 18 years of age), there are as many or more pupils enrolled in the grade immediately *below* the expected span as there are pupils enrolled in each of the expected grades (figure C–3).

Considering these differences, a new table of standards was constructed for the nonwhite pupils. This table of standards describes more accurately the performance of the nonwhite pupils and meets the following minimum criteria for the selection of expected grades of performance for each single year of age: expected levels of performance (1) should encompass all measures of central tendency, (2) should also encompass the majority of pupils at each age level, (3) should assure that no one of the deviant grades has more pupils enrolled in it than any one of the selected grades, and (4) should conform to a pattern of progression, namely, that with each yearly increase in age of pupil there should be a concomitant increase of one grade in the accelerated level of performance.

On the basis of the above specifications table C–2 of nonwhite standards was constructed.

FIGURE C–3.—NONWHITE POPULATION 7 TO 18 YEARS OLD, BY GRADE OF SCHOOL IN WHICH ENROLLED, BY SINGLE YEARS OF AGE: 1950

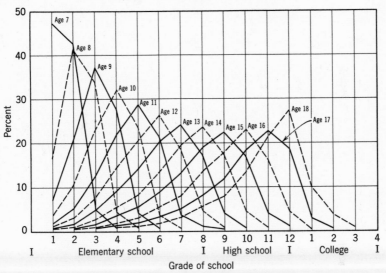

Source: Derived from *1950 Census of Population*, Vol. II, *Characteristics of the Population*, Part 1, U. S. Summary, table 112.

TABLE C–2.—NONWHITE STANDARD OF SCHOOL PERFORMANCE, BY SINGLE YEARS OF AGE: 1950

Age	Expected grades	Retarded grades		Accelerated grades
		One grade	More than one grade	
7 years old.....................	1 and 2	...	...	3 plus
8 years old.....................	2 and 3	1	...	4 plus
9 years old.....................	2, 3, 4	1	...	5 plus
10 years old....................	3, 4, 5	2	1	6 plus
11 years old....................	4, 5, 6	3	1 – 2	7 plus
12 years old....................	5, 6, 7	4	1 – 3	8 plus
13 years old....................	6, 7, 8	5	1 – 4	9 plus
14 years old....................	7, 8, 9	6	1 – 5	10 plus
15 years old....................	8, 9, 10	7	1 – 6	11 plus
16 years old....................	9, 10, 11	8	1 – 7	12 plus
17 years old....................	10, 11, 12	9	1 – 8	13 plus
18 years old....................	10, 11, 12, 13	9	1 – 8	14 plus

Source: Derived from *1950 Census of Population*, Vol. II, *Characteristics of the Population*, Part 1, U. S. Summary, table 112.

The pattern of performance which emerges indicates that: (1) for the 7- and 8-year-old pupils the expected grade levels are the same as those for the total United States, (2) the expected levels of performance for the non-white pupils aged 9 to 17 years encompass a *three-grade span* of performance which is the same as that of the United States two-grade standard *plus* the lower adjacent grade, and (3) for the 18-year-old nonwhite pupils the expected level of performance encompasses a lenient *four-grade span* that coincides to that of the United States standard two-grade span plus the *two lower* adjacent grades.

APPENDIX D

METHOD OF MEASURING THE ASSOCIATION AND IMPORTANCE OF DEMOGRAPHIC CHARACTERISTICS TO THE LABOR FORCE PARTICIPATION OF YOUTH

Rates of gross and net association and gross importance of selected demographic characteristics on the propensity to work are presented in Chapter 8. These rates were derived in an attempt to assess the extent to which variations in the selected characteristics of youths correspond with variations in their labor force membership at a *given period of time.* The measures used differentiate the aspects of *association* and *importance.*

Association is measured by the labor force participation rate of the age-sex cohort. *Degree* of association is established by the size of the rate (0.0 to 100.0), and the *direction* of association is defined with respect to the average cohort rate: Those characteristics for which the participation is above the average for the age-sex cohort are designated as *positively* associated, and those whose rates are below the average rate are designated as *negatively* associated with participation.

To measure the *net* association of one characteristic involves an application of the method of standardization. A net rate of association is computed on the basis of the assumption that the controlled factor is being held constant at its complementary level. For example, the measure of net association between labor force participation and residence in the South while holding color constant is obtained by weighting the white and nonwhite rates of participation in the South by the white and nonwhite populations, respectively, of the non-South. In effect, then, the derived net rate assumes that the color distribution of the population in the South is the same as that of the non-South.

The importance, or impact, of a rate of association is a combined function of two considerations: (1) the number of youths possessing a given characteristic, and (2) the extent of the differential rates of participation within the characteristic category.

In examining (1), it is conceivable that a characteristic which is highly associated with participation is shared by so few youths that it does not "contribute" many workers to the total active group. An example of this is found in examining participation by household relationship, where the highest participation rate for youths occurs among those who are "heads of household." However, the number of youths who are heads of household is very small; thus the importance of this characteristic to the total participating group cannot be large, despite its high rate of association.

With respect to (2), the measure of importance, or impact, is also a function of the degree of differential participation among the components of a characteristic category. In this respect it provides an indication of the heterogeneity of the groups of demographic characteristics in relation to labor force participation. It is conceivable, for example, although more so for older participants, that rates of labor force activity within one characteristic category could be about equal, thereby vitiating the importance or impact of any one component characteristic upon the propensity to be in the labor force. Particularly among male adults, for example, it is possible that participation rates would not differ much among the various household relationships. Although association would be high in each case, the importance (with respect to labor force activity) of being identified by one or another relationship would be negligible. Among youths, the relative homogeneity of behavior with respect to labor force activity differs markedly for the various characteristic categories. Thus, being identified by some characteristics is of more (or less) importance (with respect to participation) than is identification by other characteristics.

A measure of the joint functionings of both these considerations does not distinguish between each of its aspects.

In deriving this measure a method of expected cases was used. An expected labor force was computed on the assumption that participation took place at a rate complementary to that of the particular characteristic being examined. For example, to measure the impact of being "head of household" involved:

(*a*) calculating the labor force of the particular age-sex group that would have existed if all persons in the group were *not* heads of households, and

(*b*) subtracting the results of (*a*) from the observed labor force for the given age-sex group.

In order to derive a relative measure of importance among all the characteristics considered, the difference between the expected and observed figures is expressed as a percentage of the observed labor force.

Insofar as the measure was designed to assess the combined impact of size and differentiation, it does not balance the positive and negative "impacts" of each characteristic. It is applicable only to the positively associated characteristics.

APPENDIX E

SELECTED TABLES

TABLE **E-1**.—Selected Variables for Intercorrelation

	Area	Persons under 20 years old per 100 persons 20 to 64 years old (1)	Median family income (dollars) (2)	Median grade of school completed by persons 25 years old and over (3)	Percent of persons 5 to 19 years old enrolled in school (4)	Current expenditure (excluding interest) per pupil[1] (dollars) (5)	Percent of enrolled males 14 to 17 years old retarded more than one grade[2] (6)	Percent of selective service registrants who failed Armed Forces Qualification Test[3] (7)
1	United States..	59	3,073	9.3		209		19
2	Northeast........	49	3,365	9.6				
3	New England..........	52	3,246	10.4				
4	Maine..............	65	2,596	10.2	76	157	14	18
5	New Hampshire......	57	2,875	9.8	79	211	9	5
6	Vermont............	66	2,573	10.0	77	193	7	14
7	Massachusetts......	51	3,344	10.9	78	236	9	5
8	Rhode Island.......	50	3,117	9.3	74	240	10	10
9	Connecticut........	49	3,543	9.8	78	255	8	13
10	Middle Atlantic......	49	3,402	9.3				
11	New York..........	46	3,487	9.6	78	295	10	13
12	New Jersey.........	47	3,670	9.3	77	280	9	11
13	Pennsylvania.......	54	3,182	9.0	77	216	9	10
14	North Central....	56	3,277	9.4				
15	East North Central...	55	3,428	9.6				
16	Ohio..............	55	3,363	9.9	78	202	10	13
17	Indiana............	59	3,197	9.6	77	235	9	7
18	Illinois...........	49	3,627	9.3	78	258	8	9
19	Michigan...........	58	3,519	9.9	79	220	8	14
20	Wisconsin..........	60	3,256	8.9	82	230	7	8
21	West North Central...	60	2,900	9.0				
22	Minnesota..........	61	3,163	9.0	78	242	6	2
23	Iowa..............	61	3,068	9.8	78	231	6	5
24	Missouri...........	55	2,617	8.8	76	174	10	17
25	North Dakota.......	74	2,933	8.7	76	226	11	13
26	South Dakota.......	68	2,771	8.9	76	230	9	8
27	Nebraska...........	60	2,812	10.1	77	217	4	8
28	Kansas.............	59	2,823	10.2	80	219	6	6
29	South.............	70	2,248	8.6				
30	South Atlantic.......	68	2,413	8.6				
31	Delaware...........	54	3,167	9.8	74	259	12	20
32	Maryland...........	56	3,266	8.9	74	213	15	20
33	Virginia...........	66	2,602	8.5	71	146	30	34
34	West Virginia......	75	2,584	8.5	75	150	20	24
35	North Carolina.....	78	2,121	7.9	73	141	27	38
36	South Carolina.....	87	1,921	7.6	72	122	36	58
37	Georgia............	75	1,898	7.8	73	123	31	36
38	Florida............	56	2,384	9.6	76	181	19	32
39	East South Central...	76	1,793	8.3				
40	Kentucky...........	74	2,032	8.4	69	121	28	26
41	Tennessee..........	70	1,983	8.4	74	132	29	37
42	Alabama............	79	1,810	7.9	75	117	31	43
43	Mississippi........	86	1,198	8.1	74	80	45	45
44	West South Central...	68	2,358	8.8				
45	Arkansas...........	78	1,501	8.3	75	112	28	47
46	Louisiana..........	73	2,122	7.6	75	214	35	48
47	Oklahoma...........	67	2,387	9.1	78	207	14	21
48	Texas..............	65	2,680	9.3	71	209	20	22
49	West..............	56	3,430	11.3				
50	Mountain.............	70	3,101	10.7				
51	Montana............	64	3,255	10.1	78	268	9	6
52	Idaho..............	74	3,046	11.0	78	186	6	5
53	Wyoming............	65	3,482	11.1	74	263	9	7
54	Colorado...........	61	3,069	10.9	76	220	8	9

[1] Average daily attendance in full-time public, elementary and secondary day schools, 1949–1950.
[2] Retarded more than one grade in age-grade school progress.
[3] July 1950 to June 1951.
[4] Less than 0.5 percent.

MATRIX, BY REGIONS, DIVISIONS, AND STATES: 1950

Percent of persons in labor force		Percent of dwelling units--				Percent of population living in urbanized areas	Persons under 5 years old per 100 women 20 to 44 years old	Persons 65 years old and over per 100 persons 20 to 64 years old	
14 and 15 years old	16 and 17 years old	Owner occupied	Dilapidated	With television	With 1.51 persons or more per room				
(8)	(9)	(10)	(11)	(12)	(13)	(14)	(15)	(16)	
		55	9	12	6	46	56	14	1
		48	5	22	3	66	48	14	2
		51	5	17	2	58	52	16	3
5	23	63	9	1	4	12	63	19	4
8	29	58	6	9	2	16	57	19	5
14	32	61	8	2	3	(4)	65	19	6
5	25	48	4	22	2	72	50	17	7
3	31	45	4	22	2	70	49	15	8
5	25	51	4	15	2	63	48	14	9
		48	5	24	3	69	47	14	10
4	20	38	5	25	3	77	45	14	11
4	23	53	4	37	2	78	46	13	12
5	20	60	5	17	3	54	49	14	13
		61	7	11	4	45	56	15	14
		60	6	15	4	51	55	14	15
10	25	61	6	17	3	53	55	15	16
11	28	66	7	7	5	36	57	16	17
8	28	50	6	19	5	61	49	14	18
10	26	68	6	15	3	56	57	12	19
16	30	64	5	9	3	31	61	16	20
		62	8	4	5	31	60	17	21
18	35	66	6	6	4	37	63	16	22
20	34	63	6	2	3	22	62	19	23
11	30	58	11	7	7	48	53	18	24
19	34	66	8	1	8	(4)	74	15	25
22	35	62	8	1	6	(4)	71	16	26
17	33	61	6	3	4	28	61	17	27
16	31	64	7	2	4	24	59	18	28
		54	18	5	11	28	62	13	29
		52	15	7	9	30	60	12	30
5	24	59	7	23	3	54	53	14	31
8	30	56	7	27	4	60	54	12	32
9	28	55	14	7	8	30	59	11	33
5	17	55	16	2	10	15	66	13	34
12	31	53	17	1	11	13	64	10	35
19	40	45	23	1	13	12	71	11	36
17	38	47	23	4	13	27	64	12	37
10	28	58	12	2	8	39	53	15	38
		54	22	3	13	21	66	14	39
11	28	59	17	5	12	21	67	15	40
10	26	57	19	2	12	29	60	13	41
14	30	49	25	1	15	25	66	12	42
20	31	48	30	1	16	5	74	14	43
		56	17	3	11	31	62	13	44
12	26	55	25	1	13	11	69	15	45
10	26	50	21	3	12	35	66	12	46
11	23	60	14	3	9	22	60	16	47
12	30	57	16	3	12	37	61	12	48
		58	7	9	6	50	57	14	49
		59	10	1	10	20	67	13	50
16	31	60	11	1	8	(4)	67	15	51
17	31	66	10	1	9	(4)	71	14	52
18	37	54	9	1	10	(4)	65	11	53
15	33	58	8	1	8	43	60	15	54

TABLE **E-1.**—SELECTED VARIABLES FOR INTERCORRELATION

Area	Persons under 20 years old per 100 persons 20 to 64 years old (1)	Median family income (dollars) (2)	Median grade of school completed by persons 25 years old and over (3)	Percent of persons 5 to 19 years old enrolled in school (4)	Current expenditure (excluding interest) per pupil[1] (dollars) (5)	Percent of enrolled males 14 to 17 years old retarded more than one grade[2] (6)	Percent of selective service registrants who failed Armed Forces Qualification Test[3] (7)
West--Cont.							
Mountain--Cont.							
1 New Mexico.........	83	2,653	9.3	73	222	25	29
2 Arizona............	72	2,851	10.0	74	241	21	20
3 Utah..............	80	3,264	12.0	79	179	7	2
4 Nevada............	52	3,613	11.5	78	246	9	10
5 Pacific...........	52	3,545	11.5				
6 Washington........	57	3,495	11.2	77	248	7	6
7 Oregon............	56	3,376	10.9	79	281	6	3
8 California........	50	3,585	11.6	80	264	6	9

[1] Average daily attendance in full-time public, elementary and secondary day schools, 1949–1950.

[2] Retarded more than one grade in age-grade school progress.

[3] July 1950 to June 1951.

[4] Less than 0.5 percent.

Source:

Col. 1, *1950 Census of Population*, Vol. II, *Characteristics of the Population*, Parts 2–50, table 16.

Col. 2, *1950 Census of Population*, Vol. II, *Characteristics of the Population*, Part 1, U. S. Summary, table 85.

Col. 3, *1950 Census of Population*, Vol. II, *Characteristics of the Population*, Parts 2–50, table 20.

Col. 4, *Ibid.*, table 19.

Col. 5, U. S. Office of Education, *Biennial Survey of Education in the United States, 1948–1950*, Chapter II, "Statistics of State School Systems, 1949–50" by David T. Blore and William Jaracz, table XIV.

Col. 6, derived from *1950 Census of Population*, Vol. II, *Characteristics of the Population*, Parts 2–50, table 63, on basis of method described in Appendix C.

Col. 7, U. S. Office of Education, *Literacy Education*, Circular No. 376, June 1953, table 2.

MATRIX, BY REGIONS, DIVISIONS, AND STATES: 1950—Cont.

Percent of persons in labor force		Percent of dwelling units--				Percent of population living in urbanized areas	Persons under 5 years old per 100 women 20 to 44 years old	Persons 65 years old and over per 100 persons 20 to 64 years old	
14 and 15 years old	16 and 17 years old	Owner occupied	Dilapi- dated	With tele- vision	With 1.51 persons or more per room				
(8)	(9)	(10)	(11)	(12)	(13)	(14)	(15)	(16)	
9	24	59	14	1	19	(⁴)	76	9	1
10	27	56	15	2	15	29	66	11	2
15	27	65	6	5	7	33	76	12	3
15	28	49	11	1	7	(⁴)	53	11	4
		57	6	12	4	60	54	14	5
13	27	65	6	3	4	42	60	15	6
13	24	65	8	1	5	31	58	15	7
10	22	54	5	15	5	68	52	14	8

Source—Cont.

Col. 8, derived from *1950 Census of Population*, Vol. II, *Characteristics of the Population*, Parts 2-50, table 69.

Col. 9, *Ibid.*

Col. 10, *1950 Census of Housing*, Vol. I, *General Characteristics*, Chapter 1, U. S. Summary, table 17.

Col. 11, *Ibid.*, table 18.

Col. 12, *Ibid.*, table 20.

Col. 13, *Ibid.*, table 19.

Col. 14, derived from *1950 Census of Population*, Vol. I, *Number of Inhabitants*, State table 9.

Col. 15, *1950 Census of Population*, Vol. II, *Characteristics of the Population*, Part 1, U. S. Summary, table 63.

Col. 16, *1950 Census of Population*, Vol. II, *Characteristics of the Population*, Parts 2-50, table 16.

TABLE E-2.—RELATIVE PERFORMANCE OF THE SCHOOL ENROLLMENT 8 TO 18 YEARS OLD, BY AGE, COLOR, AND SEX: 1950

[In thousands]

Color and relative performance	Both sexes					Male					Female				
	Total, 8 to 18 years old	8 to 13 years old	14 and 15 years old	16 and 17 years old	18 years old	Total, 8 to 18 years old	8 to 13 years old	14 and 15 years old	16 and 17 years old	18 years old	Total, 8 to 18 years old	8 to 13 years old	14 and 15 years old	16 and 17 years old	18 years old
ALL CLASSES															
Total enrolled	21,333	13,385	3,972	3,109	868	10,838	6,795	2,019	1,566	458	10,495	6,590	1,953	1,543	409
Expected grades	15,798	10,392	2,637	2,158	611	7,711	5,118	1,255	1,026	312	8,087	5,274	1,382	1,132	299
Retarded grades	4,072	2,122	1,018	728	203	2,437	1,262	614	438	122	1,635	860	404	290	81
One grade	2,449	1,439	539	358	113	1,444	846	317	213	68	1,005	594	221	145	45
More than one grade	1,623	683	480	370	91	993	417	297	225	54	630	266	183	145	36
Accelerated grades	993	563	232	149	48	431	250	100	60	22	562	313	133	89	27
Grade not reported	471	307	84	74	5	259	165	50	41	2	211	142	34	33	3
WHITE															
Total enrolled	18,779	11,721	3,500	2,776	782	9,575	5,966	1,787	1,404	417	9,204	5,754	1,713	1,372	365
Expected grades	14,512	9,463	2,447	2,023	579	7,130	4,687	1,174	970	299	7,383	4,776	1,273	1,053	280
Retarded grades	2,993	1,514	772	553	155	1,838	921	478	342	96	1,156	592	293	211	59
One grade	1,939	1,098	448	298	94	1,176	662	272	183	58	763	436	175	115	36
More than one grade	1,055	415	324	255	60	662	259	206	159	37	393	156	118	96	23
Accelerated grades	866	479	208	135	44	382	215	91	55	21	484	264	117	79	24
Grade not reported	407	265	74	64	4	225	143	44	36	2	182	122	29	28	2
NONWHITE															
Total enrolled	2,555	1,664	471	333	85	1,263	829	231	162	41	1,291	835	240	172	44
Expected grades	1,285	929	190	135	32	581	431	81	56	13	704	498	109	79	19
Retarded grades	1,078	608	247	175	49	599	341	136	96	27	479	267	111	79	22
One grade	510	341	91	60	18	268	183	45	30	9	242	158	46	30	9
More than one grade	568	267	156	114	31	331	158	91	66	17	237	110	65	49	13
Accelerated grades	127	84	24	15	4	49	35	9	5	1	78	49	16	10	3
Grade not reported	63	43	11	10	...	34	22	6	5	...	30	20	5	5	...

Source: 1950 Census of Population, Vol. II, Characteristics of the Population, Part 1, U. S. Summary, table 112.

TABLE E-3.—RELATIVE PERFORMANCE OF THE SCHOOL ENROLLMENT 8 TO 18 YEARS OLD, BY AGE AND SEX, URBAN AND RURAL: 1950

[In thousands]

Area and relative performance	Both sexes					Male					Female				
	Total, 8 to 18 years old	8 to 13 years old	14 and 15 years old	16 and 17 years old	18 years old	Total, 8 to 18 years old	8 to 13 years old	14 and 15 years old	16 and 17 years old	18 years old	Total, 8 to 18 years old	8 to 13 years old	14 and 15 years old	16 and 17 years old	18 years old
URBAN															
Total enrolled.........	12,050	7,417	2,217	1,842	575	6,080	3,739	1,116	924	301	5,970	3,678	1,100	917	274
Expected grades.........	9,381	6,043	1,571	1,339	428	4,596	2,983	753	642	218	4,785	3,059	818	697	211
Retarded grades.........	1,713	826	435	350	102	1,032	493	262	213	63	682	333	173	137	39
One grade.........	1,116	607	258	190	60	670	361	155	116	38	446	246	103	74	23
More than one grade.........	597	218	177	160	42	361	132	107	97	25	235	86	70	63	16
Accelerated grades.........	668	361	158	107	42	294	162	69	43	19	374	198	89	64	23
Grade not reported.........	288	188	52	46	3	159	100	31	26	1	129	87	21	20	2
RURAL NONFARM															
Total enrolled.........	4,828	3,129	889	651	159	2,467	1,596	454	329	87	2,362	1,533	435	322	72
Expected grades.........	3,468	2,367	562	434	105	1,682	1,160	262	203	56	1,786	1,207	299	230	50
Retarded grades.........	1,091	596	271	177	47	655	355	165	107	29	435	241	106	70	19
One grade.........	657	406	140	85	26	386	238	82	50	16	271	168	58	35	10
More than one grade.........	433	190	131	92	21	270	117	83	57	13	164	73	48	35	8
Accelerated grades.........	160	96	37	22	5	69	42	15	9	2	91	54	21	13	3
Grade not reported.........	109	70	20	18	1	61	39	12	10	1	49	31	8	8	1
RURAL FARM															
Total enrolled.........	4,455	2,839	866	617	134	2,291	1,461	448	312	70	2,164	1,378	418	304	63
Expected grades.........	2,949	1,982	504	385	77	1,433	974	239	181	39	1,516	1,008	264	205	39
Retarded grades.........	1,268	701	312	201	54	750	415	187	118	31	518	286	126	83	24
One grade.........	675	426	140	83	26	388	247	80	47	15	288	179	60	36	12
More than one grade.........	593	275	172	118	28	362	168	107	71	16	231	107	65	47	12
Accelerated grades.........	165	106	38	20	2	68	45	15	8	1	97	61	23	12	1
Grade not reported.........	73	50	12	11	1	40	26	7	6	...	33	23	5	4	...

Source: Same as table E-2.

TABLE E–4.—Relative Performance of the School Enrollment 8 to 18 Years Old, by Age and Sex, for Regions: 1950

[In thousands]

Region and relative performance	Both sexes					Male					Female				
	Total, 8 to 18 years old	8 to 13 years old	14 and 15 years old	16 and 17 years old	18 years old	Total, 8 to 18 years old	8 to 13 years old	14 and 15 years old	16 and 17 years old	18 years old	Total, 8 to 18 years old	8 to 13 years old	14 and 15 years old	16 and 17 years old	18 years old
NORTHEAST															
Total enrolled.........	4,992	3,050	937	787	218	2,543	1,551	477	398	116	2,449	1,499	459	389	102
Expected grades.........	3,849	2,469	646	573	162	1,906	1,230	314	278	84	1,944	1,239	331	295	78
Retarded grades.........	657	296	177	145	40	403	182	108	88	25	254	114	69	57	15
One grade.........	433	224	107	77	25	265	137	65	47	15	168	87	41	30	9
More than one grade......	225	71	71	68	15	138	45	43	41	9	86	26	27	27	6
Accelerated grades.........	354	200	92	48	14	162	93	41	21	7	192	107	50	28	8
Grade not reported.........	131	86	23	21	2	72	46	13	12	1	60	40	9	10	1
NORTH CENTRAL															
Total enrolled.........	6,202	3,863	1,153	932	253	3,154	1,965	588	468	133	3,048	1,898	566	464	120
Expected grades.........	5,048	3,254	871	725	199	2,486	1,618	420	347	101	2,562	1,635	450	378	98
Retarded grades.........	772	376	201	152	43	486	236	128	94	27	286	140	73	57	16
One grade.........	540	294	131	87	28	339	184	83	55	18	201	110	48	32	10
More than one grade......	232	83	70	65	15	147	52	45	40	9	85	30	25	25	6
Accelerated grades.........	249	145	58	35	10	107	63	25	15	5	141	82	33	21	6
Grade not reported.........	133	88	24	20	1	74	47	14	12	1	59	41	9	8	1
SOUTH															
Total enrolled.........	7,480	4,814	1,398	989	279	3,778	2,434	707	493	144	3,701	2,380	691	496	135
Expected grades.........	4,767	3,293	757	557	160	2,255	1,581	344	252	79	2,512	1,712	414	305	81
Retarded grades.........	2,291	1,276	556	360	99	1,333	740	326	211	57	958	537	230	150	42
One grade.........	1,231	788	246	150	47	689	444	135	84	26	542	344	111	67	21
More than one grade......	1,061	488	310	210	52	644	296	191	127	31	416	192	119	83	22
Accelerated grades.........	282	154	60	50	18	115	65	23	18	8	167	89	37	31	11
Grade not reported.........	139	91	25	22	1	75	48	14	12	1	64	43	11	10	1
WEST															
Total enrolled.........	2,660	1,658	483	401	118	1,363	845	246	206	65	1,296	812	237	194	53
Expected grades.........	2,133	1,377	363	303	90	1,063	689	177	149	48	1,070	688	186	154	42
Retarded grades.........	351	174	84	71	22	215	104	51	45	14	137	69	33	27	8
One grade.........	246	133	56	44	13	151	80	34	28	9	94	53	21	16	5
More than one grade......	105	41	29	27	8	63	24	17	17	5	42	17	12	11	3
Accelerated grades.........	108	64	23	16	5	47	29	10	6	2	61	36	13	9	3
Grade not reported.........	67	43	13	11	1	38	24	8	6	...	29	19	5	5	...

Source: 1950 Census of Population, Vol. II, Characteristics of Population, Part 1, U. S. Summary, table 152.

TABLE E-5.—RELATIVE PERFORMANCE OF NONWHITE SCHOOL ENROLLMENT 8 TO 18 YEARS OLD, BY AGE AND SEX, ON NONWHITE STANDARD: 1950

[In thousands]

Relative performance and sex	Total, 8 to 18 years old	8 to 13 years old	14 and 15 years old	16 and 17 years old	18 years old
Both sexes, total enrolled.....	2,555	1,664	471	334	85
Expected grades.....................	1,757	1,220	281	195	62
Retarded grades.....................	607	317	156	114	19
One grade.........................	323	210	63	43	7
More than one grade...............	283	107	93	71	12
Accelerated grades..................	127	84	24	15	4
Grade not reported..................	63	43	11	10	...
Male, total enrolled.............	1,263	829	231	162	41
Expected grades.....................	827	586	126	86	29
Retarded grades.....................	353	186	91	66	11
One grade.........................	181	120	34	23	4
More than one grade...............	172	66	56	42	7
Accelerated grades..................	49	35	9	5	1
Grade not reported..................	34	22	6	5	...
Female, total enrolled...........	1,291	835	240	172	44
Expected grades.....................	930	634	154	109	33
Retarded grades.....................	253	132	65	49	8
One grade.........................	142	91	29	20	3
More than one grade...............	111	41	36	29	5
Accelerated grades..................	78	49	16	10	3
Grade not reported..................	30	20	5	5	...

Source: Derived from *1950 Census of Population*, Vol. II, *Characteristics of Population*, Part 1, U. S. Summary, table 112.

TABLE E-6.—RELATIVE PERFORMANCE OF SCHOOL ENROLLMENT 8 TO 18 YEARS OLD BY AGE AND COLOR, ON U. S. STANDARD, AND OF NONWHITE SCHOOL ENROLLMENT BY AGE, ON NONWHITE STANDARD, FOR THE SOUTH: 1950

[In thousands]

Standard, color, and relative performance	Total, 8 to 18 years old	8 to 13 years old	14 and 15 years old	16 and 17 years old	18 years old
U. S. STANDARD OF PERFORMANCE					
White, total enrolled...........	5,654	3,610	1,063	762	220
Expected grades.....................	3,954	2,685	646	482	141
Retarded grades.....................	1,387	751	351	223	62
One grade.........................	825	504	178	108	35
More than one grade...............	562	246	173	114	28
Accelerated grades..................	207	105	47	41	15
Grade not reported..................	106	69	19	17	1
Nonwhite, total enrolled.........	1,825	1,205	335	226	59
Expected grades.....................	813	608	112	74	19
Retarded grades.....................	905	526	204	138	37
One grade.........................	406	284	68	42	12
More than one grade...............	499	242	137	96	25
Accelerated grades..................	74	49	13	9	3
Grade not reported..................	33	22	5	5	...
NONWHITE STANDARD OF PERFORMANCE					
Nonwhite, total enrolled.........	1,825	1,205	335	226	59
Expected grades.....................	1,183	847	179	117	40
Retarded grades.....................	535	286	137	96	16
One grade.........................	281	188	53	34	6
More than one grade...............	254	99	84	62	10
Accelerated grades..................	74	49	13	9	3
Grade not reported..................	33	22	5	5	...

Source: Same as table E-4.

TABLE E-7.—MALES 8 TO 18 YEARS OLD IN RETARDED GRADES BY DEGREE OF RETARDATION AND COLOR, BY AGE, FOR THE SOUTH, URBAN AND RURAL FARM: 1950

[Retardation for nonwhite measured on both U. S. standard of performance and nonwhite standard of performance]

Area, standard, color, and degree of retardation	Total, 8 to 18 years old	8 to 13 years old	14 and 15 years old	16 and 17 years old	18 years old
URBAN					
U. S. Standard of Performance					
White, total enrolled...........	1,161,580	723,805	211,880	164,330	61,565
Retarded grades....................	252,215	127,735	64,230	45,800	14,450
One grade........................	157,400	89,350	35,255	24,150	8,645
More than one grade...............	94,815	38,385	28,975	21,650	5,805
Nonwhite, total enrolled........	348,235	225,925	63,975	45,645	12,690
Retarded grades....................	144,500	77,440	34,435	25,545	7,080
One grade........................	73,510	47,535	13,665	9,645	2,665
More than one grade...............	70,990	29,905	20,770	15,900	4,415
Nonwhite Standard of Performance					
Nonwhite, total enrolled........	348,235	225,925	63,975	45,645	12,690
Retarded grades....................	74,440	35,340	20,770	15,900	2,430
One grade........................	43,030	25,375	9,935	6,715	1,005
More than one grade...............	31,410	9,965	10,835	9,185	1,425
RURAL FARM					
U. S. Standard of Performance					
White, total enrolled...........	891,995	568,655	179,125	118,220	25,995
Retarded grades....................	321,370	173,840	83,910	50,865	12,755
One grade........................	175,000	109,495	37,445	21,605	6,455
More than one grade...............	146,370	64,345	46,465	29,260	6,300
Nonwhite, total enrolled........	355,690	240,930	65,050	40,355	9,355
Retarded grades....................	242,115	148,815	52,245	33,075	7,980
One grade........................	86,505	67,740	11,115	6,025	1,625
More than one grade...............	155,610	81,075	41,130	27,050	6,355
Nonwhite Standard of Performance					
Nonwhite, total enrolled........	355,690	240,930	65,050	40,355	9,355
Retarded grades....................	168,035	95,005	41,130	27,050	4,850
One grade........................	76,745	56,910	11,690	6,750	1,395
More than one grade...............	91,290	38,095	29,440	20,300	3,455

Source: Same as table E-4.

TABLE E-8.—CIVILIAN POPULATION 14 TO 24 YEARS OLD IN THE LABOR FORCE, BY SINGLE YEARS OF AGE, COLOR, AND SEX: 1950

[Numbers in thousands]

Age and color	Male			Female		
	Total	Labor force		Total	Labor force	
		Number	Percent		Number	Percent
ALL CLASSES						
14 to 19 years.............	6,223	2,323	37.3	6,367	1,438	22.6
14 years......................	1,096	142	13.0	1,042	43	4.1
15 years......................	1,077	193	17.9	1,049	67	6.4
16 years......................	1,055	308	29.2	1,026	133	13.0
17 years......................	1,030	421	40.8	1,044	233	22.3
18 years......................	1,018	593	58.2	1,097	440	40.1
19 years......................	947	666	70.3	1,108	523	47.2
20 to 24 years.............	5,233	4,230	80.8	5,862	2,513	42.9
20 years......................	931	706	75.8	1,119	524	46.8
21 years......................	1,034	811	78.5	1,155	522	45.2
22 years......................	1,067	860	80.6	1,182	514	43.5
23 years......................	1,097	911	83.0	1,195	489	40.9
24 years......................	1,105	942	85.3	1,211	463	38.3
WHITE						
14 to 19 years.............	5,478	2,005	36.6	5,575	1,294	23.2
14 years......................	962	120	12.4	909	35	3.9
15 years......................	950	162	17.1	916	55	6.0
16 years......................	924	260	28.2	891	115	12.9
17 years......................	906	359	39.6	915	207	22.6
18 years......................	895	514	57.5	963	402	41.7
19 years......................	841	589	70.1	980	479	48.9
20 to 24 years.............	4,661	3,775	81.0	5,165	2,239	43.3
20 years......................	827	626	75.7	980	473	48.3
21 years......................	920	720	78.3	1,023	471	46.0
22 years......................	951	767	80.7	1,042	458	43.9
23 years......................	980	817	83.4	1,052	432	41.0
24 years......................	984	844	85.8	1,067	404	37.9
NONWHITE						
14 to 19 years.............	745	318	42.7	792	145	18.3
14 years......................	134	23	16.9	133	7	5.5
15 years......................	127	31	24.1	133	12	8.7
16 years......................	131	48	36.5	135	18	13.5
17 years......................	124	62	50.0	129	26	20.1
18 years......................	123	78	63.7	134	38	28.0
19 years......................	106	77	72.3	128	44	34.5
20 to 24 years.............	572	455	79.5	696	274	39.4
20 years......................	104	80	76.9	138	50	36.3
21 years......................	114	91	79.9	131	51	38.6
22 years......................	117	93	79.6	140	57	40.5
23 years......................	117	93	79.9	143	58	40.3
24 years......................	121	98	80.9	144	59	41.1

Source: *1950 Census of Population*, Vol. IV, *Special Reports*, Part 1, Chapter A, Employment and Personal Characteristics, table 1.

TABLE **E-9.**—CIVILIAN POPULATION 14 TO 24 YEARS OLD IN THE LABOR FORCE, BY SINGLE YEARS OF AGE AND SEX, URBAN AND RURAL: 1950

[Numbers in thousands]

Area and age	Male			Female		
	Total	Labor force		Total	Labor force	
		Number	Percent		Number	Percent
URBAN						
14 to 19 years............	3,475	1,176	33.8	3,805	1,033	27.2
14 years........................	589	61	10.4	577	21	3.6
15 years........................	582	81	14.0	583	35	6.0
16 years........................	572	137	23.9	575	83	14.5
17 years........................	569	205	36.0	618	164	26.5
18 years........................	590	317	53.8	701	328	46.8
19 years........................	574	375	65.2	750	402	53.6
20 to 24 years............	3,470	2,704	77.9	4,056	2,000	49.3
20 years........................	588	420	71.5	766	408	53.3
21 years........................	681	508	74.7	802	411	51.3
22 years........................	704	545	77.5	817	413	50.5
23 years........................	741	597	80.5	829	395	47.6
24 years........................	757	633	83.7	842	373	44.3
RURAL NONFARM						
14 to 19 years............	1,337	448	33.5	1,358	240	17.6
14 years........................	248	22	9.0	235	10	4.1
15 years........................	244	34	13.8	236	15	6.4
16 years........................	230	59	25.6	230	26	11.5
17 years........................	221	83	37.5	227	42	18.5
18 years........................	208	119	57.0	217	68	31.3
19 years........................	186	131	70.5	213	79	36.9
20 to 24 years............	1,018	836	82.2	1,161	354	30.5
20 years........................	179	138	76.8	220	77	35.0
21 years........................	196	159	81.2	225	75	33.2
22 years........................	212	174	82.2	233	70	29.9
23 years........................	216	183	84.5	239	67	27.9
24 years........................	214	182	85.3	245	66	27.1
RURAL FARM						
14 to 19 years............	1,411	700	49.6	1,204	166	13.8
14 years........................	260	59	22.7	231	12	5.2
15 years........................	251	78	30.9	230	17	7.3
16 years........................	253	113	44.5	221	23	10.6
17 years........................	239	132	55.4	199	27	13.8
18 years........................	221	157	71.3	179	43	24.2
19 years........................	187	161	85.9	145	43	29.5
20 to 24 years............	746	690	92.5	645	159	24.6
20 years........................	163	147	90.4	133	39	28.9
21 years........................	157	143	91.6	128	36	27.9
22 years........................	151	141	92.9	131	32	24.3
23 years........................	140	131	94.0	128	28	22.0
24 years........................	135	127	94.1	125	25	19.7

Source: Same as table E-8.

TABLE **E–10.**—CIVILIAN POPULATION 14 TO 24 YEARS OLD IN THE LABOR FORCE, BY SINGLE YEARS OF AGE AND SEX, FOR REGIONS: 1950

[Numbers in thousands]

Region and age	Male			Female		
	Total	Labor force		Total	Labor force	
		Number	Percent		Number	Percent
NORTHEAST						
14 to 19 years.................	1,483	435	29.4	1,530	409	26.7
14 years.........................	250	15	6.0	239	5	1.9
15 years.........................	252	21	8.3	245	8	3.1
16 years.........................	250	45	18.0	243	28	11.6
17 years.........................	249	76	30.5	251	62	24.8
18 years.........................	247	126	51.1	273	138	50.6
19 years.........................	236	152	64.7	279	168	60.2
20 to 24 years.............	1,356	1,050	77.4	1,528	814	53.2
20 years.........................	240	171	71.1	289	172	59.6
21 years.........................	269	201	74.5	304	173	56.9
22 years.........................	277	212	76.7	306	167	54.8
23 years.........................	284	228	80.2	312	156	50.0
24 years.........................	285	238	83.5	318	145	45.5
NORTH CENTRAL						
14 to 19 years.............	1,781	709	39.8	1,812	467	25.8
14 years.........................	313	48	15.4	300	15	5.1
15 years.........................	308	63	20.3	298	23	7.8
16 years.........................	297	94	31.7	286	44	15.5
17 years.........................	295	124	42.2	297	76	25.7
18 years.........................	288	175	60.8	312	142	45.4
19 years.........................	279	204	73.2	320	167	52.0
20 to 24 years.............	1,565	1,299	83.0	1,688	735	43.5
20 years.........................	279	220	78.8	325	162	50.1
21 years.........................	308	248	80.6	337	156	46.3
22 years.........................	318	262	82.5	337	149	44.2
23 years.........................	330	281	85.2	343	138	40.3
24 years.........................	330	287	87.1	346	129	37.2
SOUTH						
14 to 19 years.............	2,218	910	41.0	2,282	409	17.9
14 years.........................	398	61	15.4	385	16	4.2
15 years.........................	391	86	21.9	384	25	6.6
16 years.........................	384	136	35.4	378	45	11.9
17 years.........................	365	176	48.2	371	71	19.2
18 years.........................	358	221	61.8	390	116	29.8
19 years.........................	322	229	71.3	375	134	35.8
20 to 24 years.............	1,693	1,387	81.9	1,943	705	36.3
20 years.........................	310	240	77.3	390	144	37.0
21 years.........................	337	271	80.6	379	142	37.6
22 years.........................	345	283	82.0	389	144	37.0
23 years.........................	351	295	83.9	392	140	35.7
24 years.........................	350	299	85.3	393	135	34.3
WEST						
14 to 19 years.............	719	253	35.2	741	152	20.6
14 years.........................	128	19	14.9	123	7	5.5
15 years.........................	128	24	18.8	125	9	7.4
16 years.........................	123	33	27.2	120	15	12.6
17 years.........................	117	42	36.3	120	24	20.0
18 years.........................	115	61	53.1	124	44	35.5
19 years.........................	108	73	67.6	129	53	41.3
20 to 24 years.............	637	509	79.9	711	275	38.6
20 years.........................	109	81	74.2	132	54	40.9
21 years.........................	124	97	78.2	137	56	40.5
22 years.........................	128	102	79.4	141	56	39.5
23 years.........................	135	111	81.7	147	55	37.3
24 years.........................	141	119	84.5	154	55	35.4

Source: *1950 Census of Population*, Vol. II, *Characteristics of the Population*, Part 1, U. S. Summary, table 155.

TABLE **E-11.**—ESTIMATES OF 1950 EXPECTED STUDENT LABOR FORCE BASED ON 1940 RATES,
BY AGE, AND 1944 RATES

[Numbers in thousands]

Age	Population attending school (1)	Student labor force (2)	Rates (2)/(3) (3)	Population attending school (4)	Student labor force (5)	Expected frequency (3)x(4) (6)	Difference (5)-(6) (7)
	1940			1950			
Total, 14 to 19 years old..	9,160	370	.040	8,470	1,270	350	920
14 and 15 years old............	4,350	90	.021	3,970	370	85	285
16 and 17 years old............	3,360	140	.042	3,110	540	130	410
18 and 19 years old............	1,450	140	.097	1,390	360	135	225
	1944						
Total, 14 to 19 years old..	7,930	1,460	.184	...	...	1,570	-300

Source: Col. 1, *1940 Census of Population*, Vol. IV, *Characteristics by Age*, Part 1, U. S. Summary, table XV.

Col. 2, Civilian labor force estimates for 1940 have been revised by the Bureau of the Census for comparability with the Current Population Survey (unpublished). On the basis of these revisions, in Lester M. Pearlman and Leonard Eskin, "Teen-Age Youth in the Wartime Labor Force," *Monthly Labor Review*, Vol. 60, No. 1, table 2, it was found that 8.7 percent of the total labor force (including Armed Forces) was attending school. On the assumption that the school attendance rate in the Armed Forces was the same as in the civilian labor force this percentage was applied to the 1940 revised civilian labor force for those 14 to 19 years old. The resulting figure was distributed according to the age distribution of employed students given in *1940 Census of Population*, Vol. IV, *Characteristics by Age*, Part 1, U. S. Summary, table XV.

Col. 4, *1950 Census of Population*, Vol. II, *Characteristics of the Population*, Part 1, U. S. Summary, table 122.

1944 rates, Pearlman and Eskin, *op. cit.*, table 2.

TABLE **E-12.**—EMPLOYMENT STATUS OF PERSONS 14 TO 19 YEARS OLD, BY SCHOOL
ENROLLMENT, AGE, AND SEX: 1950

[In thousands]

Employment status and sex	Enrolled in school				Not enrolled in school			
	Total, 14 to 19 years old	14 and 15 years old	16 and 17 years old	18 and 19 years old	Total, 14 to 19 years old	14 and 15 years old	16 and 17 years old	18 and 19 years old
Total.................	8,482	3,972	3,109	1,401	4,302	296	1,065	2,941
Labor force.................	1,293	367	552	374	2,666	78	570	2,018
Employed.................	1,167	344	495	328	2,184	70	457	1,657
Unemployed.................	126	23	57	46	482	8	113	361
Not in labor force..........	7,188	3,605	2,557	1,026	1,634	218	493	923
Male...................	4,336	2,019	1,566	751	2,078	150	543	1,385
Labor force.................	860	277	359	224	1,658	60	396	1,202
Employed.................	776	262	324	190	1,279	55	313	911
Unemployed.................	84	15	35	34	379	5	83	291
Not in labor force..........	3,474	1,742	1,206	526	419	90	146	183
Female.................	4,146	1,953	1,543	650	2,224	146	522	1,556
Labor force.................	433	90	193	150	1,008	18	174	816
Employed.................	391	82	171	138	905	15	144	746
Unemployed.................	42	8	22	12	103	3	30	70
Not in labor force..........	3,714	1,863	1,351	500	1,215	128	347	740

Source: *1950 Census of Population*, Vol. II, *Characteristics of the Population*, Part 1, U. S. Summary, table 122.

TABLE **E-13.**—INDUSTRIAL DISTRIBUTION OF EMPLOYED PERSONS 14 TO 24 YEARS OLD,
BY AGE: 1950 AND 1940

[In thousands]

Year and major industry group	Total, 14 to 24 years old	14 and 15 years old	16 and 17 years old	18 and 19 years old	20 to 24 years old
1950					
Total..............................	9,566	382	918	1,968	6,298
Agriculture, forestry, and fisheries.....	1,367	161	270	295	641
Mining....................................	118	1	3	17	98
Construction..............................	431	3	24	77	327
Manufacturing.............................	2,454	64	134	480	1,776
Transportation, communication, and other public utilities.........................	667	4	21	115	527
Wholesale and retail trade...............	2,038	59	261	476	1,242
Finance, insurance, and real estate......	401	1	13	110	277
Business and repair services.............	223	2	13	40	168
Personal services........................	532	44	76	110	302
Entertainment and recreation services....	151	12	37	33	69
Professional and related services........	740	7	32	147	554
Public administration.....................	254	1	3	31	219
Industry not reported.....................	190	22	31	38	99
1940					
Total..............................	8,935	210	663	1,808	6,254
Agriculture, forestry, and fisheries.....	1,932	143	317	438	1,034
Mining....................................	127	(1)	2	18	107
Construction..............................	242	1	9	41	191
Manufacturing.............................	2,240	19	86	405	1,730
Transportation, communication, and other public utilities.........................	358	1	11	54	292
Wholesale and retail trade...............	1,616	17	93	341	1,165
Finance, insurance, and real estate......	220	(1)	4	39	177
Business and repair services.............	147	1	7	27	112
Personal services........................	925	17	93	224	591
Entertainment and recreation services....	106	2	11	26	67
Professional and related services........	554	2	11	91	450
Public administration.....................	273	(1)	1	57	215
Industry not reported.....................	194	7	19	46	122

¹ Less than 500.

Source: *1950 Census of Population*, Vol. II, *Characteristics of the Population*, Part 1, U. S. Summary, table 132; *1940 Census of Population*, Vol. III, *The Labor Force*, Part 1, U. S. Summary, table 80.

INDEX

Abrams, R. H., 35, 137
Acceleration of students, 80–82
  as a cumulative process, 81
  defined, 66–67, 148, 152–154, 156
  increase in rate at age 18, 81–82
  number of students for U.S., 80–81
  by region, 81, 82, 172
  in rural-farm areas, 81, 82, 171
  in rural-nonfarm areas, 81, 82, 171
  by sex, age, color, 81
  in urban areas, 81, 82, 171
  variations in, 80–82
  white, nonwhite, 81, 170, 173
Additional workers, as related to employment of youths, 113
Age-grade school progress, *see* School progress
Age groups, defined, 1
  interdependencies of, 7
  population by, 1950, 11–15
  population trends in, 7–9, 133
  significance of, 1–2, 131
Aged population dependency ratios, 11–12, 167
Agriculture, employment in, 106, 108–111, 179
Ayres, L. P., 137, 149

Bakke, E. W., 106, 138
Becker, H., 36, 137
Bernert, E. H., 3, 137, 148
Birth rate, and elementary school enrollment, 61
  and family formation, 132
  and school enrollment, 60
  during war years, 8
Bossard, J. H. S., 35, 42, 137
Bowles, G. K., 3, 137
Broken families, 33–39
  burden on women, 36
  children among, 36
  children as restraints upon family disruption, 39
  divorce as a factor, 35–36
  by marital status of family head, urban and rural, 36
  married parents living apart, 35

size of, 37, 38
trends in, 39
widowhood as a factor in, 35, 36

Carleton, R. O., 106, 138
Carlisle, J. C., 65, 70, 137
Carr-Saunders, A.M., 84, 137
Child labor laws, effect upon labor force participation of youth, 85, 112, 113
  effect upon school enrollment, 43, 113
  State requirements, 114
  and student labor force, 60, 112
Child and youth dependency, and adult educational attainment, 30–31
  defined, 20–21, 131–132
  distribution of children under 18, 40
  and educational attainment, 25, 29, 30–31
  and family income, 22–23, 25, 29, 30, 31
  and housing, 30–31
  and labor force participation, 30–31
  and migration, 29
  among nonwhite population, 17, 19, 29
  problem of, 21, 31
  regional variations in, 12, 13, 19, 21, 132
  rural-urban variations in, 13–16, 29, 132
  and school enrollment, 30, 31
  and school expenditures, 25, 29, 30, 31
  and school performance, 25, 29, 30, 31
  by States, 21, 22, 166
  and unequal school opportunities, 25, 30
  among white population, 17, 19, 29
Child and youth group, color variations in, 17–18
  defined, 1
  population trends in, 7–9
  rural-urban variations in, 13–17
  size and distribution of, 9–13
Children and youth, in broken families, 33–39
  as dependents, 20–32
  and educational attainment, 52–60
  by family size and income, 40–42
  in the labor force, 59, 60–61, 85–130, 134–135, 176, 177, 178, 179
  living arrangements of, 30, 31, 33–42